Paradise Alley

by

John D. Sheridan

1903-1980

GW00503542

A SEVEN TOWERS PUBLICATION

David Doran

2013

Published 2012
By
Seven Towers 4, St Mura's Terrace,
Strangford Road, East Wall, Dublin 3, Ireland.

This edition second printing; first printing 100 copies,

limited, Pride of Place Edition.

www.seventowers.ie

info@seventowers.ie

ISBN 9780957151093

Introduction

This introduction accompanies a new publication of the novel *Paradise Alley* by John D. Sheridan. The novel is being republished word for word as it was originally published and so contains some words no longer in common usage and spellings that may no longer be used. The single change is the removal of a word that, while used in the original context as a descriptive term, may cause offence if used in a similar manner today.

John Desmond Sheridan was born on 7th July 1903 at 29 Park Road, Glasgow, Scotland to Donegal parents. When he was still a young child, his family returned to Ireland and eventually settled in Hollybank Road in Drumcondra. His father, Thomas, like Mandy Logue, Anthony Domican's cousin in *Paradise Alley*, was a Fruit and Vegetable salesman; also like Mandy, spent some time in Glasgow. John D. Sheridan went to school at O'Connell's Christian Brothers School on the North Circular Road and trained as a teacher at St Patrick's College, Drumcondra as well as studying at UCD. During his life, he wrote a number of novels, including *Paradise Alley* and *The Magnificent MacDarney* and published numerous poetry collections, including *Stirabout Lane*. Some of his poems were placed for a time on the National Education Curriculum. He also wrote a biography of Clarence Mangan and a number of humorous works. In addition, John D. Sheridan worked as Director of Books at the Educational Company of Ireland Limited, and he wrote a humorous column for the *Irish Independent* newspaper, a selection of which were published as *I have been busy with words: The Best of John D. Sheridan* (Mercier Press 1979), selected by Gay Byrne, and Gay Byrne also released a recording of John D. Sheridan's work. John D. Sheridan died in 1980.

71 Leabra Road,
Phibsboro',
Dublin.
16th July '43.

The Ploy Clerk,
Dublin District.
(Roll 14514)

A Chara,
I enclose my University Parchment of the B. A. degree and hope that you will return it to me when I have been registered in the office as a graduate. The special degree increment will not be due until September 14th.

Yours faithfully,
John O'Sheridan

(East Wall B. N. S.)
14514

Letter written by John D. Sheridan while he was a teacher at East Wall National School (ED12/31722, © National Archives of Ireland)

From 1927 to 1932 John D. Sheridan taught at the National
School on East Wall Road, a school variously known over the
years as the Wharf School, East Wall Convent and East Wall
National School. Founded in 1895 by the Sisters of Charity in
Seville Place in Dublin, the school comprised an infants' school
(opened in 1898), a boys' school and a girls' school. The infant
school was the convent proper and the teachers were sisters
from the Seville Place Convent and the boys' and girls' schools
were national schools. The original school building was built
in 1895 and housed the three schools until the 1930s. Due
to overcrowding in the schools, a new boys' school was built
in the 1930s on St. Mary's Road in East Wall, and the boys
were transferred there in July 1938. Today the Sean O'Casey
Community Centre stands on the site, the school having
eventually migrated back to a new building on the East Wall F
site.

There is still a school on the old school site, the current builuing
having been built in 1961, and it is now called St Joseph's Co-
Ed National School. It was the original school on the East Wall
Road that was the model for the school in Sheridan's 1945
novel *Paradise Alley*. And, it is as part of the celebration of the
school, coinciding with the finding of the school archive, and the
retirement of the most recent principal, Mr. Seamus Murphy,
after 37 years in the school, and under whom the school got its
current name, that this new edition of *Paradise Alley* is being
published. The association of the author, and the book, with the
school has been preserved in the memory of the former pupils,
and passed on to the East Wall History Group by a former pupil of
the girls' school, Rita L'Estrange.

Recognising the fact that *Paradise Alley* is a work of fiction and
that all the characters are fictional, it is clear that the author was

influenced by his personal biography, his experience in the school and the history of the country, the city, and even the school before his time there and there are many similarities between the school and life in *Paradise Alley* and the school and life in East Wall of the time.

In his description of the school in chapter four of *Paradise Alley*, Sheridan says:

> Between the Tolka and the Liffey, on an artificial peninsula which started life as a sandbank, lies Paradise Alley and the North Wall docks-a place of wharves and ships, sheds and granaries, tangled railway lines and sea-serving canals, cattle yards, coal yards, timber yards, and backyards. Its days are filled with the rattle of lorries and steam-waggons, the whirring of cranes and winches, the swelling scream of whistles; and at night the follow-my-leader clanking of rolling-stock introduces a new note into a symphony that has for metronome the suck and surge of the tide against the quays. Paradise Alley is a short street on the Tolka side of dockland, and it runs along the shore of the little back bay that the North Wall peninsula cuts off from the Liffey estuary. On one side it is bounded by the low sea wall, and on the other by the wall of St. John's School, the wall of Jenkinson's soap factory, and the wall of Ryan's building yard. Beyond Ryan's yard it takes a sharp turn to the right (so that it is not an alley at all), changes its name to Donegan's Wharf, and connects a succession of warehouses, coalyards, stables, cattle lairs, and public-houses with the quays proper.

This description evokes the area around the East Wall school in the time of the book's story and at the time when John D. Sheridan taught at the school. East Wall Village is on reclaimed land, the reclamation of which created an artificial peninsula between the Tolka and Liffey rivers. Until the middle of the 20th Century, the Tolka entered the sea on the East Wall Road just beyond the school, on the North Strand side, and the Liffey

The old school taken from East wall Road © Curtis Collection, East Wall.

In *Paradise Alley,* our hero, Anthony Domican came to the school in 1903, and was appointed principal in 1936 and retired in 1944. Looking at the immediate vicinity of the school during *Paradise Alley's* storyline times, and John D. Sheridan's time in the school from 1927 to 1932, the 1903 *Thom's Directory* lists 2 manure companies (Goulding and Ulster) and one fertilizer (Goulding) company. These are listed consistently in the directories up to 1945, with some new ones added and then lost over the years, for instance in 1916, *Thom's* lists 3 manure companies and 3 fertilizer companies, reduced again by 1936 to Goulding's, and 1939 and 1945 Directories also list one fertilizer works. Any of these could, of course, have caused chapter one's "yellow cloud that rose from the chugging outflow pipe of the manure factory." *Thoms* Directories from 1903 to 1945 also lists Crowe's saw mill and stores next door to the school. And by the 1939 *Thoms* the Rathborne oil manufacturer had become the candle factory, just a short distance from the school. Also listed in the vicinity of the school from 1903 to 1945 are numerous petroleum, oil and colour factories, Port and Docks shipyards and dry docks and the Merchants Warehousing and Carting Companies, one of whose steam carts was crashed into, with some ceremony and much later embellishment, by the Archdeacon driving his motor car in chapter sixteen.

And after that, in the same chapter, there is the more romantic description:

> The tide was full, and a boy was sailing a small, brown varnished dinghy a stone's throw from the sea-wall. Howth was bareheaded in the sun, and the sky was blue and white. "Look at it," said Father Dunphy, taking in the whole scene with a proprietary sweep of his umbrella. "Where would you find the like of it in any *city?* The sea coming right to the very door. I envy you, Mr. Domican.

And in the opening chapter of the book, Anthony Domican describes his final look at the view from the window:

> Behind it he could see the nodding masts of the little sailing boats that were anchored outside the school, and behind them the low grey line of the Bull Wall and the misty outline of Howth Head.

Charlie O'Leary, a former pupil at the school in East Wall, who remembers Sheridan, and who gained fame himself as an FAI referee and as the popular Ireland team kitman, says the following about the wharf which was just the other side of the "low sea wall" on East Wall Road:

> When we looked out the wall was only this height [indicating less than 3 feet from the ground]. And when we looked out, they way you would know the make of motorcar, well we knew the names of all the yachts from Clontarf and we'd sit on the wall, particularly for one or two big races . . . and they all raced, they sailed to come all the way around past the tavern and we'd all be sitting on the wall . . . and not long after the Merchants Road, about fifty yards further on, there was a slipway and that's where all the boats were brought in to enter the sea there.[1]

He also remembered that that the slip was "where you learnt to swim . . . from paddling up . . . every kid from down there learnt to swim."

Another pupil, and former company team footballer who emigrated to Coventry and then New York, Larry Kane also remembers learning to swim at the Wharf:

> We used to get cans, they were big cans, tin cans. And you'd put them under your arms, one under each and you'd go out in the water and the cans would hold... your neck up, your head . . . you'd learn to swim that way.[2]

There are also similarities between the teachers in *Paradise Alley* and the real life people in East Wall school at the time, in

---

[1] O'Leary , Charlie, Oral History interview, Lundberg/Mooney 2011

[2] Kane, Larry, Oral History Interview, Lundberg/Mooney, 2012

particular between Domican's predecessor, Alfred Mendelssohn Rodney, and East Wall principal John Francis Homan, the predecessor to the principal in John D. Sheridan's time, Charles MacCarthy.

John Francis Homan had started as principal when the school opened in 1895. He remained in the position until 1926 when he was succeeded by Charles MacCarthy, who had worked his way up from his first position as an assistant teacher in the school having started in the school not long after Mr. Homan. Mr. MacCarthy remained principal teacher until his death in July 1932, shortly after John D. Sheridan left the school. He was succeeded as principal by John O'Hagan. Unlike his two predecessors, Mr. O'Hagan had not been in the school for long, having apparently joined only in the 1930s, not long before John D. Sheridan left the school. His principalship was relatively short and by the time the new school was built in 1938, Mr. Herlihy, who seems to have served in the school under both Homan and MacCarthy, took the helm. Mr. Homan and Mr. MacCarthy were both from Cork and Mr. Herlihy, like Mr. Sullivan, Domican's successor in *Paradise Alley*, was from Kerry.

Like Arthur Mendelssohn Rodney in *Paradise Alley*, Mr. Homan was a well educated man, having come to the school from a private school in Kilkenny. He liked the boys to read Shakespeare, as witnessed in the pupil's book list during his time in the school, and also liked the boys to stay back after school to help with odd jobs, as well as paying them for academic achievements. "He awards the money prizes during the year, and the average spend annually totals about £5.[3] Mr. Homan also tried to institute some after school training in typing and related business skills and also in violin lessons, which were all available to current and past pupils for a small fee.

---

3 ED12/21770, 16 September 1911, National Archives of Ireland

Mr. Rodney in chapter eight of *Paradise Alley,* is criticized for his unorthodox teaching methods – Canon, later Archdeacon, Brady, the school manager at East Wall school, says about Mr. Homan in a letter in October 1911 that "I constantly interceded when I thought there was a question of reducing his status and believe that, but for my excellent reports about him and for the indulgence of the Inspectors he would have lost his V. G. [school rating] . . . some years ago."[4] . This is echoed in a letter from Mr. MacCarthy written in 1920 where he states, referring to Mr. Homan's teaching methods, that "what the principal does with and for his own pupils is a matter for his own conscience".[5] A 1921 Departmental memo notes that in 1914, Mr. Homan was "severely reprimanded and warned in regard to general unsatisfactory performance of duty, failure to take a proper share of the school work, defective organisation, and unpunctual attendance".[6]

Mr. Homan, like Rodney, and as noted above, also had a well documented problem with punctuality, that was noted by the manager, the other teachers, and the inspectors:

> ALFRED MENDELSSOHN RODNEY was a bachelor, and he lived at Dalkey with an unmarried sister who could not get him up in time in the mornings. When he caught the train he should have caught he arrived in Paradise Alley about nine-fifteen, but when he travelled by one of the later trains, as he did two mornings out of three, he did not arrive until half-past ten or later. (chapter eight)

The notes on Mr. Homan indicate frequent complaints about his lack of punctuality and irregularity of attendance, including in 1903 when "Mr. Homan did not arrive till 10 o'clock instead

---

4   Ibid, 22 October 1911

5   Ibid, Letter Sept 16 1920

6   Ibid, report 10 Jan 1921

of 9.30. Explained he was detained by special private business"
and in 1908 when "Mr. Homan did not arrive until 10 o'clock and
would give no satisfactory explanation as to cause of his lateness.
Manager's attention drawn to this by Inspector."[7] In the Senior
inspector's report of 11 November 1911, James (Seamus) Murphy
says of Mr. Homan:

> The Manager informs me that he as
> heard lately from the assistants that Mr.
> Homan is rarely on time in the mornings.
> This is borne out by the experience of
> inspectors . . . Mr. Homan allows himself
> a margin of 10 to 30 minutes in the
> morning. On the morning of my visit . . .
> he did not enter the school room till 9.40
> but stated that he had been delayed
> a few minutes at the door talking to a
> sister of one of the pupils.[8]

An Inspector's report for the 22 November 1911 states ". . . it has
also been shown that . . . Mr. Homan has, more than once, failed
to attend school at the proper hour in the morning". The report
requests that the Manager "impress on Mr. Homan, the need for
strict punctuality".

Punctuality is still an issue in 1920 when, in a letter on 11
November 1920, Mr. Homan himself claims the manager told him
that the inspectors had written to him complaining about the
'unpunctuality' of Mr. Homan's attendance.[9]

There is also evidence that Homan, like Rodney, was not as
stringent about some aspects of paperwork as the authorities
would have liked him to be.

and if he [Rodney] was asked for

---

7   Ibid November 1911

8   Ibid, 11 November 1911

9   Ibid 11 November 1920

> drawing-copies which he hadn't got he
> would stroke his beard and explain that
> the boy who had been told to burn last
> year's copies had burned this year's as
>
> well. (chapter eight)

This is echoed somewhat in a note from December 1909 which says "manager requested to inform Mr. Homan that written evidence of proper preparation for class lessons is essential and will be looked for in future ("Teacher makes practically no preparation for class lessons")[10]. The reference in the above quote from *Paradise Alley* to Mr. Rodney stroking his beard is also interesting. The late Kevin O'Byrne who, like his father before him was a pupil at the national school in East Wall, remembered his father's stories of Mr. Homan's penchant for stroking his long silver beard[11].

Also, in the same passage as the quote above is taken from, reference is made to Mr. Rodney's knowledge "of the strange but effective methods used by teachers in China —where he had once served as a war correspondent". Though he did not claim to be an expert on schools in China, Homan had visited Japan, in his case in 1905, and in 1906 he wrote an article on methods of discipline in schools in Japan[12]. Some complaints in relation to distribution of classes, work, and class sizes that were made over the years about Mr. Homan can be traced back to his lessons learnt in relation to Japanese schools, where teaching methods, according to his article, prefer larger centralized schools.[13] There is no indication from the article that Mr. Homan went there as a war correspondent, though he does open his article with a discussion about the war:

---

10   Ibid noted in November 1911 report

11   Oral history and *East Wall Festival Brochure 1975*, East Wall for All Archive

12   Homan, JF, "Japanese Schools – their lesson", *The New Ireland Review, Vol XXV,* May 1906, pp136ff

13   See ED12/21770, National Archives of Ireland

> At first nearly all the conversation turned
> on the war[14], for the Baltic fleet was in the
> pacific[15]

and later in the article, he refers to being cited in Japanese newspapers:

> It might have been the special interest
> I took in the Normal School that
> caused me afterwards to be amusingly
> described in the newspapers as a
> Professor of the "Dublin Normal School."

It also appears that Mr. Homan traveled to France during the First World War on his own initiative, which may relate to the war correspondent accolade for Mr. Rodney:

> Six years ago . . . [I] redoubled by efforts
> to get out to France, until at last I got
> my passport for Verdun. Would to God
> I could have left my bones there rather
> than be harassed as I am here.[16]

Extract from school timetable ca 1930, showing a list with John D. Sheridan and his colleagues © East Wall History Group/School Archive.

---

14   Likely to be a reference to the Russo-Japanese War

15   Homan, "Japanese Schools", p 136

16   letter 7 Jan 1921, ED12/21770, National Archives of Ireland

Like Domican in *Paradise Alley*, the teachers had sympathy with the boys in the area, and involvement in the local community. Charlie O'Leary says the following about school principals during his time:

> When I went first, Mr. MacCarthy was the headmaster . . . then when he left, Mr. O'Hagan was headmaster there and he was the Director of Shamrock Rovers and then Mr. O'Herlihy took over. Mr. O'Herlihy, the Kerry man, a big Kerry gentleman. He was marvelous. When the Corporation scheme started, he went [to form a sense of community] and he formed the garden guild [where prizes were given for the best gardens].

Mr. Domican himself may also have a counterpart, or at least a muse, in the East Wall school. Although he clearly did not instigate the fight with Touser Kennedy in chapter four, the likelihood of such a fight may not have been far removed from reality within the school in East Wall. In an affidavit sworn by principal Charles MacCarthy on 6th February 1932, he says the following about assistant teacher Leo McCann, a contemporary of Sheridan's at the school:

> On one occasion, when he had beaten a boy who showed the marks of the ill treatment he had received the boy's father came to remonstrate with him and the parent reported to me that Mr. McCann said "Get out you bastard" and that Mr. McCann also attempted to kick him.[17]

This is one of a number of complaints about Mr. McCann in the affidavit. A full investigation into the issue never took place due to the death of Mr. MacCarthy.

---

17   6 February 1932, ED12/19070, National Archives of Ireland

This story maybe the genesis of Domican's experience with Touser Kennedy in chapter four:

> Anthony found out all this the first day he slapped Tiddler. It wasn't much of a slap, as slaps go, and Tiddler had deserved it, but it caused a sensation. Tiddler yelped round the room and swore that his father would come down to give Anthony 'a baitin'. ... Anthony wanted to run but he had no place to run to, and then, suddenly, his panic was replaced by a wild elation and the battle fury came on him. ... It was less like a fight than like a conjuring trick. Touser went down like a bag of flour, and he lay where he fell. A trickle of blood welled out about his face, and his head lay against one of the iron desk-legs.

There are other colourful stories about the school in East Wall that may also have served as inspiration to Sheridan. Charlie O'Leary recalls two particularly colourful incidents, one relating to a boy who was expelled, and one that makes you wonder where Nedser Bolger got those bigger apples referred to in chapter five:

> '. . . boy from Ballybough. He was the only boy I saw expelled from the school . . . when I was in fourth class . . . Mr. Feeney . . . he was at the blackboard and [the boy] he said something, I forget what, Mr. Feeney turned around and said what was it you said . . . whatever it was it wasn't nice anyway and Feeney shouldn't have done it but he had a little stick . . . it would be about three quarter of an inch in diameter, he threw it at him . . . [the boy] caught it and threw it back . . . Feeney he went to duck below the chair and [the boy] ran up and dived on him and battered the head off him. Feeney held his hand back and

wouldn't touch him. We were all afraid of [the boy] to go out and tell the Man . . . So the next day [the boy] came back with his mother and the whole school was brought out to the back yard . . . and Mr. O'Hagan stood there with your man and with his mother and said 'I wish you to apologise to the whole school, to Mr. Feeney in front of the whole school.' He said 'Sorry Mr. Feeney, I'm sorry I didn't mean it', then he said 'Right, now go on home and don't come back here again'.

and

[When the Wharf area opposite the school was being filled in] that was called the sloblands at the time and people would say 'Do you live near the Sloblands' . . . and you didn't want to tell them . . . But then companies started dumping there – and the big fruit market would come with their dump and around that period of time fruit was terribly dear, it wasn't all that easy to buy, there was a lot of poverty back there as well and when the food lorries was coming, people would get in there, you'd get the odd good apple . . . Mr. Sheehan was the teacher, very particular . . . Second Class, I think it was, Mr. Sheehan was a spotlessly clean man, he was that clean you wouldn't see a hair astray with him . . . [he said to a boy] 'are you eating something?' He said 'Yes sir', 'What are you eating?' 'An apple sir', 'How many have you?' 'I've two sir', 'Give me a look at the other one'. So he brought it up. 'That looks very nice ... You can carry on eating yours but I'm going to eat this one'. Then he said 'That is a beautiful apple, where did you get that one?' 'Down the dump sir'. Sheehan nearly got sick.

The issue of over crowding, leading to the building of the new school was very much an issue for the East Wall school over a number of years, in a similar manner to that related in *Paradise Alley.*

The following extract from a draft letter written by the principal of the school in 1959, describes the changes that led to the building of the new school:

> In about 1938 some new houses, under a Corporation scheme, were completed. To obtain one a married couple to have a family of at least six young children. This meant an increase of roughly four thousand children, as far as our schools were concerned in a sudden jump from two hundred forty boys to roughly five hundred fifty. To meet the emergency a twelve roomed school was built in 1939[18], giving employment to fifteen teachers

However, as indicated throughout *Paradise Alley* the issue of overcrowding and the building of a new school/provision of more school space was under discussion for many years. Indeed the increased attendance at the school was being discussed as early as 1921[19]:

> . . . the attendance at the school has so increased that the average necessary for a third assistant has been restored . . . The schoolhouse is vested in trustees; and the manager, I may add, is prepared to enlarge it, on the usual conditions, with a view to providing adequate accommodation for the increased attendance.

Tommy Devlin, a pupil at East Wall school in the 1930s also remembered that before the new school was built, due to the overcrowding some of the boys attended class in a single room in Barber's Lane off Church Road – "It was a temporary thing."[20] Charlie O'Leary, too, remembered classes being held in a room in the social club at the back of Merchants Road.

18 The Corporation houses were built in 1936; the principal of the girls' school at the time of the building of the new school, Sr. Margaret Ivers, and former pupils in the new school all state that the first boys started in the new school in 1938.

19 ED12/21770, 11 March 1921, J P Dalton Inspector, National Archives of Ireland.

20 Devlin, Tommy, Interview, East Wall Oral History, Mooney 2012

The sheds described in *Paradise Alley*, and the short classes moving back and forth between the sheds and the main building also have their counterpart in the school in East Wall during the time Sheridan was in the school. In *Paradise Alley* (chapter thirteen), these sheds are described as follows:

> The floor of the sheds was the sloping, concrete floor of the playground, and the two twilight windows—one to each shed—were so small that in more primitive times they would have been exempt from window-tax. These additions, which held about forty boys each—the way a sardine-tin holds sardines—made school organization a nightmare. No class could be expected to stay in one of the sheds more than half-an-hour at a time, so all the classes changed rooms at the end of every period and the school spent about one-eighth of the day on the march.

A letter from the school inspector in April 1931 about difficulties between Mr. McCann and the principal Mr. MacCarthy notes:

> I think the unsatisfactory accommodation has something to do with this unpleasantness. The constant changing of classes from the main building to the hut in the playground, and the wretched conditions obtaining in this hut must jar on nerves.[21]

Other aspects of school life recorded in *Paradise Alley* also have real life counterparts. For instance, Domican in the book laments that the boys had to leave the school at fourteen, likely, given the number of times it is mentioned in the book, also to be Sheridan's view:

Chapter eight:

---

21   18 April 1931, J J Doody, Inspector; ED12/19070, National Archives of Ireland.

Paradise Alley children left school at fourteen (the statutory leaving-age for a generation lucky enough to have been born in a humane age which recognized the tremendous possibilities of popular education) and they carried with them into the adult world the vast amount of knowledge and skill which can be acquired during eight years at school, and the fully-developed intellect which, as is implied in the official regulations, every child is bound to possess "on the last day of the quarter in which he attains his fourteenth birthday."

Chapter sixteen:

They left at fourteen (getting jobs as messenger boys, or no jobs at all) because the State laid it down that at fourteen a boy was as far as the master could put him. The experts said fourteen and the parents took them at their word. It never occurred to them to ask at what age the children of the experts left school. Their strong suit was humble faith. A boy could learn a lot in eight years if he put his mind to it.

Chapter seventeen:

He was thinking of Paradise Alley and the slums about it, of boys who left school at fourteen and faced a labour market which had no room for them, of sandwich-men in flittered boots, of the recruiting station at Newry, of the whole horrible mess that was called a social system.

Chapter twenty three:

It was my sorrow, during my years here in Paradise Alley, to see most of my good-quality pupils leave school for ever at fourteen, and forsake books for grocery baskets and carrier bicycles. Many of them, indeed, left me for no more

profitable occupation than that of holding
up the nearest factory wall.

This sentiment was shared by the principal in the 1950s who says, in his letter of 1959:

> There is the type who take the children
> from school at fourteen years and place
> them in blind alley occupations.

It is also shared by Charlie O'Leary who says he loved school and hated leaving:

Mr. Boland (left of boys) and Mr. Herlihy (right of boys) at new school, St. Marys rd. © Curtis
Collection, East Wall

We stopped at fourteen whether we liked it or not . . .

Tommy Devlin remembers leaving at fourteen also:

I left when I was fourteen – everyone did.

Tommy also remembers going to the new school:

We didn't know ourselves going there – beautiful.

Larry Kane noted the difference between schooling in the city and in the country, and seems to underline the statement in *Paradise Alley* about how important schooling was:

> My mother was very smart and she was very well educated. She was . . . into books . . . She went to a good school in Longford where there was only a small class, and she had a brilliant teacher, only about 12 people, 12 kids in the class. And there were 52 in here, in class here.

Paradise Alley also records the other difficulties in for the pupils and their families in the area, including the poverty in the docklands:

> The children of the poor were unintelligent. They inherited dullness from their parents. So the intelligence-testers said, the research educationists, the new psychologists. A fat lot they knew. The children of the poor were as intelligent as anyone else, but they didn't get a dog's chance. They didn't get food, or living space, or proper rest. They didn't get woolly vests, or seaside holidays, or cod liver oil, or bedtime stories.

It wasn't only woolly vests and cod liver oil the children lacked.

Chapter three, referring to the large dockland labourers who had moved to Dublin from the country says:

> . . . and they did not pass on their physique to the children they reared in tenement rooms and on starvation wages.

The recognition of poverty in the area is a common theme throughout the book and, in fact, prompted the author of the obituary for John D. Sheridan in *The Irish Times* to note the debt owed to *Paradise Alley* by *Strumpet City.* In other chapters Sheridan says:

Chapter one:

> Their environment in Paradise Alley
> was one huge barrier to development-
> mental, physical, and moral. It
> made poverty and misery an almost
> inescapable inheritance.

Chapter four:

> They lived in tenements along the river, or in
> pea-pod houses off the quays

Chapter sixteen:

> Paradise Alley had taught them the
> truths of their religion, linking up with
> the teaching of home and chapel;
> it had given them what character
> training it could against the down-
> dragging influence of the slums and the
> degradation of congenital poverty.

and:

> The bulk of Anthony's pupils had been
> under-sized and under-nourished, and
> they had grown up to under-paid, casual
> employment. The sanatorium and the
> graveyard took their toll.

and – talking about attendance:

> Bad weather, broken boots, and sickness
> claimed a good share of the balance.

Charlie, Larry and Tommy all remember the poverty. Charlie talks about people looking for fruit in the sloblands dump as "around that period of time fruit was terribly dear, it wasn't all that easy to buy, there was a lot of poverty back there as well". Lar remembers sharing out food on his road:

It was very tough. What saved us was my grandmother . . . she was always sending up food [from a farm in the country] . . . like potatoes, vegetables . . . and my mother was very good, she'd share them with the neighbourhood, you know, bring it down to the neighbours . . . A lot of poverty, a lot of poverty.

An eleven year old Tommy Devlin (2nd row from back, 5th child from right) with his classmates after their production of Ali Baba and the Forty Thieves in the new school on St Mary's Road. © Curtis Collection, East Wall

Tommy Devlin remembers the school lunches:

There used to be milk and a bun. And you went over to the bicycle shed . . . At the back of the houses on Caledon Road, there was a shed along there. We used to go over there to get the bun and milk. All the kids then were suffering from malnutrition with no food.

Larry Kane also remembers the illness and even death that affected the children:

My little girlfriend, more like my playmate, she died of tuberculosis. Doris Kelly. That was very painful. I came home one day and she wasn't there. She wasn't sitting on the steps anymore. Every day when I came home from school Doris was sitting on the steps and she

was very good at reading, you know, and I was
having difficulty and she'd help me and one
day she wasn't there. I said to my mother . . .
'what happened to Doris, where is she?' She
was always there, every day . . . And my mother,
she was in an awful state . . . she knew the
family very well. She [Doris] had tuberculosis.
We weren't allowed see her, you know. And
she died. Of course, there was a lot of that .
. . different things, tuberculosis, pneumonia.

The tenement houses, infill houses, sheds and stables of the
dockland area, and throughout the city, are well documented.
In fact dockland slums were still being talked about in the late
1990s in debates in the Dàil about the Docklands Development
legislation. As well as this slum housing, there were newer
houses, often built by businesses, which were an improvement
on the original slums, but brought about their own poverty. The
descriptions of these in *Paradise Alley* include the 'two-pair backs"
of chapter one. Some of the two pair houses were the Merchants
Cottages built by the Merchant Warehousing Company, where
2up-2down houses were built to provide accommodation for two
families, one upstairs and one downstairs. The two-pair backs
refers to the two back yards, where each family in the single
house had their own back yard, each containing a separate family
water closet.

Two life long residents of the Merchants Road – Maisie Lynch
who has lived there since the early 1920s and Teresa Mason
whose family have lived there since the late 1920s—remember
overcrowding in the Merchant's houses:

> The Roes' [reared fourteen children in
> the two rooms]. And the Flemings . .
> . had . . . I don't know how many they
> had and the Larkins . . . there were loads
> of them. The Roe's had the most . . .
> children.[22]

While talking about the slum problems in the docklands, Sheridan also gives a nod in the novel to the development of the suburbs with which the government will attempt to address the city slums:

> The most paying crop for land about Dublin
> these days is houses

(Lenihan, chapter seven)

Paradise Alley also includes a view of the wider area around the school – the workers in the dockyards, the railway, the packers on the quays, the local pubs – the Anchor Tavern in *Paradise Alley* surely a nod to the Wharf Tavern, now Seabank House– the Guinness Wharf at the Custom House, the fields around the city, including at Rialto and Dolphins Barn, as well as as far away as Rush in north county Dublin, where the produce exported at the Docks and sold at the market, was grown. Also included, are the social clubs, and the football clubs. The football clubs feature throughout the book, from the first throwaway remark about the 'fullback at Shelbourne' to Mr. Dooley's involvement in Strand Rovers United, and his football playing son, and of course the Quay Wanderers and the later fundraising efforts for the clubs. East Wall has, in fact, a footballing history to be proud of: as well as being the training ground for referee and Republic of Ireland kitman, Charlie O'Leary, East Wall was also home to Shelbourne player Ben Hannigan, Republic of Ireland and Rangers star Alec Stevenson, Liam Tuohy and the famous Lawlor family, with generations of famous footballers. In the 1930s, Seaview United and St Barnabas teams shared the ground in Church Road (where the Catholic Church now stands) and both won the Leinster Junior Championships (St Barnabas 1930 and Seaview 1931). Charlie started his refereeing days in the famous Street Leagues, which Martin Lawlor also remembers fondly from family stories. Ben Hannigan remembers playing with a rag ball in Shelmalier Road in East Wall, and having to stop the game every five minutes to re-tie the rags.

Bringing the football back directly to the school, as Charlie O'Leary remembers, former principal Mr O'Hagan was a director of Shamrock Rovers, and Tommy Devlin remembers the sporting teachers too:

> I remember Mr. Seán Moran; I think he played for Home Farm. When he retired, I think he took up social work or something . . . There were the two Waterford hurlers, the Feeneys, Mick and Seán, I think.

When talking about his students, Domican sees another side of them:

> But they had energy, cunning, a limited and conditional loyalty, and a zeal for life.

> (Chapter four)

And at the very end of the novel, as he looks forward to helping his former pupils to look forward for themselves:

> And he felt reasonably sure that he could hold them, not because of anything in himself, but because of something in them, something that poverty, and under-nourishment, and bad smells could not kill.

It might have pleased Sheridan, and the fictional Domican to know that many of his students went on to become successful, in football as well as other areas, and that, far from their intellects being dulled, many years after leaving school at fourteen, and even after the death of Sheridan, they still remember their time at the school clearly, and continued to be curious and to inform themselves. Their stories and memories are informing the history of the area around the school.

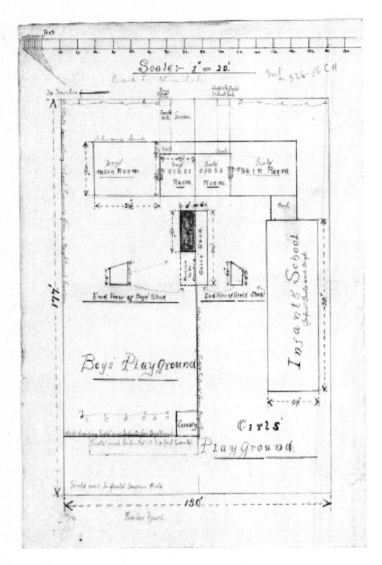

Plan of school circa 1916 with proposed extension, file ED920748
© National Archives of Ireland (note timber yard and sea wall
marked in)

Sheridan also throws a wider net in the book, looking at the
history of the times he is writing about, and the wider history of

Ireland. We see produce coming and going in the Docklands from as far afield as Palestine, the British Navy arriving, and the army barracks being provisioned in the early part of the 20th century. We see recognition of the emigration of the Irish, and the work they undertook across the pond with the reference in chapter sixteen to the former pupils working in Boston – "some of the best were driving street cars in Boston, navvying in Liverpool or Manchester, stoking ships round the Cape". We also see the tensions that were part of daily life in Ireland, with the story of Lord Leitrim—a Dubliner by birth, the Member of Parliament for Leitrim and a notoriously brutal Donegal landlord who was murdered in Fanad in 1878, being told alongside stories of Irish serving and dying in the First World War ("lying quiet in Flanders fields"); and surely pupils from the East Wall school were among the more than six thousand Dublin men who died between 1914 and 1918 and later in the Second World War. Both Dooley's and Domican's sons were to serve.

> The first of the Dooleys to ever take the shillin'. Sure me father, God rest him, would turn in his grave if he knew it. All me people was Fenians—no British Army for the Dooleys. But it's the best thing ever happened Jem. I could never make any hand of him, but the barrack square soon fixed him up and made a man of him. He's a sergeant in the Irish Guards this minute (chapter nineteen)

The reference here is to the "Saxon Shilling" or later "King's shilling", a derogatory reference to the pay of those who joined the British Army. At a time of low wages and high unemployment in the city the army was an attractive option, particularly with separation allowances being paid to soldiers wives. The army also provided the opportunity for the unskilled to learn a trade, while getting into the crafts was normally a closed system[23]. Later, despite the neutrality of the Irish Free State during the Second World War, many Irish Men did join branches of the British military. Over three and a half thousand were to lose their lives.

Domican's son joined the RAF and 10 Irish men fought with the RAF in the Battle of Britain, including Dubliner Brendan "Paddy" Finucane, so famous that "model airplanes of his Spitfire with the vivid green Shamrocks were sold all along Piccadilly Circus." [24]

Paradise Alley also refers to different religions in the city with the experience of the devout Catholic Domican living with the Scottish Protestant landlady as described in chapter three.

> Mrs. Mason, the landlady, was a Scotswoman, a sea captain's widow and a very righteous body. She kept her house shining and decorated its walls with flaming texts from the Holy Book, admonitions to sinners, statistics of deaths from alcoholic poisoning, potted proverbs, and framed questions like "Are you washed in the Blood of the Lamb?" She made no secret of her belief in the maxim "Be just and fear not" and she told the world that the Lord was her Shepherd. She regarded herself as a missionary in a heathen country and had a notion that some day Rome would burn the house over her head. In the meantime she was content to make a frugal living by feeding heretics.

The friendly indulgence of one religion for the other shown in the book is also remembered by Charlie O'Leary who recalls his Church of Ireland friend who went to Catholic devotions with him every week, because it was something to do rather than being left out on his own.

---

23   Yeates , Padraig, *A City in Wartime* Gill and Macmillan, 2011

24   Hyler, Glenn T., www.acesofww2.com

Sheridan also addresses the political tensions extant in the first decades of the twentieth century, tensions that led to the 1913 lockout that is described in the book:

In chapter nine:

> Strikes were the order of the day.
> Dray-horses champed in their stables,
> the trams stopped running, plate-
> glass windows shivered into starry
> fragments. In the side-streets platoons
> of policemen waited.

In chapter ten

> The strikes dragged on. The strikers
> pawned their blue serge suits, their
> brown boots, their china mantel-dogs,
> their bedclothes. They fought hunger by
> going hungry.

and Canon Dunphy also in chapter ten:

> Think of the terrible times we're living
> in—strikes and baton charges and hearts
> full of hate. The poor people! It's the
> women and the children who suffer
> most in violent times like these. God
> alone knows what will be the end of it

The period is an important one in the history of Dublin City – and East Wall along with other docklands communities were at the centre of the events. The Lockout was the culmination of years of growing conflict between the business classes (represented by the Employer's Federation) and the workers organisation the Irish Transport and General Workers Union (ITGWU). Dublin Port was a key battle ground in 1913, many local firms and employers becoming involved, locking out their workers who refused to sign a pledge denouncing the ITGWU. Men at many shipping companies refused to handle 'tainted' goods from locked out companies, and these in turn were sacked and locked out.

This included the Merchants Warehousing Company, T and C Martins, Brooks Thomas, Heitons coal merchants, the Port and Docks Board, the London and North Western Railway Company (LNWR) and the City of Dublin Steam Packet Company. Sheridan describes this is *Paradise Alley:*

> The farm labourers were on strike, the
> carters were on strike, the dockers were
> on strike, and in Kimmage and Rialto
> cabbages were going to seed or rotting
> in the ground.

In chapter seven Anthony Domican engages in a conversation regarding wages and living conditions in the city. His sympathetic attitude leads to him being accused of speaking "Rank socialism- Beresford place stuff". Beresford place was the location of Liberty Hall, the headquarters of the ITGWU. Through the discussions (between Anthony Domican, Mandy Logue and the Lenihans) Sheridan very much sums up many of the opposing attitudes that were prevalent at the time, and illustrates the values and prejudices of a particular class. Many observers at the time could sense that events were building towards a climax, and there was a sense of a powder keg ready to explode. Domican makes a grim pronouncement: "I know Paradise Alley and places like it and I can tell you that ugly things are brewing."

In chapter nine Anthony Domican finds himself caught up in a police baton charge that had begun at Beresford Place and spreads onto Abbey Street where he is lucky to avoid injury:

> Anthony was caught one night in
> a baton charge that began outside
> Liberty Hall. He was one of a crowd that
> stretched round into Abbey Street, and
> he was jammed like a match in a full
> box. When the charge began he was
> carried off in the rush, but when the
> crowd thinned a little he was able to

> stand his ground with difficulty and he
> saw the police running and heard the
> thud of the batons. It was a sickening
> sound, and a terrifying one. One man
> went down near him, an old fellow with
> a wheezy, asthmatic way of breathing.
> His hat rolled from his bald head and a
> trickle of blood followed it.

Anthony managed to escape without injury, though, in the actual event that is recalled in *Paradise Alley,* which took place on 30 and 31 August, *others* suffered the fate, and worse, of the old man he saw. The *Dublin Disturbance Commission 1914* published a report containing eye witness accounts of these incidents, including many from "respectable" bystanders. The photographs of the police baton charges on Sackville Street (now O'Connell Street) are infamous. It is an indication of the savagery exhibited at the event that while the baton charges lasted for less than five minutes between four and six hundred citizens were injured within this short timeframe.

Thomas McDonagh (a proclamation signatory in 1916) saw "the police batoning the people and striking them on the head... I saw sometimes three policemen attack a single individual. I saw them attack an old woman with a shawl over her head and baton her brutally. I saw them attack a small man who had lost his hat ...I heard the continual rapping of batons on people's heads." The account of one bystander, a business man, is very evocative of the description given of events in Paradise Alley:

> I was surrounded by a forest of batons...
> I put my hands up. I was anything but
> militant. A constable made a dive for me...
> and I said-'Oh! For Christ's sake have you
> no mercy?' ... He made a dive, I swerved,
> and I partly got into the arms of another
> policeman. The next thing happened
> was – I got a bash on the head... I was
> partly thrown on the ground and I got
> a strike on the back, and went down a
> second time."

The same witness earlier described being

"Driven by a stampede"

of panicking citizens, and used the description

"We were like herrings in a box."

And the description below from the Commission's report of the death of James Nolan from Spring Garden Street in the North Strand is echoed in Sheridan's description of Domican's experience:

> One of the constabulary walked from the centre of the road onto the sidewalk and without the slightest provocation felled the man with a blow from his staff. The horrible crunching sound of the blow was clearly audible fifty yards away. The drunken scoundrel was ably seconded by two of the metropolitan police who, as the man attempted to rise, beat him about the head until his skull was smashed in several places.

In chapter ten Domican is with Canon Dunphy on the quay at North Wall and he describes the interaction between the Canon and a "little man" over children of strikers being transported to England.

> "Why can't you let the chislers go where they'll get enough to eat?" shouted a voice.

> "Because I don't know where they're going," said the Canon. "The best and safest place for any child is his father's house."

> "Listen to him," shouted the man with the voice like a gale of wind. "What kind of houses have the fathers and mothers of Dublin? Rooms without a stick

of furniture in them—grate without fires—beds without bedclothes—and larders without a bite in them. Is this kind of a home the best place for a growing child? Judge for yourselves, mothers of Dublin?"

The events described here are also real events, based on what became known as 'the kiddie scheme'. Some of the actual history of it is recorded by Sheridan in chapter ten, when he describes the support for the strikers from the English unions. The proposal to relocate the children of strikers to homes in England, the so called "Dublin Kiddies scheme" originated with Dora Montefiore, a London based socialist. She later explained: "When I read of the dire distress in Dublin consequent on the prolonged industrial trouble, and when I hear from the lips of Jim Larkin … what straits the workers and their families were in, after seven weeks of slow starvation, I bethought me of the plan, tried already successfully by workers in Belgium and during the Lawrence strike in the United States, of removing the children from the strike area and placing them in the homes of workers in other parts."[25]

When this suggestion was put to Larkin he was very quick to give his approval, and steps were taken to put it in place. A "Dublin Kiddies Scheme" committee was set up, and an appeal was sent out in the socialist, progressive and trade union press. According to Montefiore, within a week 300 responsible homes had been offered. Fearing some opposition, she pointedly drew attention to the fact that many of those offering homes were Catholic.

---

25   Montefiore , Dora *Our Fight to Save the Kiddies in Dublin-Smouldering Fires of the Inquisition –*. Pamphlet 1913- Marxists Internet Archive

Boys at the old school east Wall Road © Curtis Collection, East Wall

The plan was for the first group of 50 children (accompanied by a number of women) to first attend Tara Street Baths to be cleaned and dressed in new clothes, travel by train to Kingstown (now Dun Laoghaire) and board the steamer to Holyhead. The group was accosted firstly at the Baths by a group of priests and supporters, and then prevented from reaching Westland Row station. Parents were harangued and bullied, and some children were taken away by the priests. A second attempt was made to travel with 16 children on a later train. In the station and on the train the women were continuously intimidated and even assaulted by the priests. Ten children were too frightened to leave the train and only a small number finally made it aboard the *Scotia*, still being pursued. After some of these were either snatched away or fled off the ship, the attempt was finally abandoned in failure. Montefiore's companion Lucille Rand was arrested on the pier, and was charged with the kidnapping of a 14 year old boy. The children were taken by the priests back to Westland Row station, were they were greeted by cheers of "God Bless Our Priests."

Despite this setback, it was decided to immediately send the next group of 15 children that evening from North Wall. Jim Larkin addressed a crowd of workers from the window of Liberty Hall and told them that he depended on them to ensure the children sailed to Liverpool.

> Soon after seven the little procession started, almost like a forlorn hope, from the steps of Liberty Hall, each child being carried on the shoulders of a stalwart docker, Miss Neal and two Irish girls having a bodyguard, who were to see them safely on to the boat. These precautions were not unnecessary, for the priests and Hibernians were down at the boat before our little party arrived, and the same scenes of violence took place as had disgraced the morning's proceedings.[26]

The Manchester Guardian, 24 October 1913 reported on the events of the following evening:

> There were scenes of great excitement in Dublin to-night due to the expected deportation of more children by the outgoing steamers. A large crowd of people gathered at the North Wall previous to the hour of departure of the steamers. In the vicinity of Liberty Hall the "Larkinite" forces assembled in considerable numbers, and there was much tension. The Laird line steamer for Glasgow was the first due to depart, and a large number of people, headed by several priests, were keeping a look-out. Feeling was clearly strong in this group against the deportation. But it was soon seen that no children were being taken over by this boat. The crowd next visited the Burns steamer Tiger, but there was no sign of children among the passengers, and the departure of the vessel without any youngsters on board was signalised by an outburst of cheering from the priest-led crowd. The hymn "Faith of our fathers" was sung, and in a vigorous speech a member of the party denounced

26   Ibid

the conduct of the Larkinites in assailing
the clergy.

As with the Canon's work in *Paradise Alley*, the work of the
Catholic Church in Dublin was successful in preventing the
majority of the children being shipped to England, and the kiddie
scheme was eventually abandoned.

In his chapters on the strike, lockout and the kiddie scheme,
Sheridan makes sure to give both sides of the story. In
chapter nine he says "The police were not the enemies of the
people. They were of the people". In chapter ten, he gives the
businessmen's side of the strike.

> The strike was costing Mandy money.
> The salerooms of Liverpool were stacked
> with stuff that he was itching to sell—
> American apples, Spanish onions, bananas
> from Jamaica and the Canaries, tufted
> pineapples from Calcutta. His supplies were
> not cut off completely, but the little he could
> handle under police protection wouldn't
> fill his ledgers. The Glasgow trade, too, had
> dwindled to nothing.

Also in chapter ten, he makes sure both sides of the kiddie
scheme argument are voiced in the debate on the docks, in the
different voices and the different opinions given (and where
there is a possibility that the mention of the 'little man' on he box
opposite the Canon is a nod to his fellow Scotland-born Irishman,
James Connolly). Domican, howeve, also tells us "There is tyranny
on both sides, but he tyranny of the workers is the tyranny of
desperate men".

As well as events and people recalled in *Paradise Alley*, it is true
that there are some obvious lacunae. The man who reports the
events of 1913 in such detail, who mentions the different religions
and gives a nod to the familial confusion when the child of a
family of 'Fenians' joins the British army, does not cover the 1916

rising, the War of Independence or the Civil War, and does not mention DeValera's government and the effect of the change of regime on the experience of being a national school teacher. Equally the author who is clearly Catholic, who refers the need for a fair wage and proper treatment of the workers to Pope Leo XIII's *Rerum Novarum* doesn't mention the Eucharistic Congress which took place in Dublin in 1932. Whatever the reasons for these apparent omissions – be they political, personal or artistic – they have left us with a book that focuses almost exclusively on the school, people and immediate surroundings of Paradise Alley and hence, of East Wall itself.

However, as close as the novel may be to events in the real East Wall, and as much as John D. Sheridan was influenced by these events, as we said earlier, Paradise Alley is a work of fiction, and John D. Sheridan was a writer of poetry and fiction. So the last words in this introduction should go to the novel and the novelist who captured the victory mixed with sadness that went with being educated and an educator in the area; who captured life at the time in a manner that is complemented and lauded by those who lived through it; who gave us the image of the terrified Dooley in the car with the Canon, and who left us with memorable phrases:

> a few weeks in which to get the picture
> of his life into focus-before Sullivan and
> the others distorted it with high praise.

from chapter one, and the opening sentence of the novel

> He gathered the roll books into the
> press and locked away for the last time
> the sloping attendance marks that
> were like tombstones to the dead days

*****

Sarah Lundberg and Joe Mooney Dublin June 2012

Paradise Alley

by

John D. Sheridan

CHAPTER ONE

HE gathered the roll books into the press and locked away for the last time the sloping attendance marks that were like tombstones to the dead days. The monthly return lay on the table in front of him. It was the last one he would ever fill in. From now on it would be Sullivan's job to collect the signatures of the other teachers, see that all absences were duly entered, and bring the completed form down to the Archdeacon. But the Archdeacon, God help him, hadn't so many monthly returns to sign either. He too, like Anthony himself, and the old school, was nearing the end of his tether. They were all finishing up together.

St. John's National School, Paradise Alley, Dublin.
   Roll No. 14567.
   Anthony Domican, Principal.

As he stood up from the table a great, unwieldy seagull lobbed onto the window-sill. Behind it he could see the nodding masts of the little sailing boats that were anchored outside the school, and behind them the low grey line of the Bull Wall and the misty outline of Howth Head. That was the best way to look from Paradise Alley—to lift your eyes and stare into the distance. If you looked straight down you saw the low sea wall, the muddy foreshore that the tide was so slow in covering, and the yellow cloud that rose from the chugging outflow pipe of the manure factory.

The seagull was late, and the lunch-time crumbs had been scooped up long since by his more punctual fellows. Perhaps, Anthony thought, it had as bad a time sense as he had himself. Until now he had never realized that he was growing old. Every summer, when the last year's Infants had marched in from the convent next door, clutching their little slips of age and identity tightly, he had given Time a post-dated cheque. And now, when he had, as the Rules and Regulations put it, reached "the end of the quarter in which he attains his sixty-fifth birthday" (it seemed incongruous to think of the staid Department taking any notice of a man's birthday), the cheques had come in together and his store of youth was withered and shrunken.

He felt old.

It would be more fitting, he thought as he went out into the street, if he could lock the door behind to symbolize his passing, but Mrs. Malone would lock the door. There was no statutory retiring age for Mrs. Malone. She would go on brushing and scrubbing until she dropped.

He crossed the railway bridge and the canal, but instead of calling on the Archdeacon, as he had intended, he kept straight on past the new school and out on to the quays.

He would bring the monthly return down to the Archdeacon after tea and drop it into the Education Office on his way home. There was no hurry. There would never again be any hurry. His time was his own.

Men touched their hats to him: men loading ships, men driving lorries, men standing outside public houses. They were all his old pupils. Some of them were the sons of old pupils. Was he as old as all that?

He fell to thinking then of the new school, with its eighteen classrooms, an assembly hall, a playground as big as a barrack square, and, *mirabile dictu,* a teachers room.

All he had ever had in Paradise Alley was five rooms and two crazy, concrete-floored, unheated, death-trap, overflow sheds. The magnificence would all be Sullivan's. A good chap, Sullivan, though a little excitable, The capitation money would be useful to him.

It had taken a long time to get the new school out of the Canon. Donkey's years. The Canon had hated the thought of gathering money from his poor parish, bargaining with archiects and contractors, coaxing the Education Department to put its hand deep in its pocket. Ten years before—and he had been on old man even then—he had pleaded that it was a job for his successor. If he started it would kill him. But it was finished now and the Canon was still at the wicket. (He was an Archdeacon now, of course, but Paradise Alley called him "the Canon" as often as not).

A man of God, the Canon, if ever there was one; crotchety and kind by turns, but in love with his people; gentle with sinners but merciless where plain chant was concerned. "The little la-la" he called it, "ad-or-e-e-moos-moos, not muss."

"If the children are taught to sing their hymns properly," the Canon used to say, "they won't have Dublin accents."

Anthony could laugh at it all now, but it had been different in the old days.

"They must have Dublin accents," he had told the Canon time and time again. "Surely you don't expect to have Cahirciveen accents?"

There you go again," the Canon would say. "Trying to be funny."

He had never let anything go with the Canon. That was the way to get on with him. They had argued for forty years, and looking back on it neither of them would have had it otherwise.

The Canon was sorry to see him go. He knew that. And the Canon was as proud as Punch of his new school, though at times he seemed to forget that only for the nagging of Anthony Domican it wouldn't have been started yet.

But to do the Canon justice, be had made a good job of it—a palace of green and white, with wide, rubberoid-floored coridors, and red EXIT signs in the assembly hall.

The Canon was tickled at the EXIT signs. "As good as a picture house," he had said.

And the Canon, gangrened foot or no gangrened foot, would preside at his presentation and make a whale of a speech. Sullivan would be sending an account of it to the newspapers, no doubt, and he knew the kind of account Sullivan would write.

"A very pleasant function took place in the Regal Hotel, Dublin, on Thursday … when Mr. Anthony Domican, N.T., was entertained at a banquet given by some of his colleagues, friends, and grateful ex-pupils, and presented with a substantial cheque to mark his retirement from the Principalship of St. John's National School, Paradise Alley,

Dublin, where he laboured with such success for forty years...

"The presentation was made by the Very Rev. Archdeacon Dunphy, P.P., who, in an eloquent and graceful Valedictory oration, paid well-deserved compliments to the guest of the evening . . ."

God help us!

" Senator M. Logue said it was a signal honour for him to propose the health of his friend and kinsman . . ."

You've come a long way, Mandy since we knocked out the captain of the *Ayr Maid* on the quay at Milford—a long, long way.

"Mr. Edward Bolger, T.D., speaking on behalf of the ex-pupils, associated himself cordially with the remarks of the previous speakers. It was a long time since he had first made the acquaintance of Mr. Domican..."

"The divil of a long time, Nedser, and yet not so long. I remember the cow's lick that straggled down over your bumpy forehead. I remember your red and white face and your button nose. You were like a ventriloquist's doll. " Mr. Adrian O'Sullivan recounted the sterling qualities of his predecessor...."

Adrian was a great respecter of traditions. All the old, moth-eaten phrases would roll off his tongue in a cascade of rich Kerry vowels.

".... taught for some time in his native Donegal before coming to Paradise Alley in 1903 .... appointed Principal in 1936.... zeal and conscientiousness.... enduring work for God and Ireland.... A man of culture and scholarship.... many of his pupils occupy prominent positions in Church and State. The large and representative gathering testifies in no small measure to the esteem and affection in which he was held by everyone with whom he came into contact."

Maybe he was anticipating a little. That was a bit of the funeral notice— "large and representative cortege."

The funeral stuff would come later. But in one sense part of the funeral was over already, for it was like dying a little to leave Paradise Alley: the place had become part of him.

The send-off would be like a shovel of clay on his coffin.

Many of his pupils now occupy prominent positions in Church and State." Flapdoodle. One was a curate in Toowoomba, another missioner in the Philippines. He had turned out a dozen postmen, and two or three civil servants who had risen from boy clerkships to heights only a little more dizzy. But these were the exceptions. The lucky ones got trades: the unlucky became publichouse porters, private soldiers, billiard markers.

Precious little he had done for them ....taught them to sign their names, to add and subtract....Battle of Clontarf, 1014.... Derby and Nottingham coalfield...."like signs give plus, unlike signs give minus.'" It wasn't his fault. He couldn't have fed them and dressed them. He couldn't have taken them out of their two-pair backs and given them decent houses. He couldn't have paid for them in secondary schools and put them on for medicine or apprenticed them to accountancy. The children of the poor were unintelligent. They inherited dullness from their parents. So the intelligence-testers said, the research educationists, the new psychologists.

A fat lot they knew. The children of the poor were as intelligent as anyone else, but they didn't get a dog's chance.

They didn't get food, or living space, or proper rest. They didn't get woolly vests, or seaside holidays, or cod liver oil, or bedtime stories. They became men and women before their time, so that their mental development was telescoped and stunted. Intelligence was a function of the soul, but its proper development depended on physical factors. His own experience had proved it. He had seen, every six years or so, batches of bright, normal children march in from Sister Ita, and he had seen them grow dull and listless as they grew old. They couldn't attend. They couldn't concentrate. They got no chance. Their environment in Paradise Alley was one huge barrier to development—mental, physical, and moral. It made poverty and misery an almost inescapable inheritance.

"Many of his pupils occupy prominent positions in Church and State."

Aye, indeed. One was stand sacristan in St. Stephen's. Another had been hanged in Pentonville. A man could do a lot of harm in forty years. It was a long time, and he had a few weeks now to remember, a few weeks in which to get the picture of his life into focus—before Sullivan and the others distorted it with high praise.

CHAPTER TWO

ANTHONY DOMICAN came of a family of teachers.

His father, Black Donal, had been Principal of Lurgameelon, at the foot of flint-faced Errigal; and his grandfather, Sean Domican, was a poor scholar who had come back from Salamanca unpriested. The Domicans had a name for learning. Black Donal could read and write both Gaelic and English, and he taught his senior pupils cube root. He had the Latin, too, as befitted the son of his father, and a smattering of Greek.

Black Donal married Sarah Logue from the bottom of the Fanad peninsula, and a year later his sister married John Ruadh, a brother of his wife's: so that Anthony Domican and Mandy Logue, the first-born of the two marriages, were cousins twice over. The Logues were a dealing family. Buying and selling was in their blood, and even in the dark days when the Gael had nothing but a few acres of mountainy ground and a cow apiece the Logues sold butter and eggs to the breed of the planters. And it wasn't easy making a living in Fanad of the stony fields and scraggy beasts. The whole peninsula wouldn't have fetched the price of a decent dowry.

John Ruadh had a small farm on the shores of Mulroy, that lovely, twisted labyrinth of in-thrusting Atlantic water. His house, at the time of his marriage, was just a room and a kitchen, but John built a loft bedroom over the room but under its roof, a tiny, jutting-out bedroom off the room, and a still tinier bedroom in the kitchen. The kitchen bedroom was a room within a room—it was for all the world like a big varnished crate in the corner. But the first addition that John Ruadh built was a shop. He built it off the kitchen and opened a door on to the street. It was a tiny shop and it would not, on its own, have supported a family, but John got a living from the farm, and the shop was something over and above. The farm gave him shelter, and food, and clothes, but the shop gave him money to come and go on. The farm was his daily bread, the shop his vocation. Most of the other Lahardan men had to hire out their sons and daughters to the big farmers in the rich Lagan valley, and had to go themselves to the harvest in Scotland every year that they might have a wheen of pounds to put by against the winter and the spring sowing. John Ruadh and his family stayed at home.

When Anthony's mother was a young bride she usually spent a week in Lahardan in September, and her sister-in-law, John Ruadh's wife came to Lurgameelon for a few days at Easter. John would drive her over on the sidecar and spend the night there, for it was a long journey and the mare couldn't do it two ways in one day. And a night was about as long as John cared to spend in Lurgameelon, for he and Black Donal hadn't much in common. They were opposites, in temperament as in colouring. The teacher was nervous, and given to moodiness: the shopkeeper high-spirited and full of stories. But from the beginning the two sons Anthony Domican and Mandy Logue, took to one another, though they too were opposites. Anthony Domican had his father's colouring. He was a tall, black-haired boy with broad shoulders and a slender body. Mandy had the short, stocky frame, the blunt nose, and the red hair that went with the Lahardan Logues. Mandy grew up followed by a long line of brothers and sisters. Anthony's only brother died in infancy.

Before very long the Logues came no more to Lurgameelon, for there was always a young Logue in baby clothes, and sometimes two, and it was not easy for the mother to make the journey. But Anthony Domican spent every summer in the boisterous house on the shores of Mulroy, so that, years afterwards, when he looked back on his boy-hood, it was of Lahardan he thought and not of lonely Lurgameelon. Sometimes his father complained. "What call has he to be running to Lahardan so often?" he would say. "Sure the Logues have a big enough houseful of their own without being bothered with the likes of him."

"It does him good," his mother would answer. "This is a quiet house for a young fellow, and there's plenty of company for him over there. He'll be no bother to them—one more or less makes no difference in Lahardan."

And neither it did. The Logues always had their fill of porridge, potatoes, butter, oatmeal scones, and herring from the bay, and although, like their neighbours, they ate meat only about three times a year, they were sturdy and well fed. It was porridge and potato men who did the rough, navvying work for the young towns of the Clyde valley, loaded ships in New York and San Francisco, and supplied bulk and sinew for the police forces of two continents. There was plenty of food in the Lahardan household, but there wasn't much space. Anthony slept with four of his cousins in the low, loft bedroom, right against the thatch. There were two beds there, side by side, and the five boys punched and pummelled before they went to sleep. John Ruadh slept in the kitchen, and when shouted threats failed to bring silence in the loft he would drag on his trousers, grumble his way upstairs, and flog the foot of the bed with the ends of his braces.

*　　*　　*　　*

When Mandy Logue was eighteen he announced that he was going to America.

"America, how are you! "said John Ruadh. "Anyone would think to hear you that your folk hadn't a decent way of living on them. Why would you go to America and you with a shop and farm at your back?" "There's nine of us for the shop and the farm," said Mandy. "And be the time the youngest is fit to leave I won't be a chicken. Some of us will have to clear out and better the eldest nor the youngest. That's why I'm for the States."

"And what the hell will you do when you get there?"

Lie on your belly and hack coal out of the ground, or dig subways in the city of New York? A fine life that would be for one that got the rearin' you got. A fine life indeed. I'll break every bone in your body before I let you go. And where in the name of God you got the notion I don't know. But you didn't get it from Anthony Domican, I'll go bail. Trust a Domican to have some sense under his hat! You won't find Anthony Domican wanting to go to the States before he has grown man's hair on his face." John ranted for a full week, and then changed his tactics.

"Sure if you don't want to stay at home, son, there's no need to," he coaxed. "You could become a shop boy in Derry. You could start to deal in cattle. And sure if you went for a while to your Uncle Donal you might pass the King's Scholarship and go to training up in Dublin with Anthony next September. Master O'Donnell will be goin' out on pension in three or four years and the school would be yours for the asking."

But Mandy wasn't open to suggestions. His mind was made up. He was going to America whether his father liked it or not, and he went ahead with his preparations.

Mandy sailed in May, and the following September Anthony entered the training college in Dublin. He left it two years later, a certificated teacher, and after a month at home he was appointed Principal of Loughhuidhe National School, a tiny, one-roomed building about two miles from Mulroy and three from his cousins in Lahardan. His aunt wanted him to stay at Lahardan, but he knew that there wasn't room for him there so he looked for lodgings nearer the school.

He found them with Dinny the Cobbler. Dinny had a high regard for book-learning, and he was proud to have the Master of Loughhuidhe under the same roof with him. He even hinted that there was no other house in the locality fit for the honour. "Sure you couldn't stay in an ignorant house, Master," he told Anthony. "It wouldn't be right." Anthony ate and slept in the "room": Dinny and his wife confined themselves to the kitchen, which was also the cobbling shop.

Every night, when the kitchen was full of patient customers who dared not ask when their shoes would be ready, Dinny cut and hammered, and "put out spells." He could spell 'fuchsia—hardy shrub,' 'ferrule—the ring of a stick,' and 'hemorrhage—bleeding from the lungs, arteries, or veins.' Dinny did not stick to his last. In spite of Dinny's chatter Anthony found Loughbuidhe a lonely place. Lahardan was near enough in the summer but it was a good walk in the winter time, and even Lahardan wasn't the same with Mandy away.

But Mandy wasn't long away. He spent three years Philadelphia and then wrote to say that he was coming home. His father, who had been angry when he went away, was angrier when he heard he was coming back. "What in blazes is takin' him home?" he said. "Sure it wasn't worth his while goin'. Troth it wasn't. I was thinking all the time that me bould Mandy would find the States too hard for him. And now he's runnin' out of it. We're shamed for life." The truth was that John Ruadh had thought nothing of the sort. He had been quite sure from the beginning that Mandy would get on in America, and he had done his share of boasting on the stone dyke outside the chapel after Mass on Sundays. Mandy wasn't stayin' long in any job. Be me sowl, no. Mandy wasn't the one to stick in a rut. Mandy would be a wealthy man before he was finished. John Ruadh may have been glad that his son was coming back to him: he was certainly a little disappointed that he was coming back so soon.

Mandy Logue wasn't the sort of returned Yankee that Fanad was used to. It had seen exiles come home to die, Or to get a last look at the old folk, but they had all been stern, hard-faced people with mouthfuls of shop teeth and specks of gold when they parted their lips. Mandy came Younger than many a one who was still thinking of going, and Fanad wondered what had brought him back so soon to the land of porridge and potatoes. But Mandy, when he came, gave no reasons to Fanad, nor to his parents. He came home the way a hired boy might come home from the Lagan or a grown man from the harvest in Scotland, and he kept his reasons to himself. Anthony was the only one he confided in.

"I hadn't a minute there. I worked like a black during the day—no stoppin' for a blather or a smoke in the States. You get good money, but by heavens you have to earn it. It was good fun for a while, but I hadn't time to bless myself, and I began to think that maybe I'd be happier at home." "But you'll be just as discontented as ever after a month or two at home. You'll never settle down on the farm." "I'm not going to try," said Mandy. "I'll just look round me for a while. There must be many a way of making a living even in this poor country."

Mandy was not long looking about him. Within a month he had taken an empty store on Milford quay and nailed up above the door the sign

M. LOGUE, GENERAL MERCHANT.

It was a great, dusty, tumbledown place, full of rats and cobwebs. " It has a roof on it so it'll do me rightly," said Mandy. "I'm not going to waste money on paint. If it holds stuff that's all I want"

"What kind of stuff?" asked Anthony

"Anything I can lay my hands on that will sell for good money in Derry or Glasgow—we'll see as we go along."

"We?"

"Aye, why not? We should do well together. I get notions, but they're sometimes wild notions. I need someone to brake me. The firm must have a head on it."

It wasn't hard to get eggs, fowl, and potatoes, but the prices the Derry merchants gave didn't leave much profit for M. Logue, General Merchant.

"We've made three pounds seventeen so far," he said to Anthony after the first month. "A man could save more than that in a week in the States. We'll have to do something about it. These Derrymen aren't working for the love of the thing. I collect the stuff from all over the country, have all the trouble, and make a few shillings—they dump it on the boat and make as many pounds. Why shouldn't we sell direct to Glasgow?"

Anthony could see nothing against the idea, but he was not greatly interested. He had not Mandy's love for buying and selling. He wasn't a Fanad Logue. He liked seeing mosaics of eggs in boxes, knobby sacks of potatoes, and fat turkeys with the feather stubs still on them; he liked invoices and envelopes, and ladders of figures; he liked the colour and smell of merchandise, and the rattle of the carts that brought Mandy's crates to the railway. But he hated driving a bargain, and he saw the other fellow's point of view as clearly as he saw his own. He was chary of new ventures and loath to commit himself. He never felt uneasy about Mandy's new ventures, however, for he felt that Mandy had an instinct in matters like these, and he seldom threw cold water on his cousin's suggestions. He saw in Mandy a side of his own nature which had never developed, and in endorsing Mandy's wild notions he tasted adventure by proxy. It was Mandy who thought of going to Glasgow, but it was Anthony who made him go.

"Why waste time?" he said. "The sooner you go the sooner you'll have the Derrymen's profits in your pocket."

"I'll go the morra," said Mandy, and thought for ever after that the notion had been Anthony's. Mandy spent a fortnight in Glasgow and made arrangements with merchants and shipping agents. He saw the Clyde and the big shipyards, he saw the sleepless, belching chimneys, but because he saw them as accidentals, as the background of his dreams, as a frame for the plans he was whittling, he saw them less clearly than Anthony did at home in Lahardan. Anthony taught in Loughbuidhe during the day and managed Mandy's store in the evenings, but whether he was sliding a pointer along a map or nailing a label on a box of eggs he heard the eerie hoot of steamers going down the dark Clyde and saw the red glow where the great furnace fires of Shettleston seared the night sky. Mandy's two letters told him nothing about Glasgow. He knew all about Glasgow already. He had been hearing about Glasgow since he had first come to Lahardan on holiday. Scotland was nearer to Fanad than Derry was. Fanad had reaped her harvests and built her sewers, and the 'model lodging house' was well known in the homes about Mulroy. Dinnv the Cobbler was one of the local authorities on Glasgow.

"A fine town," he told Anthony, "and a young town. I mind the time when you could cross the Clyde in the bare feet at low water."

Dinny and men like him had seen Glasgow grow and had helped her to grow. They had served her with pick and shovel, and she had given them in return food, and shelter, and a grudged toleration. And in the bad days, when Lord Leitrim was evicting whole countrysides, and turning the people out of their holdings when the corn was ready for the scythe and the potatoes swelling under the brown earth, it was to the city of the Clyde that the dispossessed carried their memories and their hates. They had to take what they could get and be thankful for it, and what they got was the heavy work, the sore work, the mud-grovelling, rain-soaked, back-breaking work that the Scot wanted done for his growing city. They settled down with the all-conquering patience that is bred in stony fields, and they built schools and paid teachers so that the next generation of Glasgow Gaels might be free of the pick and the shovel.

The story of Lord Leitrim was as much Glasgow's as it was Fanad's, and the last chapter of it, which was written in blood along the shores of Mulroy, woke a wild and unchristian joy by the banks of the Clyde, where men bent by labour thanked God that vengeance had come in their time. There were blacker charges against Leitrim than evictions and rent-raising, and it was husbands and fathers who waited for him by the shore road and, when their crude muzzle-loaders were useless against the steel of his waistcoat, gathered about him and smashed his skull with the butts of their guns. Nor did the anger of the people cease with his death, for when they brought his coffin to Dublin there were men who thought that the sewage waters of the Liffey would be a more suitable resting-place for the despoiler of a countryside than the quiet vaults of St. Michan's, and only for the batons of the police the mob would have had its way.

Mandy Logue was amongst kinsmen in Glasgow, and he came home with tales of the clannishness and mòrtas of it's Donegalmen.

"They have little now," he said to Anthony, "but the day is coming when they'll have more. I might settle down there myself." But he didn't settle in Glasgow. Be stayed at home and helped to feed her. He sent her potatoes, eggs, fowl—anything that the people had to sell. But the people hadn't much to sell. It was a poor countryside, and the was little to spare when the home mouths were filled.

*   *   *   *

Most of Mandy's merchandise went by Derry, but once a fortnight he sent a load by the *Ayr Maid*, a little cargo steamer that called at Milford on its way from Sligo and Galway. If Sandy Murchison, the big, red-bearded skipper had had his way the *Ayr Maid* would never have crept slowly up Mulroy, but Anthony had a contract with her owners and Murchison had to do as he was told. "You and your pig tatties," he would say to Mandy. "Why don't you keep them at home and fill your ain empty stomachs? If there was a heid on anyone in Campbell, Douglas, and Company I wou'dna have to face this tormented stretch of wather every fortnight."

Mandy was making money, but he was not satisfied. He was thinking all the time of the great, hungry, hammer-crazed towns along the Clyde, and he knew that Fanad couldn't feed them. "If you could see the Glasgow quays of a morning," he used to say to Anthony. "The Dublin boat comes up the river with the gulls about her rigging, and the lorries are waiting. As soon as the gangways are off they start to unload her. Manalive, you wouldn't believe it—cauliflowers, cabbage, leeks, scallions, turnips, carrots, spuds! Thousands of pounds' worth. And that's not just one morning. It's every morning!'

"Why don't you get them to grow that kind of stuff about here?"

"Where would they grow it?" asked Mandy patiently.

"On the sides of the hills is it? Sure any land they have is wanted for corn and potatoes, and they haven't half enough as it is. Vegetables? The only vegetables they can grow about here is an odd lock o' kale to feed the beasts in the winter?

"You were born in the wrong part of Ireland, I'm thinking. If you lived in Dublin you wouldn't have any bother filling the *Ayr Maid*."

"You don't need to be born in a place to make a living in it," said Mandy. The notion was in his head even then.

It was Anthony who suggested sending holly to Glasgow for the Christmas trade, but the idea came first from Dinny the Cobbler.

"You could sell anything in Glasgow," Dinny said one night. "Any mortal thing. If you had a creel o' eggshells or a burden o' benweeds you'd find folk ready to give you money for them. I saw a man gettin' two poun' ten there once for a load o' holly. Troth I did. Fifty shillings for a horse-load!" Mandy was enthusiastic when Anthony suggested that there might be money in holly.

"You're right," he said "We should have thought of it long ago. This is a hungry country but it grows a sight of holly. I'll write to McConnell and see what price it's likely to go."

For a full fortnight after that Mandy and Dinny went to the Long Wood every morning to cut holly. They left home before daylight, and they hid their slashers and hatchets when the morning's work was over.

Anthony helped them on Saturdays. It was sore work and he wasn't much good at it, but it was a welcome change from noisy Loughbuidhe.

"It's good to be out in the open air" he said to Dinny one morning when they had finished cutting. "I don't know why I ever started to teach."

"Have sense, Master" said Dinny. "There's more to farm work than fine, frosty mornings. There's claber, and hardship, and a struggle to find the rent. Where would I be but for the few shillings I make at the cobbling? Oh, no, Master. Stick to your rostrum and don't envy them that earns their meat be the sweat o' their brows."

The holly was loaded on carts by night and taken quietly to Mandy's store, but it did not escape the eye of Red Shuvlin. "Where are you goin' wi' all the holly?" he asked as Dinny carried in a big bundle. Dinny got rid of his load before he answered.

"Father Dan asked us to get him a lock for the Crib."

"Och, away outa that wi' you," said Shuvlin. "Sure you have more holly there than the whole diocese would use in a lifetime."

Dinny became confidential.

"You'll not tell a soul?"

"Divil a one, Dinny. Sure it's as safe with me as if you told it to the priest in the box."

"Well this is how it is. The holly is for beddin' turkeys."

"You must take me for a right lug," said Shuvlin.

"Sure as death," went on Dinny. "You see, when turkeys is bein' fattened for Christmas they must eat and eat or they won't be worth a hait. If they lie down they won't eat, so they must be kept standin' up. That's why they bed them on holly!'

Shuvlin was not convinced.

"Sure it would tear the feet off them."

"Not at all" said Dinny. "The turkeys I'm speakin' about are shod like horses."

Mandy made sixty pounds on the holly, and wanted Anthony to take half of it. He said it had been Anthony's idea, but Anthony said it had been Dinny's idea, and that his own work in the Long Wood wasn't worth half-a-crown.

In the end, after much wrangling, Anthony took ten pounds, which was only slightly less than what he got for three months' work in Loughhuidhe. Dinny got five pounds, and thought himself overpaid.

*   *   *   *

Mandy went to Dublin two years after his return from America. He wanted to have his share of the big money that could be made by feeding Glasgow, and he felt that Fanad wasn't the place for him. Anthony went to Dublin, too, just because Murchison of the *Ayr Maid* threw off his blue jacket on Milford quay one June morning.

Murchison mightn't have bothered, for it was the last consignment he was ever to take aboard for Mandy Logue, though the red-bearded Scotsman didn't know it at the time. And the fight should really have been Mandy's, for the potatoes were Mandy's, and it was Mandy who insisted that they should be stowed in a particular place in the hold. But Anthony, for some reason which he could never fully explain, had made the fight his own. The quarrel flared up suddenly, but it had been brewing for months.

"Don't give any orders on this boat, Logue," said Murchison.

"I'm only telling them where to put my potatoes," said Mandy.

"Well, keep your mouth shut. For two pins I'd throw you and your tatties into the tide-aye and any other Papist idolator that wants a coolin'."

He looked as if he could do it, for he was well over six feet, and heavy with muscle. Mandy was five inches smaller and a good three stone lighter, but he was a red-haired Fanadman, and he returned the challenge with interest.

"If you step off your flea-bitten tub, you firkin o' foul you, I'll smash your Scotch pus for you. I've had enough of your bullying."

Murchison vaulted the low rail and faced Mandy; He spoke quietly.

"Away home wi' ye, laddie. I could fight a dozen like ye, and if I started I might hurt you sore."

"Hurtin' is a game two can play at. Let's see if you can fight as well as you can boast."

"Have it your ain way," said Murchison. "But dinna blame me if your mither disne ken ye when I've finished wi' ye."

He threw off his cap and jacket, and folded his sleeves on broad, hairy arms. The deckhands and the men on the quayside gathered about.

"Wait a minute," cried Anthony. "I'll handle this."

"Stand back, Anthony." Mandy didn't want a champion. "I'll handle it myself."

Anthony pushed him aside and faced Murchison.

"Maybe you'd better tackle someone nearer your own height?"

"It makes no differ to me," said the Scotsman. "One or both. It doesn't matter. You'll have further to fall than the wee fellow."

The "wee fellow" still wanted to fight, but the men held him back.

"Let the Master do the fightin'" one of them shouted. "He's bigger not you. The captain should strike his match."

Anthony peeled off his coat and folded his sleeves. The Scot had the advantage of height, weight, and reach, and although Anthony was a trifle broader in the shoulder he hadn't half as much meat on him.

Murchison was a fighter, and he tried to get to close quarters at once. Anthony kept his distance. His right fist landed twice on the captain's nose, drawing blood but doing little damage. The man had a face like granite.

Anthony got two more blows home, and then Murchison dropped his guard and came for him head down. Anthony fended him off as best he could, but one of the Scotsman's wild punches caught him full on the ear and made his head sing.

The next time Murchison came rushing in Anthony struck heavily, left and right, to the body, and the big fellow winced in pain. He could take punishment on the face but he was fleshy amidships, and after two more body punches he became wary and tried to box. Anthony felt a little bit confident then, for the first time. He was scared of the wild punches. Anthony landed another left to the body, and then, when Murchison dropped his guard instinctively, he lashed a venomous uppercut to the point of the jaw. The blow would have dropped any ordinary man in his tracks, but Murchison was no ordinary man, and though he stumbled he recovered immediately and came in with both fists flailing. Anthony was taken unawares. One blow seemed to break the bridge of his nose. Another struck sparks from his right eye. Through a haze of pain he saw Murchison coming to pin him against the wall of the shed and pulp his head on the tough stone. He straightened his left arm with his full weight behind it, and prayed that the blow would check the rush and give him breathing-space. But he had no need of breathing space. Murchison measured his length on the cobble-stones, and he didn't get up again until he was helped up.

"I gie you best, laddie," he said, grinning wryly and spitting out a bloody tooth. " Gie us your hand, man. You're a bonnie fighter. It's not many a man can boast that he stretched Davy Murchison."

Dinny the Cobbler wet a handkerchief in the salt water and sponged the captain's face. It was a labour of love.

"Och, I'll do rightly," said Murchison. "I was never an oil-painting. Come on, now, every mither's son o' ye and take a swig o' the bottle. Win or lose there's nothing like a dram."

A month later the sign M. LOGUE, GENERAL MERCHANT, was taken down from over the store and there was a vacancy for a Principal in Loughbuidhe National School. Anthony had had his first bit of adventure that June day on Milford quay, and had liked the taste of it.

CHAPTER THREE

ANTHONY DOMICAN was bursting with certificates when he went down to St. John's Presbytery to be interviewed by Father Dunphy. He had a letter from the Principal of the Training College certifying that he was a young man of excellent character and high ability, a letter from Father O'Donnell of Loughbuidhe certifying that he had taught there with conspicuous success and had observed at all times a due sense of decorum, and a document which certified that he had completed his probationary period and satisfied the Department's inspectors. He also had a certificate that he could play the harmonium (though all he could play was one Benediction service and The Bluebells of Scotland), a certificate in rural science, and a birth certificate.

The world was his oyster.

Going down the quays he interviewed Father Dunphy, and answered the few questions which his glowing testimonials left unanswered. There was nothing to be afraid of. He knew his trade and he had a fine record. Any manager would be lucky to get him. He was not quite so confident when he sat in the dusty parlour waiting for the real Father Dunphy.

The priest came in humming a little faraway tune. He was a small man in the middle forties, and he wore a stained soutane from which several buttons were missing and a biretta that wasn't on straight. His face was small, but broad, his nose had a tilt to it that gave him a look of awareness, and his mild eyes were as blue as a hedge sparrow's egg. The song did not die away completely until he had shaken hands with Anthony.

"Ah Mr. Domican. How are you, Mr. Domican? It was good of you to call. Sit down, Mr. Domican." The voice was low-pitched, quiet, and distinct.

"I got your letter, Mr. Domican. I have it here."

He took a bundle of letters from his pocket and searched through them. "Ah, here it is"—this with an air of discovery. Then he put on his glasses and read through the application as if he was seeing it for the first time.

"Ah, these applications!" he went on, as if they were things which should be put down by legislation. "I got dozens and dozens of them, and all from excellent men—excellent men. It's really amazing the amount of talent that is available in the country. You were teaching in Donegal, Mr. Domican?"

"I was, Father."

"And what made you leave it?"

Anthony said that he thought there might be more opportunities in the city.

"I see, I see," said Father Dunphy. "This must be the flight from the land that I hear so much about. Well, well. You got First Division leaving training?"

Anthony nodded modestly.

"Though I was never very keen on First Division men myself," went on the priest. "Give me a middle man every time, a pass-by-the-grace-of-God man. They're better workers, more dependable."

Anthony said nothing. There seemed to be nothing to say.

"But of course," said Father Dunphy, "my predilection may be based on pure jealousy. I wasn't a gun in Rome. By no means. Just an ordinary, stupid student. However the point is scarcely relevant so we won't labour it now. I see you have a certificate in rural science."

" Yes, Father."

"A very useful subject, I think?"

"Yes, Father."

"In its proper place, of course," added the little priest, blandly. It isn't much use in Paradise Alley. Our school garden is made of concrete. We find that it wears better than anything else." The door opened then, and the frowsy, middle-aged housekeeper who had admitted Anthony came in without knocking.

"There's a person in the dining-room," she announced.

"Dear, dear! What an awkward time. Tell me this, Ellen—is the person of the male or the female persuasion?"

"It's a man," said Ellen. "Come about a christenin'."

"I'd better go and see him, I suppose. Will you excuse me, Mr. Domican?"

The priest went out, but the housekeeper remained.

"Good lodgings in Hope Street," she rapped out.

"Widda woman be the name of Mary O'Riordan. Very clean. Good food. Number six. Anyone will show you. Father Dunphy likes his teachers to live in the parish." Having said her piece she turned and went out, like a stolid, small-part actress. Her hands and her apron were in keeping with the dust of the room and did not augur well for the cleanliness of 6 Hope Street and its widda woman. Anthony peered through the glass of the bookcase and scanned the titles within. There were big, leather-bound theological works there, the poems of Scott and Moore, and a complete set of Dickens. Father Dunphy came back and found him standing.

"Do you read much, Mr. Domican?" Anthony didn't know how to answer this one. He felt that if he went one way he would he catechized, and that if he went the other he would be admonished. So he compromised and said "A little."

"Did you ever read Emerson on Self-Confidence?"

Anthony had not only read him, he could quote him and he did. "In every work of genius we recognize our own rejected thoughts. They come back to us with a certain alienated majesty." He would have gone on to the end of the fifty lines he had memorized for the oral test in his first year examination, but in view of what had happened already he judged it wiser to temper his display of learning, Father Dunphy gave a thin whistle. " So you read Emerson! Well, well. A meaty fellow, Emerson, but his theology is all wrong, of course. Now where were we? Ah, your certificates. I see you play the harmonium?"

"Yes, Father."

"Good." Then he added, contradicting himself: "It's not much of an instrument, of course—a makeshift—and these training college music certificates—well, I've seen them before."

Anthony swallowed in silence. He was thinking of the din in the college lecture hall, where a dozen men, most of whom had never seen a note of printed music before coming to college, had got off a few set pieces by sheer tactual memory, so that in due course they might be able to apply for vacancies where "instrumental music" was essential. Father Dunphy looked over his glasses.

"I suppose," he said, "you couldn't play Schubert or Beethoven?"

Anthony was only a young man looking for a job, but he had his limits.

"I could," he said solemnly, "—on a barrel-organ:'

The hedge-sparrow eyes twinkled once and then dimmed again.

"Well now that's very satisfactory," said Father Dunphy, rising. "I think you'll be very happy in Paradise Alley. You'll be able to start on Monday week, I suppose. You'd better see Mr. Rodney, the principal, in the meantime."

Anthony Domican was very young then. He didn't know Father Dunphy as he was to know, years later, Canon Dunphy, and, still later, the Venerable Archdeacon Dunphy—though the Archdeacon seldom got his highest title except on formal occasions, and held the second one so long that most of his parishioners forgot that he had ever been plain "Father." When you knew the Canon and his little ways you loved him in spite of them; when you didn't, he could be very aggravating. Anthony was rather dazed when he came out of the presbytery. Ellen was waiting for him. She pretended to be tying up a shrub but she was really trying to make sure of a respectable lodger for the widda woman.

"Mind what I told you. Hope Street. Number six, anyone'll show you. Riordan's the name"

There was a fresh wind coming up from the bay when he came out on to the quays. The tide was full, and the water sucked along the sides of the anchored ships and smacked against the ferry-steps. Cranes swung out with a run and a rattle and dumped their packages on the quay. Sack covered wicker baskets were being hoisted aboard the Glasgow steamer, and the packers, men and women, were snicking the stumps off cabbages with short, black-handled knives. Deep-chested horses tugged heavy lorries over the cobble-stones, and dockers came out from the quayside taverns wiping their mouths with the back of their hands.

Anthony had eyes and ears for everything. This would be his background from now on—the great, teeming port of Dublin. This would be his territory—from the Guinness Wharf at the Custom House to the Burns and Laird sheds, and on down then to the very Point of the Wall. These muscular, corduroyed men were the fathers of his pupils, and this was what the boys of Paradise Alley would become in their turn—great, strapping, swearing dockers who could lift a sack or drink a pint with any man alive. (He was to modify this prophecy in time, for the great chests and thighs of the dockside were not bred in Paradise Alley, and the giants who loaded Dublin's ships were Dubliners only by adoption. They came from Wicklow, and Cavan, and Tipperary, from the Kingdom of Kerry and the County of Mayo, and they did not pass on their physique to the children they reared in tenement rooms and on starvation wages). It was all so different from the quiet mountain valley where his father taught, and from lonely Loughbuidhe, that a wave of home-sickness came over him. It was the middle of August and the corn was changing colour in the little stony fields about Mulroy. But the home-sickness did not stay with him long. He was young and full of dreams, and he had a job in his fist.

* * * *

In spite of Ellen's advice Anthony kept clear of the widda Riordan and stayed with Mandy in a house in Drumcondra. The lodgings were clean and comfortable, the food was good and well-cooked, and although Anthony thought that twelve shillings a week was extortion, Mandy told him that he couldn't get good digs for less. Mrs. Mason, the landlady, was a Scotswoman, a sea captain's widow and a very righteous body. She kept her house shining and decorated its walls with flaming texts from the Holy Book, admonitions to sinners, statistics of deaths from alcoholic poisoning, potted proverbs, and framed questions like "Are you washed in the Blood of the Lamb?" She made no secret of her belief in the maxim "Be just and fear not" and she told the world that the Lord was her Shepherd. She regarded herself as a missionary in a heathen country and had a notion that some day Rome would burn the house over her head. In the meantime she was content to make a frugal living by feeding heretics.

Mandy was a month with Mrs. Mason before he got anything to do, and although he paid his board regularly and didn't break up the furniture she wasn't too pleased with him. There was no place in Mother Mason's esteem for a young gentleman who did no work, and she hinted that Mandy would find a headline in the Bible. Anthony, being a school master, and a "steady man," she regarded as a rock of virtue, and she tried to enlist his help in the fight for Mandy's respectability.

"Could you no try to get some sense into Mr. Logue's poor heid," she used to say. "My, O, my, Mr. Domican, it's terrible to see a young laddie who hasnie a steady job."

She needn't have worried. Mandy didn't want a job. He worked for a month in a shipping office, so that he could get to know gaffers and stevedores and learn how vegetables were packed. He was feeling his way, spying out the enemy's country, and as soon as he had learned all the quays could teach him he got a job as a salesman in the vegetable market. He was a very minor salesman and he didn't earn much more than he gave to Mother

Mason, but he was satisfied. He would have worked willingly for nothing, and he would have been dear at the price.

He learned the technique of buying and selling, the most profitable lines, the names of the biggest growers. In the evenings and at the week-ends he cycled round Santry and Swords, Kimmage and Rialto, Rush and Malahide, to see the fields that were to make his fame. His attack on the vegetable trade was planned like a campaign, and the battlefield was mapped and reconnoitred before he fired the first shot.

When at last he rented a stand in the market he wanted to christen the firm "Logue and Domican, Fruit and Vegetable Merchants," but Anthony stood firm.

"Very well," said Mandy. "Have it your own way for the present. It'll be no bother changing the signboard when you change your mind. You'll come in with me yet and be glad to get away from school mastering—it's a pauper's trade."

He spent a lot of time planning the lay-out of his billheads and he finished up with "M. Logue, Fruit and Vegetable Merchant, Potato Factor, and Commission Agent." And as soon as the first batch was printed he sent a hundred of them home to Lahardan, where they were put on display on the counter of his father's shop. Lahardan, however, did not think very much of Mandy's venture. Had he been planning to sell furniture, cod, meat, sewing machines, or flake meal, Lahardan might have seen in him even then the makings of a merchant prince, but the only vegetables which grew along Mulroy, save for the few carrots, parsnips, and turnips in the priest's garden, were the tall, coarse, spindly cabbages which were fed to the beasts.

"Be me soul, I dunno," said Dinny the Cobbler when he saw the billheads and heard the news. "I don't think anyone could make a living be selling kale!"

CHAPTER FOUR

THE Dodder joins the Liffey from the right, and at the last minute, becoming a tributary only when the taste of the salt water is in its mouth: but the Tolka, as if it remembered that Saint Mobhi built a monastery on its banks, and that the valiant grandson of Brian died, with a Dane in each hand, in its waters, keeps its independence to the last and enters the sea a little to the left of the Liffey. Between the Tolka and the Liffey, on an artificial peninsula which started life as a sandbank, lies Paradise Alley and the North Wall docks—a place of wharves and ships, sheds and granaries, tangled railway lines and sea-serving canals, cattle yards, coal yards, timber yards, and backyards. Its days are filled with the rattle of lorries and steam-waggons, the whirring of cranes and winches, the swelling scream of whistles; and at night the follow-my-leader clanking of rolling-stock introduces a new note into a symphony that has for metronome the suck and surge of the tide against the quays..

Paradise Alley is a short street on the Tolka side of dockland, and it runs along the shore of the little back bay that the North Wall peninsula cuts off from the Liffey estuary. On one side it is bounded by the low sea wall, and on the other by the wall of St. John's School, the wall of Jenkinson's soap factory, and the wall of Ryan's building yard. Beyond Ryan's yard it takes a sharp turn to the right (so that it is not an alley at all), changes its name to Donegan's Wharf, and connects a succession of warehouses, coalyards, stables, cattle lairs, and public-houses with the quays proper.

Paradise Alley National School, when Anthony Domican came to it in 1903, was a three-roomed one-storey building. In later years two more rooms were built at right angles to the main structure, and still later two wooden sheds were Built against the wall of the playground. The sheds, which lasted well into the nineteen thirties might have been preserved in the interests of students of social progress, but were eventually sold for firewood. They presented no difficulties to the demolition gang, as they consisted simply of one side-wall, two end-walls, a galvanized roof, and a partition. The second side-wall was the high pebble dashed wall of the playground itself, and a fine example of the way in which an existing structure can be utilised when schools are being enlarged. Quite an amount of wood was saved, too, by dispensing with a floor, and though the bare footed scholars —who numbered about one in five—found the concrete of the yard a little cold under their feet in winter-time, they never complained. They were not used to luxury, and the school sheds were only a little bit worse than the draughty tenement rooms in which they lived. The upper door of the sheds ended a good two inches from the concrete, so that when the rain seeped in on wet days, when the pupils sat on the desks and put their feet on the seats, beneath which the stream gently flowed. In order to give each class in the school a chance to sample these airy premises the time table provided for a change of room every half-hour, so that children who had been made sleepy by the fumes of the coke fires in the other rooms were freshened up at intervals by the wind and the rain. These improvements, which increased the capacity of the school (and increased its death-rate by a negligible ratio), did not, however, come until much later. In 1908, when Anthony Domican signed the Paradise Alley roll for the first time, the school consisted only of the three rooms which bordered the sea road. In one of these rooms, separated from the other two by a narrow corridor which was wood-lined at the bottom, glass-lined at the top, and dotted at child-height with coatpegs, Alfred Mendelssohn Rodney, the Principal, taught fifth, sixth, and seventh standards. In the second, a slightly smaller room, Tom Lehanty taught third and fourth. In the third, the smallest of the three, Anthony taught first and second.

Teaching in Paradise Alley was very different from teaching in Loughbuidhe. The children were more precocious, less disciplined, harder to teach, and poorer. Poverty in Loughbuidhe meant ragged clothes and bare feet (though in summer every child went barefooted by choice and custom), but in Paradise Alley it meant cold and hunger. Intelligence ripened slowly in Loughbuidhne—the way God meant it to ripen: in Paradise Alley misery spurred it on to premature development. But, fortunately, Anthony's pupils were not all under-nourished. At least half of them got nearly enough to eat. The first time he stood before his class in Paradise Alley he learned something which he had never learned in Loughbuidhe- that children are the most observant creatures on God's green earth. The burning, concentrated stare of fifty pairs of eyes pierced him through. His appearance was recorded like a photograph in every mind. They saw, each and every child of them, the pattern of his suit, the deep black of his hair, the whole long length of him. He was itemized, inventoried, analysed; and all he saw was a blur of faces.

It was almost a week before they listened to him properly. They devoured him, not his words. They were more interested in his accent than in what he was saying. They stored up impressions which they were to discuss amongst themselves at lunch-time and with their parents in the evening, and until his newness wore off he could do little teaching. But they were, on the whole, a lovable batch. They lived in tenements along the river, or in pea-pod houses off the quays; they could curse as well as their fathers could, and they had learned many things before their time; but they had energy, cunning, a limited and conditional loyalty, and a zeal for life. He never forgot his first batch of pupils—Muckser, Joeboy, Smasher, Magaldy, Bottleneck, Larboy Lynch, and Tiddler Kennedy; especially Tiddler. The Kennedys were given to alliteration, for Tiddlers Father was known as Touser and his uncle as Taffystick. Anthony found out all this the first day he slapped Tiddler. It wasn't much of a slap, as slaps go, and Tiddler had deserved it, but it caused a sensation. Tiddler yelped round the room and swore that his father would come down to give Anthony 'a baitin'. So Tiddler got two more slaps. He wasn't hurt, but he was obviously astonished, and so were the rest of the pupils. Anthony asked Rodney about it at lunch-time, and Rodney shook his head regretfully.

"I should have warned you," he said, making it sound like a final farewell. "Touser Kennedy has a fearful reputation. You had better go gently with his offspring."

Tiddler didn't come back after lunch. Tiddler wasn't Used to being slapped, and was showing it. His absence had the quality of a threat, and as Anthony walked up the quays that evening be had the uncomfortable feeling that people were nudging each other and talking about him. There were no absentees from Anthony's class next morning, and each time the wind blew the outer door open every head turned. Just before playtime door banged and this time it wasn't the wind. Heavy boots stamped up the corridor, and the door of the classroom was thrown open with a violence that knocked a picture off the wall.

But no one appeared. Touser liked to dramatize his approach.

"Come out here you long stockin' of a country schoolmaster till I bate you good-looking. Come out here, mountainy-man and I'll learn you something for a change."

The avenger entered the room ponderously, magnificently. He was bigger than the captain of the *Ayr Maid* and as solid as a Clydesdale. His fleshy face was red from drink and anger. As he walked slowly up the classroom he flung his coat amongst the wildly expectant pupils, spat with relish on his spade hands, and announced that he was going to tear the 'murderer' into little pieces. Anthony wanted to run but he had no place to run to, and then, suddenly, his panic was replaced by a wild elation and the battle fury came on him. Once again he was standing on Milford quay, and as the enormous hands reached out to strangle him he struck hard to the point of the chin. It was less like a fight than like a conjuring trick. Touser went down like a bag of flour, and he lay where he fell. A trickle of blood welled out about his face, and his head lay against one of the iron desk-legs. If he's dead, thought Anthony, I can plead provocation and self-defence. There was no sound in the room but the ticking of the clock and the thumping of Anthony's heart. He called one of the boys.

"Go out to Mr. Rodney's room, and ask him to lend me four of his biggest boys."

Touser opened his eyes just before the burial party arrived, but he moaned and closed them again. Anthony and the four seniors lifted him from the floor, dragged him out into the corridor, and dumped him on the footpath outside the school Muckser Madigan followed carrying Touser's coat, and he placed it, with due reverence, over the face of the fallen.

Touser recovered in about five minutes, and by that time he had caused a traffic block. When he got to his feet he had the help and advice of errand boys, lorry drivers, cattle drovers, and shawled women. He showed no inclination to renew the combat, and he suffered himself to be led off in the general direction of the Anchor Tavern. Nor did he bear Anthony any ill will, for he sent Tiddler to school the following morning with a note which read: "dere sir you done rite when you cloct me slap Tommy any time he need it yr obednt serv danl Kennedy." The tale of Touser's downfall lost nothing in the telling. The children brought it home with them at lunch time, women standing at open tenement doors told it to coalmen and bakers, the dockers brought it back with them to the quays. That evening when Anthony walked home, past the great cliff buildings from which grain was funnelled into waiting lorries, past the manure-works and its chugging, yellow-vapoured exhaust pipe, past the wash-lines of the tenements, he felt again that people were nudging each other and talking about him. They were waiting for him as for a public procession. He was the new teacher who had guzzled the life out of Touser Kennedy, walloped him round the school, beaten the lard out of him with his own studded belt, and, finally, left him for dead on the cold pavement. Not a word of a lie. God's truth. Didn't the chislers see it all, and didn't Mangan and Mulligan stop the lorry when they saw him lyin' on the pavement. Anthony Domican was firmly established in dockside folklore. He was Jem Roche and John Fitzsimons, a man to be pointed at, a man to touch your cap to. If you looked crooked at him he'd paste you up agen the wall.

Rodney came into Anthony's room as soon as Touser had been carried out. He was a man in the fifties; bald, low-sized, and bearded. He wore a long-skirted, cutaway, old-fashioned coat, a wide-winged collar and a black cravat. Rodney was every inch a Principal.

"Dear me, Domican!" he spluttered. "This is a terrible business. What will Father Dunphy say? What will the Office say? We might even have a legal action. We might have this fellow Kennedy down again to-morrow— that is, if he recovers. Anything may happen."

"Anything," said Anthony.

"I'll back you, of course—to the hilt—but I wish it hadn't happened. You should be more circumspect, young man."

Tom Lehanty, the first assistant, took a different view. Lehanty was a stout, medium-sized man of forty-five, quiet voiced, inoffensive, and packed with humour.

"I'd have given a quarter's salary to have seen it happen," he said,

"Touser Kennedy I Be the Lord Harry!"

"Rodney isn't so pleased. He's wondering what the Office will say. I might get the sack."

"Divil a sack. Sure Touser will be too ashamed of himself to make any complaint, and even if he does complain what can he make of it? He's an established public menace. He came down here in what the bobby next door to me would call 'an attitude calculated to provoke a breach of the peace,' and he got what he was looking for."

"And what about Father Dunphy? Will he get to hear about it?"

"Will the sun rise to-morrow? Sure Father Dunphy gets to know everything, and he'd want to be deaf, dumb, and blind not to hear about this. But don't let that worry you. Father Dunphy knows the Kennedys. And don't let Rodney make you panicky. You have nothing to be afraid of,"

"Still I'm sorry it ever happened."

" I'm not sorry I'm delighted. Why, the noise of the Blow you struck to-day will echo in every school in Dublin. You have lit a fire which will never be extinguished, and We all share in your glory. Don't for any sake, wish the deed undone. Of course, your methods wouldn't suit all of us. Non-combatants like me have our own ways of handling obstreperous parents."

"And how do you manage it?"

"I'll tell you. Some oul' fella comes down to ask me why I punished Tommy Ryan. If I think he's open to reason I try reason. But if he looks like a man who'd put my eye in a sling I say "Tommy Ryan!"-surprised like, did I punish Tommy Ryan? That's strange. I don't remember punishing Tommy. He's the cleverest boy in the class-plenty of brains- an outstanding boy. But he's not too fond of work. A bit lazy you know. If he only worked a bit harder he'd be a brilliant scholar. And sure after that I have the man purring like a cat at milking time. He didn't mean to complain like-he only thought he'd call down like-Tommy is a good boy like but sort of lazy like. And he ends up by begging me to punish Tommy oftener and beat a bit of sense into him . It's a technique which is guaranteed to soothe the most savage parental breast.

Father Dunphy arrived shortly before three. He was wreathed in smiles, he hummed his little tune, and he dabbed at the floor with the point of his umbrella like a man feeling his way.

" How are you, Mr. Domican?" he said, shaking hands.

"You're looking very well. Very well."

"And how are the boys?" He turned to the class and grounded his umbrella like a rifle. "Sit down, boys, sit down. Johnny, you're just as fat as ever. You must be eating too much suet pudding, Johnny. Is Tommy Riordan in to-day? Ha, I thought not. I missed his black head. I don't like boys to be absent from school. Hands up all the boys who are never avoidably absent from school." Every hand in the class went up.

"That's good," said Father Dunphy. "If you come to School regularly and say your prayers you won't go far wrong. And don't forget Confessions this evening. Hands up every boy who will be in the church this evening at a quarter to five." After several other questions, each of which led to the raising of hands, he turned to go. Anthony waked to the door with him and two boys opened it for them. "Come out to the hall with me, Mr. Domican- that's right. What's this I hear about Mr. Kennedy meeting with an accident? I hope he wasn't too badly hurt!'

"I hope not," said Anthony, looking straight into the blue, child-like eyes that gave nothing away.

"Please God he'll be all right," said Father Dunphy. "We'll both say a prayer for him. Won't we now?"

Anthony restrained an impulse to raise his right hand. "Ah, yes, we'll pray for him." Father Dunphy was examining the ground very intently. "I didn't know you were a pugilist, Mr. Domican."

"I'm not, Father. I have no qualifications in boxing."

"No, no. There was no mention of the noble art in your testimonials. Rural science, yes . . . harmonium, yes . . . first division, yes . . . but nothing about boxing."

Anthony turned on an unwinking stare.

"They didn't teach it in the training college!'

"I suppose not," said Father Dunphy placidly. "There is something to be said for fisticuffs, no doubt, but it's scarcely an academic subject. There is a time and a place for everything. Order is the big thing, the grand thing, and order is simply everything in its own place. Isn't that right?"

"It is, Father."

"Certainly it is. Walk down to the door with me now. Order is the big thing, and blood-letting disrupts order."

"I'll be frank with you, Father. If you're speaking of this Kennedy business- well, I'm sorry it happened but I have no apologies to offer. If I hadn't hit him he would have made mincemeat of me. What should I have done? Jumped out of the window?"

The little priest patted him on the shoulder.

"My dear boy. You're quite excited! I'm not blaming you-not blaming you at all. I'm speaking in perfectly general terms. But you know my difficulty. I'm the manager of the school and I have my responsibilities. There's the Archbishop, and there's the Education Office. I have to answer for everything."

"I'm sorry if I made things difficult for you, Father, but Kennedy is the one to blame."

They were standing outside the front door then and Father Dunphy was making triangles in the gravel with the point of his umbrella.

"Of course he is to blame. I know that, Mr. Domican.

But you know what the official mind is. I hope there will be no repercussions. Please God there won't. Kennedy is fond of the bottle, but he's a decent enough big slob of a man."

The tide was full, and a boy was sailing a small, brown varnished dinghy a stone's throw from the sea-wall. Howth was bareheaded in the sun, and the sky was blue and white.

"Look at it," said Father Dunphy, taking in the whole scene with a proprietary sweep of his umbrella. "Where would you find the like of it in any city? The sea coming right to the very door. I envy you, Mr. Domican. My house is facing the wrong way, and whenever I open my windows I'm choked with coal dust!'

He shook hands then.

"Good-bye, Mr. Domican, and God love you. You'll be very happy here, I know. I'm glad you're getting on so well."

"Thank you, Father."

"Take care of yourself, my boy."

The priest walked a yard or so, then turned and came back.

"All the same, though," he whispered, "you must have hit him a terrible wallop."

CHAPTER FIVE

THE firm of M. Logue, Fruit and Vegetable Merchant, Potato Factor, and Commission Agent, gave employment in the beginning only to Mandy himself and a porter named Corny Madigan. Mandy stood at the market gate at six in the morning and bought vegetables from men who had started off with their laden carts shortly after midnight from the sandy, sea-warmed peninsula of Rush-a place of small, intensively-worked farms and red-necked, broad shouldered, industrious men. Rush brought Mandy sprouts, carrots, parsnips, lettuce, peas, and early potatoes. His main-crop potatoes came from Louth and Armagh, and his cabbage from fields in Kimmage, Rialto, Santry, and Dolphin's Barn. His fruit he bought from the Liverpool agents, who called with their price-lists every morning and, wired their orders to Merseyside. In the beginning Mandy didn't buy very much from anyone, but within a couple of years he was buying cabbage by the field and taking potatoes in fifty-ton lots from the Portadown factors. By that time he had a second porter, two salesmen, and a lady clerk who worked in a six-by-ten hut.

During his first year in the market he heard that a navy flotilla was to spend a fortnight in Kingstown, and through a friend in Glasgow he got the contract for the Officers' Mess. The navy was fond of cucumbers, so Mandy wired to Covent Garden for thirty boxes. Anthony was in the market when the cucumbers arrived. It was a Saturday morning, and there was little business doing. As soon as the cucumbers were unloaded and stacked, Red Stacey, an enormous Corkman who was auctioneer for Melville and Crabtree, walked over to Mandy's stand. He took his pipe from his mouth, spat in the direction of the boxes, and said

"Cucumbers?"

"Yes," said Mandy.

"Have you sold many cucumbers since you started?" asked Red drily.

"Never stocked them before," said Mandy

"And you'll never stock them again, believe me. If you had thirty cucumbers instead of thirty boxes of them you wouldn't sell them in a month of Sundays, if you take my advice you'll pack the whole lot of them back to London right now. You'll never sell them," Mandy tried to look as green as the cucumbers.

"I don't know about that."

"Well, you'll know before long if you don't take my advice. I'm only telling you for your own good. If you keep them cucumbers you'll lose a hatful of money."

"There might be a demand for them," said Mandy.

"There might indeed," laughed Stacey. "And there might be a demand for robins' eggs and tin whistles. You'd never how. All right, me bucko! Have it your own way. But don't say afterwards that we didn't warn you. You can't sell fancy stuff in this market."

But Mandy did sell fancy stuff. He sold not only cucumbers but asparagus, seakale, artichokes, and spinach, and he sold them well. The navy had a delicate palate and it didn't quibble about prices. The petty officer who brought down the cheques on settling day got a couple of pounds for his trouble, but though this item did not appear on any of the invoices it wasn't Mundy who paid it. The market began to have a new respect for Mandy. He was a deep one. You couldn't be up to these northerners. They would steal the eye out of your head and tell you that you looked better without it. The trouble about the navy was that it didn't stay very long in one place, so when the warships sailed away from Kingstown Mandy turned his attention to the army. He made some discreet enquiries, distributed a few pound notes, and got the contracts for the Sergeants' Mess in Portobello and the Officers Mess in Beggars' Bush. And this was only the beginning. As time went on he got business from barracks all over the country, from the Curragh and Fermoy, from Templemore and Tipperary. The army, like the navy, paid well and did not study price lists too keenly. It wanted American eating apples- York Imperials, Newtown Pippins, Ben Davis; it wanted Jaffa oranges; it wanted figs, raisins, dates, bananas, and pineapples; and it paid up promptly on the third of each month. The non-commissioned officers who did the buying expected a little commission, and they got it. It was all very pleasant and gentlemanly.

Mandy might if he had wished, have indulged in bribery on a much bigger scale, but his conscience would not allow him to rob even a mighty organisation like the army, and he pretended to be stupid when mess sergeants hinted that the system of prerequisites was capable of expansion. One Sergeant, a little cockney, adopted more direct methods. He arrived on the twenty-ninth of the month with a bundle of invoices which did not tally with any goods which M. Logue had supplied to the Officers Mess.

"Where did you get these from? " asked Mandy. Bill flicked the peak of his cap and winked.

"Use your bloomin 'ead, guvnor. You puts 'em down on the bloomin' account, I initials 'em and no one's any the wiser. Get me? Fifty-fifty when I brings down the cheque"

"But I couldn't do that," said Mandy.

"Why not?" Bill was very surprised. "There's no danger—none in the wide world. Easy as falling off an ammunition waggon."

"But it's not honest."

"Gorblimey, guvnor, if you're honest you shouldn't be supplying the harmy. No one ever refused me before. 'Struth, it's a knockout. When I thinks of the perks we used to get in India—rice merchants, tea merchants, butchers —the whole bloomin' lot. Course I respect a man wot as' 'is principles, though I never 'ad any myself. No 'arm done, guvnor. Mum's the word."

Before the coming of the lady clerk Mandy brought his books home to Mrs. Mason's in the evenings, and Anthony gave him a hand with the accounts. He also helped in the market on Saturday mornings-though Saturday was a quiet day-and intermittently during the holidays. Mandy gave him a fawn-coloured coat, a salesman's book, and a leather money-bag, but he couldn't give him the instinct for business that went with the Logues.So although Mandy pressed him time and again to give up teaching and learn the tricks of the fruit and vegetable business Anthony knew that his place was in Paradise Alley. But, during his second summer holiday, he gave the market a month's trial. He rose early, he booked orders, he sold barrels of apples and loads of york cabbage, but he felt all the time that he was merely a dummy in Mandy's shop window. Anthony saw the colour and drama of the market—pippins from Oregon, oranges from Spain and Palestine, crates of strawberries from the Bann valley.

Mandy saw one thing only-money coming in, money going out, and the balance always on the right side. Anthony was a spectator in the market. He liked it as a child likes a pantomime. He liked watching the lumbering farm labourers leading their pyramid-piled carts of cabbage to the auctioneer's hammer; he liked to listen to the quick backchat of buyers, sellers, porters, and vanmen; he liked reading the lettering on the tissue papers in which the oranges were wrapped-*Pedro Suarez y hijos, Naranjas, Sevilla.* But Mandy wasn't a spectator. It was his play, and he was acting in it. If Anthony had gone into partnership with Mandy the firm of Logue and Domican might have been no less successful than the firm of Logue and Sons (the 'sons' came later) was afterwards to become. Anthony knew his own assets; he was careful, prudent, and pessimistic. But he knew also that the qualities which he had to bring to the proposed partnership could be bought with any sober clerk at a few pounds a week. His place was in the wings, and he knew it. He liked to watch Corny Madigan knock the first hoop off a barrel of American apples, tap up the second, prise out the pieces of the lid, and expose a level circle of fruit. He liked watching the hawkers judge a case of onions by prodding the outer rows with knowing fingers, and listening to the raucous, fluent auctioneers who sold loads of cabbage as quickly as a kerbside quack could sell a bottle of corn cure. He liked going round to the Daisy Market, an annexe of the main building, where you could buy cups, buckets, tweed caps, legs of mutton, bags of coal, children's toys, alarm clocks, last year's magazines, overmantels, or lead piping. But because he didn't like buying and selling he refused to let his name go up on Mandy's signboard and clung tightly to Paradise Alley.

He stayed in Paradise Alley, but he got to know the market and the people who worked there-people like Red Stacey, who auctioned from seven to ten in the morning and then ate half a pound of steak for his second breakfast. Red "took stock" every evening for Melville and Crabtree, subtracting the numbers of cases and boxes sold during the day from the numbers which had been in stock the previous evening. Daily stocktaking was absolutely essential, for during the busy hours the trade was so fast and so furious, the tangle of vans, porters, directions, bargainings, and bids so bewildering, that the salesmen's pencils could not always keep pace, and it was quite possible for one or more uncharged items to be loaded on to customers' vans. Whenever discrepancies were revealed the porters would be called in to scratch their heads and remember what they had loaded for Fagan of John Street, Mrs. Magthorpe of the Coombe, or Big Bunty of Ranelagh. Sometimes the scratching revealed the destination of the missing items, but if it didn't the loss wasn't Melville and Crabtree's. Stacey had a very simple way of dealing with mysteries of this kind- if it was a case of oranges short, for instance, he simply charged an extra case of oranges to every customer who had bought anything during the day. All but one, as a general rule, deducted the surcharge, and that one paid up in due course. Sometimes more than one customer paid for the missing package, but this, in Stacey's opinion, was all to the good. Occasionally, barristers on their way to the Four Courts from Green Street, doctors from Merrion Square, bank managers, and other visitors from the outside world stopped at Melville and Crabtree's and bought cases of fruit for their private houses. Most of them paid cash, but some of them simply gave their names and addresses and got space in the ledgers. It was difficult to get money from people like these, for they were too respectable to sue, and the market collectors got little shrift at the tradesmens' entrances. Red Stacey had a special way of collecting small debts like these-he sent for 'The Horse Hourigan.'

The Horse spent most of his time in or about Donohoe's public-house. Drinking was his profession, but his practice never equalled his thirst, and though he earned more than his share of pints by holding horses, polishing the windscreens of motor-cars, and running errands, and still more by plain cadging, be was never, except at festivals like Christmas, too drunk to collect accounts for Melville and Crabtree. The Horse, when he visited the homes of the mighty, never, descended to the basement level of the tradesmen's entrance. He knocked at the hall-door, and as soon as it opened he placed one foot on the step and announced business as if he was speaking to someone on the far side of the street. The man of the house wasn't at home? That didn't matter. The Horse was willing to wait, but he wasn't willing to wait on the doorstep. He waited in the hall and smoked patiently. But when the Horse smoked he spat almost all the time and with a deplorable sense of direction. So although the man of the house might not be at home, whoever was at home-wife, child, or maid- scraped up the money somehow and got The Horse off the premises.

* * * *

On the morning when Anthony went early to the market he had breakfast about ten o'clock in Delahunty's restaurant in Roper's Lane. It was a rough and ready place: the tables were covered with oil-cloth, the cups were as thick as a man's lip, and the tea was strong as the country carters wanted it. But it was clean, and near the market, and it suited men who were hungry and in a hurry. One morning when Anthony was breakfasting in Delahunty's a small, middle-aged man who was at the same table asked him what county he came from.

"I knew it was somewhere in the north," he said when Anthony answered, "but I wasn't sure whether it was Derry or Donegal."

His own accent was Scots, and he spoke with clear, chiselled consonants. He was dressed in black, with a white shirt, a stiff high-necked collar, and a thin, old-fashioned tie. His face was lined and rugged and great creases played about his mouth as he chewed his bread and butter.

"My name is Devern," he went on "and strangely enough, I'm a Donegalman myself. I was born in Fanad, on the shores of Mulroy. Do you know that part?"

"I ought to," said Anthony. "I spent every summer there since I was able to walk-with cousins who lived in a place called Lahardan."

"I don't remember many of the place-names," said Devern. "I left there when I was five."

"An early start."

"It was early and it was sudden." Devern buttered a slice of bread carefully. "And I've never been back. I'm nearly sixty years in Glasgow."

"You weren't the only Donegalman who went to Glasgow."

Devern considered the remark for a little while. "Aye, many's the one took a single ticket on the Derry boat. And many's the one went the way I went-with the hunger drivin' him and nothing with him but the few duds on his back. Leitrim was a right scoundrel, by all accounts. I remember seeing his black cattle knee-deep in my father's corn the day he threw us out. The harvest the poor man sowed-God be good to him-was ripe for the cutting the day he was evicted. We had but one cow, but we drove her to Derry and put her aboard the boat. There's things a man disne forget in a hurry."

They waked back to the market together. Anthony stopped at Mandy's stand.

"Is this where you work?" asked Devern.

"Now and again," said Anthony. "I give a hand on Saturdays, and sometimes during the holidays. Mandy Logue-that red fellow over there-is my cousin. He comes from Mulroy. But I'm a teacher."

"A teacher! Do you tell me. Well, I never got much schoolin' myself until I grew up and went to night classes. Maybe you have work to do now, so I'll not be keepin' you, Mr.____. "

"Domican," said Anthony.

"I enjoyed our little chat, Mr. Domican, and I'd like to continue it. Maybe you'd have dinner with me to-night? You'd be doing me a great favour. I'm staying at the Gresham. Could you come along about seven?"

"I'd like to, Mr. Devern."

"Thanks very much, Mr. Domican. And if your cousin would care to come he'll he very welcome."

Red Stacey appeared as soon as Devern went.

"Don't tell me you've roped in old Charley Devern." he said. "After Logue selling the cucumbers I'd believe anything of you northerners. You'd make a living where I'd starve."

"Who's Devern anyway?" asked Anthony.

"Who's Devern?" Stacey put on a look of innocence.

"Maybe he's the Shah of Persia. Maybe he's full-back for Shelbourne. Or maybe, again, he's one of the minstrels at the Tivoli. You never could tell."

"Devern" said Mandy when Anthony asked him.

"He's the biggest name in the Glasgow vegetable trade. He buys more than the rest of them put together. And he's asked us to dinner! Angus Gordon, his buyer, is leaving him, I hear, and he might be looking for someone to take his place. This is the chance of a lifetime."

Devern gave them a good dinner, and seemed inclined to talk. Mandy said very little. He spoke modestly of his own business and was very deferential to his host.

"Aye, I've done well," said Devern in answer to a question of Anthony's. "I'm worth a good deal of money now, and I started with next to nothing."

He twirled the stem of his wine-glass.

" But I'm a lonely man," he went on. "My wife died five years ago, my only son is in South Africa, and my daughter is married and living in London. I see her three or four times a year maybe."

"You must have had a struggle in the beginning," said Mandy.

"There was a lot of luck in it, too Mr. Logue. It was sheer chance that sent me into the vegetable business."

He looked up then, as if asking permission to go on.

"As I was telling Mr. Domican to-day, my father and mother were evicted by Lord Leitrim nearly sixty years ago. I had two brothers then- one was killed afterwards in a mine explosion-the other went to America forty years ago and was never heard of since. I was only five at the time.

"We went to Glasgow and brought our one cow with us. My mother herded the cow on the grass round the pitheads and sold the milk. My father and one of my brothers got work in the mines. I was sent to school. But as soon as I was fit for the mines down I went. I was leading pit ponies and mine trucks before I was twelve. In the winter months we never saw the light of day except on a Sunday."

"How long were you in the mines" asked Anthony.

"More than ten years," said Devern. "It was hard work, but by the time I was able to swing a pick I was making good money. I had fifty pounds in the bank before I was twenty-three. It was a lot of money in those days. But I wasn't satisfied, I wanted to be buying and selling. It was in my blood. So one day-I was on the night shift at the time- I went to an auction at a farm outside Glasgow and bought a field of potatoes for thirty pounds. I didn't know the value of them. I just bought by instinct-the way I would have bought scrap-metal or corsets. "When I was turning to pay the auctioneer, and wondering what under God I'd do with the spuds, a big stout man comes rushing up. He was a baker, and he wanted the spuds badly- they put spuds in bread in those days. So I sold him half the field for twenty pounds, on condition that he carted all the spuds into the city at digging time and left half of them at my store."

"It was a good one," said Mandy.

Devern laughed and lived his victory over again.

"And the best part of it was," he went on, "that I hadn't a store. Damn the one. But I rented one when the time came, and I hired a horse and cart and hawked my potatoes from door to door. I was still working in the night shift at the mine, so I didn't get much sleep. Then the housewives began to ask me why I didn't bring them carrots and cabbage as well, so I started going to the market in the morning to buy vegetables. That meant going straight from the mine to the market, so I gave up the mine."

"You did right," said Mandy.

"It seems so," said Devern. "I put another horse and cart on the road after a while. I opened a shop, and then another. Things went well with me. Now I have ten shops and a big wholesale business as well."

There was no boastfulness in what he said. He was a lonely man, and he wanted to talk.

"Do you come often to Dublin?" asked Anthony.

"I used to, but since I sent over Angus Gordon to buy for me I haven't come so often. Angus will be leaving me soon to start up on his own, so I just took a run over to look about me and get the feel of the market You know Angus?"

Mandy nodded.

"I do, Mr. Devern. You couldn't be in the vegetable trade in Dublin and not know Angus Gordon. A good man, I'd say."

"He's all that," said Devern. "But for this last while back he has been giving more attention to his own plans than to the business of Charles Devern. Not that I blame him, of course ."

"Of course not," said Mandy.

"A man must look after himself," said Devern, "and Gordon will do well on his own. He has plenty of push in him. A fine lad is Angus, and I wish him well. But I'll have to get a new buyer."

"So you will, Mr. Devern," Mandy tried to look as If this was a consequence he hadn't foreseen. "But you won't have any difficulty finding a buyer."

Devern shook his head.

"I'm not so sure about that. I can pick and choose, I know but it won't be easy to find the right man. He must know the business, he must have his head screwed on well, and he must be honest. No, it mightn't be so easy after all to replace Angus Gordon." Devern was making letters on the table-cloth with a spoon. "I've been figuring things out this way," he went on. "When a buyer comes here to Dublin from Glasgow he's always a stranger, and the stranger has to pay the highest prices. When Angus started to buy leeks, for instance, the prices of leeks always went up, for the growers knew that he wanted leeks and they stiffened their prices. But supposing the man who was doing my buying in Dublin — suppose he was in the trade here himself- then he would be buying leeks in any case and things would be different. The growers wouldn't know what was scarce in Glasgow and they wouldn't shove up the price. My man could make a fair profit for himself and still sell me leeks at less than what I'm paying for them now. Do you follow me?"

"I see your point, Mr Devern."

"But you don't see what I'm getting at?"

Mandy came out into the open. "I see one thing, Mr Devern. If you want someone here on the spot to buy stuff for you I'll give you as fair a crack of the whip as anyone else, and I think I could do at least as well for you as Angus Gordon."

Devern looked at him for a few seconds before he spoke.

"I think you will," he said at last. "Anyway, I'm willing to give you a trial."

Mandy stretched out his hand. "You won't regret it, Mr. Devern."

Neither of them regretted it. Devern got good value, and Mandy's earnings jumped. He never made less than five pounds a week on the stuff he sent to Devern and sometimes the figure was as high as fifteen.

The firm of M. Logue, Fruit and Vegetable Merchant, Potato Factor, and Commission Agent grew at a rate which left Glasgow's far behind. Mandy soon had five salesmen, four porters, and another lady clerk. He was an employer of labour, a man with money in the bank. Mrs. Mason began to think more highly of him, and to wish that she was a little younger or he a little older. Her creed was a simple one. She believed that in the home cleanliness was next to Godliness, and that in the market-place success was the seal of virtue and a sure sign of predestination.

CHAPTER SIX

JOE DOOLEY, the "Priest's Man," rang the bell for masses and funerals, cleaned the presbytery windows and the church gutters, and did the interminable sequence of small repairs which were necessary in order to keep Paradise Alley National School from falling asunder. Dooley mended presses and maps, put slates on the roof, replaced rotten floor-boards, adjusted the cisterns, cemented holes in the playground, and put screws in sagging desks. In all these tasks he showed more courage than skill, and he was the unhandiest of handymen. No one but Father Dunphy would have kept him and paid him.

Dooley, however, was quite unaware of his own failings. He considered himself as indispensable as a curate, and much more and though he never gave himself airs he gave himself orders, and wore a tight, boxer's haircut that was like a tonsure. When Father Dunphy was made Canon Dunphy, and later Archdeacon Dunphy, Dooley advanced himself proportionately in an ecclesiastical hierarchy of his own, and though he gave his employer credit for these promotions he seemed to believe that he himself had played some part in the winning of them.

He was a small, thin man, with a scraggy brown moustache and gapped, tobacco-stained teeth. His face was puckered and wrinkled, and when he laughed he squeezed his eye almost shut. He talked in rapid bursts and separated his phrases with 'hawhs.' Dooley's 'hawh' stood for 'what' but not for a question. It signified simply the polite intention of making every statement of fact or opinion depend upon the corroboration of the listener. Thus Dooley might say: "Had a terrible toothache last night-terrible thing a toothache, hawh-tossin' and turnin-you know how it is, hawh-wonder they wouldn't invent something that would cure it, hawh." The 'hawhs' were little knots that knitted the loose ends of his conversation together. Father Dunphy always paid a formal visit to Paradise Alley on Friday evenings and on these occasions Dooley came in his wake. When the priest walked up the classroom and shook hands with the teacher Dooley stood at the door, smiling and nodding his head; making it quite clear that though he knew his place was in the background he shared the manager's high opinion of the staff. But when the conversation turned-as it often turned-to rickety blackboards or loose window-panes, Dooley took control. He surveyed the offending article from all angles, tapped it and tested it, announced that "a bit of putty and a few belts of a hammer "would probably set it right, and then held a conference with himself to see if he could fit the repair into his programme for the following Monday morning. It was not often that anything new came into Paradise Alley. Cracked blackboards were riveted miraculously, holes in almost indecipherable maps were bridged with canvas, missing window-panes were replaced by temporary pieces of cardboard-which wore out in time and were themselves replaced by other temporary pieces of cardboard. Dooley sawed and hammered; he salvaged and buttressed; he staunched and made do. Without him Paradise Alley would have collapsed like a pack of cards and blown into the bay: with him it managed to postpone dissolution from week to week. Dooley didn't worry. He flexed his long limbs as if they were sections of a carpenter's rule and tackled jobs that a competent tradesman would have declared impossible; and when by brute force and ignorance he effected a bungling compromise with sagging wood or warped metal he screwed his thin face into a grin, stuck his clay pipe between his gapped teeth, and said that patience, perseverance, and a few belts of a spanner would bring a snail to Jerusalem.

Dooley was in Anthony's room the day Nedser Bolger first came to Paradise Alley. There were only six children in the first standard side of the room that morning; the rest had passed into second, and Anthony was waiting for the promoted senior infants from the convent who were to take their places. Dooley was waiting for them, too, though ostensibly he was fitting a piece of an orange box into the door of a press.

"You're a long time here now Mr. Domican," said Dooley, interrupting the meditation that preceded every stage of his work.

"About four years, I suppose, hawh."

"Six," said Anthony.

"Well, you'd be talkin'." Dooley stopped to consider.

"Isn't it the divil how time passes?"

Having got rid of this great thought he showed by detaching himself from his equipment that be expected Anthony to pursue it further, and when no comment was forthcoming he shook his head, as if he agreed that the subject was too deep for speech, and closed the incident by saying " Stupendous! " Then he took up his hammer and plank, and in an effort to ease the change from the contemplative to the practical order, looked out the window.

"Be the janey, Mr. Domican, here they come-the chislers from the convent, hawh. Sister Ita must have sent them in."

Anthony looked out the window at his seventh batch of raw recruits. It was always a little pathetic to see them march out the convent gate and up the street, dressed in their Sunday best and all agog with the adventure of going to "the big school." He saw them leave babyhood behind and enter Paradise Alley. Leading the procession was a tall, pale, deep-browed child, whose face seemed familiar. He was carrying a sheaf of transfer certificates. Anthony sat down at his desk and waited. He heard the front door opening, the thump of feet in the hall, and the voice of the Principal. The Principal's welcome was a feature of days like this. He greeted the ex-Infants in his special-occasion, sergeant-major voice, told them that they were welcome to St. John's, and added considerably to the terror which the more nervous of them felt at leaving the kindly nuns. The door of the classroom opened and they marched in two by two. One of them walked up to Anthony's desk and laid the certificates on it.

"The chislers' ages," he explained. "Sister Ita sent them in."

But it wasn't the tall, deep-browed child whose face had seemed familiar. It was a boy with an oversize head and bright, prominent eyes, a ventriloquist's doll of a boy. His mouth was big, his nose red and button-shaped, and his hair was clipped tight to the skull. He smiled at Anthony and all the world, and wiped his nose with a ragged sleeve. Most of the other wore jerseys and trousers, but the leader wore a suit of shoddy grey tweed. It was badly-made, torn, and dirty, but he wore it with an air of assurance. His-unwashed legs we're bare to the ankles and his stockings hung concertina-like over his muddy boots.

"And who may you be?" said Anthony.

"Edward Bolger, sir. Everyone knows me. Isn't that right, Mr. Dooley?"

Dooley laid down his hammer and straightened himself.

"Ha ha! me boy. You'll be learned manners before you're much older. Sister Ita was too soft for the likes of you. But it'll be a different story here, I'm telling you. If you speak without being spoken to the masters will break

Every bone in your body. You might sing it." He took up a saw and waved it. "Lay it on thick, Mr. Domican. Don't stand any nonsense from Nedser Bolger. Bate the badness out of him."

Dooley might have elaborated on this advice, but one of the seniors came in just then to tell him that Mr. Rodney wanted him.

"I'll finish the press for you in the afternoon, Mr. Domican," he said, gathering up his equipment. "And mind what I'm telling you, young Bolger-there'll be sparks bet outa yeh here. Am I right, Mr. Domican? Sparks no less."

This prophecy had no effect on Nedser Bolger, but it frightened some of the other children, who looked timidly at Anthony and at each other and wondered what fearsome experiences were soon to replace the catechism-chanting and plasticine worms which had filled their days in the convent.

"Tell me this, Bolger," said Anthony, when Dooley had gone. "Did Sister Ita give you these certificates?"

"No, sir," said Bolger. "She gev them to Shakespeare and Shakespeare gev them to me."

"You shouldn't call names," said Anthony. "How, would you like if someone tacked a nickname on to you?"

"Divil a hair I'd care-sure they call me Leathergob sometimes. Shakespeare doesn't mind either-'twas me christened him-he's the dead spit of the statue out in the convent."

Anthony began to enter the names in the roll-book, and he felt that Nedser had won the first round. He was to find out later that Nedser seldom lost a round. He was irrepressible, unself-conscious, abundantly sure of himself.

Nedser was a born showman and loved the limelight. If he wasn't asked his poetry he would mope all day. Poetry was the only thing he bothered to learn. He was good at mental arithmetic, but this excellence was simply the result of his preoccupation with reality. All the other subjects he barely tolerated. Little by little he became to Anthony what a more efficient Dooley would have been to Father Dunphy. He gave out and collected the exercises, looked after the chalk, sharpened the pencils, counted the pens. He did all the messages and got Anthony bigger apples and more biscuits for two pence than Anthony himself could have got for fourpence. Once a fortnight or so he was reduced to the ranks, but none of the others who took his place could fill it half so well, and Anthony was always glad to have him back. Bolger moved up from first to sixth and Anthony moved up with him, class by class. He got to know this batch of pupils very well but he knew none of them as well as he knew Bolger, and to know Bolger was an education in itself. Nedser was always in trouble in school and out of school. He knocked at doors, he spilled garbage bins, he fought in the yard, he blotted his copies. But no experience was too much for him, no failure left him dispirited. He thrived on disgrace and gave no man best. He took a pride in demolishing the mighty and was worth a regiment on inspection days. One of his victories in this class of tournament was fixed in Anthony's memory. The inspector was speaking about railways, and he branched into a little lecture on the wonderful power of steam. "Did you ever see a kettle boiling?" he asked Nedser.

"No, sir," said Nedser.

"Come, come, my boy." The inspector decided to make himself crystal-clear. "Doesn't your mother boil water in her kettle three times a day?"

"Yes sir."

"And yet you say that you never saw a kettle boiling?"

"I do sir."

The inspector smiled pityingly.

"Hands up every boy who ever saw a kettle boil."

Every right hand in the class went up and a few lefts as well, for some of the duller pupils were so delighted at the easy question that they wanted to endorse their assent; every hand except Nedsers.

"Now," said the Inspector, "you seem to be the only boy in the class who never saw a kettle boiling. Surely you must often have seen steam coming from the spout of a kettle?"

Nedser grinned in triumph.

"I did, sir, but that's not what you asked me at first- you asked me did I ever see a kettle boiling-well I didn't, and neither did you. It's not the kettle that boils-it's the water." The whole class burst out laughing, but it was an uneasy laughter and it soon died out. It was bad manners to contradict a visitor, and high treason to contradict an inspector. Nedser would be walloped. But Nedser didn't look as if he expected to be walloped. He flashed Anthony a Jack-the-Giant-killer look that said plainly: "You told us to speak up boldly to inspectors—I didn't let you down."

The great man took it quite well.

"What's your name?"

"Nedser Bolger, sir."

"Well, Nedser, you certainly have logic on your side. All I have on mine is the idiom of the language."

"Yes sir," said Nedser.

Alfred Mendelssohn Rodney didn't think much of Nedser and saw in him only a troublesome, untidy boy, who passed from class to class by the skin of his teeth and brought disgrace on the school.

Rodney had all the jargon of old-fashioned parsing at his finger-tips and could analyse verses from the Bible at sight; he was foolproof at compound proportion, the length of the Mississippi, the height of Ben Nevis; he could quote whole passages of Gladstone and declaim Emmet's speech from the dock; he was kindly after his fashion, and an excellent teacher; But he knew little about boys and next to nothing about boys like Nedser Bolger. The boy he knew was the Child Mind of the training college, the boy who climbed to knowledge up the five Herbartian steps, the boy who froze like a statue on demand. Rodney was keen on what he called "a good legible fist," and death on blots. He insisted on neatness, conformity, and a whole hierarchy of little virtues; he wasn't big enough to see the frightening intelligence behind every word and action of Nedser Bolger's.

Nedser wrote an essay on "Spring" once. It was a mixture of spidery writing, smudges, and phonetic spelling. It had only one paragraph and scarcely any punctuation. It had no introduction and no conclusion. It owed nothing to class preparation or blackboard " heads," and was neither orthodox nor echoic. It did not, as did the neat essays produced by Rodney's class, begin by telling the reader that "Spring, the first season of the year, consists of the months February, March and April," nor did it dwell on the simple and incontrovertible facts that in spring the birds build their nests and the farmer sows his seeds. It was simply Nedser Bolger's views on spring. Most of Nedser's views on spring were a little incoherent, and all but one were badly expressed. But, this one made up for all the others. It outweighed the smudges and the spidery handwriting. It cancelled the thumb-marks and the butter stain. It shone in its ugly setting like a star in a puddle, and in a different time and place it might have won for Nedser the Mandarin's prize and a pension of 2,000 yen—for this is what Nedser wrote:

"The dandyloin makes a harp of the suns rais and the blackbird danses to the music." Anthony's heart missed a beat. He rushed into Rodney's room.

"What do you think of that?" he said

Rodney adjusted his pince-nez and took the copy very gingerly. He saw the blots, the crawly writing, the finger- prints, but he didn't see the poem.

"Disgraceful! " he said." Punish him and burn the page. Better still, burn the exercise. It might get you into trouble with an inspector."

Anthony said nothing.

"You'd better be more careful with your composition work," Rodney went on. "I have some notes I must lend you-introduction, body of essay, conclusion, and blackboard heads. I found them indispensable when I was a young teacher. As for Bolger-it's plenty of the stick he wants. Anthony went back to his own room still believing in his own methods, and in Nedser Bolger. It was boys like Bolger who made him realize the privilege and responsibility of teaching, boys like Bolger who made Paradise Alley ten times more exciting than Mandy's profitable ledgers. And every boy was something of a Bolger. Every boy was utterly unlike every other boy. Every boy had in him something that could not be explained in terms of heredity or environment; every boy was, as Emerson said, something new in Nature. Creation was not just a machine that was wound up once and for ever in the garden of Eden, nor an unending progression that began with infinitesimal living things in the primeval slime. It was a recurring miracle, and every human being was as much a special creation as if he were the only human being. There were no two alike, not even in Paradise Alley.

If teaching had meant blot-free essays and the principal towns of Kerry, Anthony would have given it up and sold cabbages for Mandy. But it meant more than that. It meant almost a sharing in creation. It meant a constant nearness to and preoccupation with the growth of personality.

You could build motor-cars to blue prints and salts to formulas, but you hadn't the blue-print of a developing personality, the formula of a soul. Teaching demanded not only skill and patience but also a blind confidence, for you worked in the dark and never knew for sure whether you had succeeded or failed. You did the best you could on the wrong side of the pattern but you never knew what plans God had in store for His Nedser Bolgers. When these thoughts terrified Anthony he scaled them down to a humbler level. Tiddler might be an enigma, but he had to be taught the multiplication tables. Muckser Madigan might be utterly unlike everyone else, but he had to be weaned from the heresy that five and nine are seventeen. In tiny things like these Anthony could test his work, revise his methods, assess progress. He could assess also, in a rough and ready way, the intelligence of individual pupils as it was revealed in their work and behaviour. Many of these assessments of intelligence had to be revised from time to time, but his estimate of Ned Bolger was a constant. Anthony was sure of him from the very beginning. Nedser did not store up knowledge and give it out on demand with the faithfulness of a kitchen tap. He was not susceptible, he took nothing on trust. Schooling did not help him very much, but it did not harm him. Anthony had learned a lot in college about that abstraction known as the Child Mind, but it did not help him to understand Nedser Bolger. Nedser knew nothing about psychology but he knew a lot about Anthony Domican. He knew, for instance, that Anthony had a weakness for poetry, and he exploited it to the full. Whenever the timetable showed a lesson that Nedser didn't like, or a lesson that might expose work left undone, Nedser would take a cutting from his pocket and walk up to Anthony's desk. "I got this poem in a paper, sir-it's gorgeous!' Nedser would read the poem, Anthony would read the poem, the whole class would read the poem, and a very innocent teacher would think that his enthusiasm for literature had been passed on to at least one of his pupils. It was a long, long time before Anthony tumbled to it.

Nedser didn't like being punished. When he was slapped he jumped round the room holding his palm under his jumper and shouting that he was going to get his father to come down to the school and "flatten " Anthony. But there was neither venom nor substance behind Nedser's threats, for ten minutes later his hand would be up with the others, and it was common knowledge that Bolger senior thoroughly approved of corporal punishment and administered quite a lot of it himself. Whenever a complaint came from the school about Nedser, Mr. Bolger answered it by saying that he was giving as much of his time as he could to beating Nedser but that he had a job to go to and couldn't be walloping all the time.

Nedser broke a window once and Rodney sent for his mother. "Oh, I know he has Mr. Domican's heart broke," said the poor woman. But we do the best we can, Mr. Rodney, indeed we do. His father has his belt wore out on him.

And we'll pay for the window, Mr. Rodney-the school won't be at the loss."

"He's a young scamp," said Rodney, "an incorrigible blackguard. This is not the first time he's been in trouble. I wish you'd take him away and send him somewhere else."

"Ah, now, Mr. Rodney, don't be too hard."

"He's a disgrace to the school. Isn't he Mr. Domican?"

"He's a bit of a bother," said Anthony," and it's not for want of brains."

"Indeed it's not," said Mrs. Bolger "He has plenty of brains, plenty."

Had she finished there it would have been better, but she didn't. She rolled her eyes, raised her hands, and added: "He has more brains than you have yourself, Mr. Rodney."

This was a very modest estimate of Nedser's brains. It would have still been modest, Anthony thought, if Mrs. Bolger had lumped him in with the Principal. But Rodney didn't think so.

"How dare you, madam," he spluttered. "How dare you! We have quite enough bother from your unruly progeny without having to listen to your ill-mannered and insulting remarks. Good-day, madam. I'll leave Mr. Domican to deal with you, and if he takes my advice he'll expel your ruffian son here and now. He's no use to any school."

"There now!" cried Mrs. Bolger as Rodney swept off.

"What am I after saying? I'm after annoyin' Mr. Rodney, God help me. Sure I didn't mean any harm. God's truth I didn't. That scamp of mine gets me into more rows! And he has his poor father worried off the face of the earth. If it's not one thing it's another. I don't know under God what'll be the finish of him, and that's no lie. I don't know what'll be the finish of him?"

She mightn't have worried. Nedser finished up in a blaze of glory.

CHAPTER SEVEN

SOMETIMES on Saturdays and Sundays Mandy hired Mikey Connolly and his sidecar and drove out into the country to buy vegetables or to inspect the progress of crops that were already his. It was a pleasant as well as a profitable way of passing an afternoon. Mikey had a good turnout, and his brood mare, though her best days were past, carried herself like a thoroughbred. A run with Mikey was always a conducted tour. He knew the history of every house and family in County Dublin. He could show you where Sarah Curran lived and where Buck Armstrong shot himself, and whenever his whip pointed his tongue wagged.

It was on one of these Saturday afternoon runs that Anthony first met the Lenihans of *Sycamore Lodge*. The Lenihan farm touched the foothills on the south-eastern side of the city, and *Sycamore Lodge* was a great, bleak-looking barrack of a house that stood in a sea of cabbages. Arthur Lenihan was a widower in the early fifties. He had a handsome, swarthy face, a big fair moustache in the peninsular military tradition, and bright, confident eyes. He wore shabby riding-breeches and gaiters, and he seemed more interested in his hunters than in the vegetables which gave him a living.

Lenihan gave Mandy and Anthony a drink in a room where everything was old and good. Silver dishes stood on a long sideboard of dull mahogany, and above them were dim oil-paintings in gilt frames.

"You must come out to the meet next week, Mr. Domican," he said when they were waiting for tea. "I can fix you up with a mount quite easily. There's no use asking our friend Logue—he sticks too closely to business."

"Thanks for the offer," said Anthony, "but I know next to nothing about horses and less about hunting. I've never hunted anything bigger than a rabbit."

"You must learn, then. It's great sport. Logue here would be a better man if he took it up—yes, and if he went on an odd skite into the bargain. That's what I'm always telling him. A few drinks now and again and an odd visit to a music-hall would do him a world of good. Dammit, Logue, you're a young man. A fellow must mind his business, I know, but he should mind himself, too. Ah, here's Alice. This is Mr. Domican, Alice—friend of Logue's."

Alice Lenihan was a tall, good-looking girl, with a well-shaped face and fine grey eyes. Her hair was jet black, and she carried herself well. Anthony credited her mentally with these good points but he did not enthuse over the total. There was a lack of sparkle in her, and she was so deliberate in speech and gesture that he saw in her even then the gracious matron she was to become.

She poured out the tea, passed the cups gracefully, and made light conversation. She talked about books for a little while then, but she got little support. Anthony could talk about established classics, but his literary small-talk wasn't up to the minute: and Mandy could not even talk about established classics. Mandy was very quiet. Lenihan spoke about peaches, sherries, brood mares, lazy workmen, and musical comedies.

They had almost finished when Mollie Lenihan came in. Mollie was very like Alice, but smaller and less statuesque, and her hair was black without being jet black. Alice's eyes were placid, and reflected her self-sufficiency; Mollie's had a warmth that brought a sort of glow about her.

Mollie attacked a cream bun as if she liked it, holding her head well back so that no blobs would fall on her knees, and she spoke with her mouth full. Alice, thought Anthony, would never speak with her mouth full.

"Are you in the vegetable business, Mr. Domican?" said Alice. Anthony got the impression that Miss Alice did not think much of the vegetable business (a wrong impression, as he was to discover later) and felt as if he had been asked if there was ringworm or lunacy in his family.

"No," he said. "I'm a schoolmaster."

"A schoolmaster!" Lenihan looked surprised. " But you don't look like a schoolmaster."

"Most schoolmasters don't," said Anthony. "Anyway, I'm young yet."

"You teach in a college?" said Alice—as if she hoped that Anthony's confession did not necessarily mean complete and final degradation.

"I teach in a dockside national school. It's called Paradise Alley."

"How interesting!" said Alice. Then she made a liar of herself by asking. "Do you find it dull?"

"Not dull. Anything but that. Tiresome and depressing sometimes, but never dull."

"I don't know how you stick those slum children," said Lenihan.

"They must be crawling with vermin."

Mollie took a hand then.

"I can't think of anything more worth-while. You have a chance to do some good-you're in contact with the common people."

Anthony took this for Big House snobbery and warm-woolies-for-the-children-of-the-lower-orders condescension. But something in Mollie Lenihan's eyes convinced him of her sincerity, and the antipathy which had been awakened in him to *Sycamore Lodge* and all it stood for softened a little.

"It's certainly worth-while," he said, "but the difficulties are tremendous. It's hard to expect bare-footed, hungry children to show any interest in schoolwork. The environment is dead against us-everything is wrong. There's so much misery and undernourishment in this city of low wages that popular education seems an anachronism at times. It has come before the decent social conditions that are necessary if it is to have any effect."

Mandy flashed a danger signal. This was no talk for a county drawing-room.

"I can't say that I agree with you about the low wages," said Lenihan. "Wages are quite high enough, and if parents didn't drink so much the children mightn't be so badly-dressed and badly-fed. The lower classes in this country are extravagant and improvident-that's what's the matter. They have no idea of thrift or cleanliness, and they don't spend their money to the best advanta.ge."

Anthony disregarded Mandy's signals.

"Precious little they get to spend. And I don't blame them for drinking-it's the only outlet they have, for their life is just one litany of misery. As for the living wage-as far as I can see it's simply a polite fiction. For nine-tenths of Dublin's workers it just doesn't exist."

"Come, come!" laughed Lenihan. "This is rank Socialism—Beresford Place stuff. After all, running a business is not a philanthropic affair, and most Dublin employers are finding it deuced hard to show a profit. Am I right, Logue?"

Mandy lied placidly.

"As for us farmers—well I know it takes me all my time to make a living. I pay the best wages I can, and I don't see any signs of hunger or revolution amongst my workers. They're quite satisfied."

"Revolutions don't advertise themselves," said Anthony. "If they did there would be no revolutions. But I know Paradise Alley and places like it and I can tell you that ugly things are brewing."

"Nonsense!" Lenihan was not convinced. "Only for the labour agitators the people would be contented enough. Oily-tongued idlers who never did a decent day's work in their lives and who want to keep anyone else from doing one. If I had my way I'd shoot every trouble-maker out of hand. Put 'em up against a wall. Why can't they leave the people alone? An employer wants a job done and he offers a certain wage. Any worker who isn't satisfied has the remedy in his own hands. If he doesn't want the job he needn't take it."

Anthony felt himself getting hot under the collar. He wanted to ask Lenihan what he paid the women who thinned his turnips and cut his cabbages, to name the family wage he gave his ploughmen and carters. But he couldn't in decency. He was the man's guest, and a guest at one remove at that, his respectability vouched for by Mandy.

Mollie Lenihan continued the argument for him.

"You're talking nonsense, dad, and well you know it. You say that no one forces a man to take a wage he feels is too small. Don't his children force him? A man might face starvation himself, but he can't stand idle and see his children starve. He must take the best job he can get, and if all the employers are paying rotten wages he must take a rotten job or go hungry. What else can he do? He has no option."

Lenihan smiled at her.

"You're a firebrand, Mollie. We must get you a soapbox outside the Custom House some Sunday."

"If you do I'll take it," she laughed, "and I'll tell all you employers a few home truths."

Anthony felt that he had provoked all this, so he interrupted with a mannerly question.

"You do a lot of market-gardening, Mr. Lenihan?"

"A good deal. As much as anyone about here, in fact, with the exception of Ryan of Kimmage and Alderman Riordan. But there's precious little money in it I can tell you. Anything that's in the business goes to the wholesalers and the shopkeepers. The farmer is the mug. He has the work and the worry, but it's Logue here and the likes of him who can set the sovereigns on their edges."

"It's not so easy for us either," said Mandy. "Anyone who believes that the Dublin farmer is as green as his cabbages has a lot to learn. You get your cheque as soon as the crop is ready, and sometimes before it is ready. Your trouble is over then. We have to take the risk of the market going against us."

Alice smiled sweetly.

"Don't mind dad, Mr. Logue. He's always grumbling without any reason. Anyone would think by him that he was on the road to the poorhouse."

"Oh, I'm not as far gone as that yet," laughed Lenihan. "We can manage to keep a drop of wine in the cellars and a few hunters in the stables. But market gardening is no gold mine, believe me, no matter what Logue may say. The most paying crop for land about Dublin these days is houses, and as soon as the city starts to grow in this direction I'll sell out to the builders and retire. This farm will be worth money yet."

"I hope you won't ever sell out to the builders, dad," said Mollie.

"It's a bad sign of the country when the city is bursting its waistband and the farmers about it can't make a decent living."

"You've been reading too many books," said Lenihan. "When I was a young man girls were content to look pretty and leave the thinking to the men. But times have changed. Nowadays the women want to rule the roost. Surely you're not going, Mr. Logue? We'll have some music if you stay, and a game of cards after dinner. What's your hurry?"

Mandy refused to stay to dinner, and they left in a welter of invitations. The girls asked them to tennis, the father offered them the loan of guns and horses. They were to come out any time and not to stand on ceremony or wait to be asked.

Mandy was very quiet as they jogged back to the city.

Afterwards, when they were back again at Mrs. Mason's, Mandy asked Anthony what he thought of Alice Lenihan. Anthony was going to tell him, but some sixth sense warned him.

"She's a good-looker," he said.

Mandy nodded and puffed at his pipe.

"Aye, she is indeed. A fine girl."

"The younger one has more go in her, I think."

"Mollie?" Mandy laughed disparagingly. " Oh, Mollie's all right, but she's a bit of a feather-head. She hasn't the dignity of Alice."

"You seem to think a lot of Alice," said Anthony. Mandy readied his pipe and put it back into his mouth again.

"I do think a good deal of her, Anthony. As a matter of fact I'm thinking of marrying her."

"Why not? I'm thinking of marrying the daughter of the Marquis of Bute myself."

"You think I'm fooling," said Mandy. " But I'm not. I'm in dead earnest."

Anthony laughed at him.

"Oh, Mandy, Mandy, you'll be the death of me. Sure you haven't met her more than two or three times."

"Four," said Mandy.

"And your mind is made up?"

"I only said I was thinking of marrying her. There's no harm in thinking, is there? Many's the one I've had a notion of in my day. But Alice Lenihan is the finest-looking girl I ever saw. There's a touch of style about her."

"I grant you that," said Anthony. "But she has a father, and I'm not so sure that the old boy thinks there's a bit of style about you. As far as I can see he'll be wanting his daughters to marry well. He's a bit of a snob."

"Larry Lenihan is all right. There's not a hait the matter with him. After all you must make allowances. His folk on both sides have been gentry for generations, and he can't help the way he was reared. What the hell do you want him to do? Chew tobacco and wear a muffler? Have a bit o' wit, man. Larry isn't a bad soul when he's let alone. It's no wonder you got him going. You were talking like a Socialist."

"I'm not sorry for anything I said, and for that matter I said nothing that wasn't said far more explicitly by Leo XIII in *Rerum Novarum*."

"In what?"

"It's an encyclical. You should read it some time. It will do you a world of good—especially if you don't believe that the working-man is entitled to a decent living-wage, decent home conditions, and a decent way of rearing a family."

Mandy lost his temper then.

"Hang it all, man!" he shouted. "Who do you think you're talking to? Rockfeller or somebody? Who's a working-man if I'm not one? Answer me that. It's men like you, who never did a hard day's work in their lives, that make decent folk discontented by talking about the rights of the working man. There's no unrest among the workers—except the unrest that is fomented by paid agitators that are making a good thing out of it."

"You may not see the unrest, Mandy, but it's there, and there's no use getting angry about it. If you were teaching in a slum school, as I am, and could see the stark poverty and misery—aye and the spirit that misery breeds—you'd know the reason why the paid agitators get a hearing. Wages in this city are well below subsistence level."

"Now look here, Anthony." Mandy tapped his argument into his palm with the dottle from his pipe. "Wages are things that fix themselves. If you want men you offer them wages—if I want the men you want I must offer them more than you're offering them—that's the case in a nutshell. It's all a question of supply and demand."

"It is, but it shouldn't be," said Anthony. "That's just the damnable part of it. Labour has become a commodity, like wheat, or porter, or scallions, and if there's a surplus of it anywhere then wages come down with a bump. And there's a still more inhuman side to the business—and it's this—even when there is no surplus of labour wages can still be kept down if the employers club together and fix things to suit themselves."

"But sure only employers can fix wages," said Mandy. "If we left it to the workers themselves every man would have ten pounds a week."

"I don't say that the fixing of wages should be left to the workers, but I do say that it shouldn't be left to the employers, or to the material forces which you call supply and demand. What I say is that the worker should have some say in determining his own wage. Employment is a contract, and there should be two sides to a contract. Human nature being what it is a one-sided contract is usually unjust. And I say this——"

"Go on," said Mandy. "Don't mind me. Keep on with the fairy tales. It's good fun."

"Well, here's the fairy tale. There should be a minimum wage—the lowest wage that will keep a family in frugal comfort—and no adult male worker should be offered less—no matter what the work is and no matter how many are after the job."

"It's great to be listening to you," said Mandy. "You're lost in Paradise Alley. It's not the place for you at all. Tub-thumping should be your trade, not schoolmastering—and it might be yet, for if Father Dunphy gets to hear of the wild notions you have there may be a vacancy in Paradise Alley."

" Don't let that worry you. Father Dunphy knows as much about the hunger and misery of the docks and the slums as anyone else—he's living in the middle of it—he can't get away from it. And if his social opinions aren't something like my own he should look up his encyclicals."

"If you take my advice, Anthony, you'll keep your opinions to yourself—for they're only wild, foolish notions. And mind what I'm telling you—Father Dunphy mightn't like to know that he has a firebrand in his school."

"I'm not a firebrand, Mandy. I'm just frightened by the look of things, and I think there's trouble brewing."

CHAPTER EIGHT

ALFRED MENDELSSOHN RODNEY was a bachelor, and he lived at Dalkey with an unmarried sister who could not get him up in time in the mornings. When he caught the train he should have caught he arrived in Paradise Alley about nine-fifteen, but when he travelled by one of the later trains, as he did two mornings out of three, he did not arrive until half-past ten or later. But whether he was late or early he was spruce and debonair, and if the season permitted he wore a rose in his button-hole.

Whenever he was later than usual he went to Tom Lehanty and explained that he had a touch of neuralgia, a slight dose of asthma, or a speck of bronchitis, and his manner conveyed the impression that these ills of the flesh were not the ordinary complaints of the vulgar but the sort of thing you would come across in the biographies of the great.

"The way he looks at you," Lehanty used to say, "you'd almost believe him."

When Rodney came in late in the morning he stayed late in the evening, a form of restitution which might be admitted by moral theologians but was not provided for in the rules of the Department. His pupils stayed in also, but they were not compelled to stay. Any one of them could have gone home with Lehanty's boys or with Anthony's boys at three o'clock had he so wished: but none of them did. Indeed the juniors would gladly have joined Rodney's boys at three o'clock, for Rodney paid overtime at the rate of a penny an hour.

And there were other ways in which Rodney's boys could earn money. When one of them brought home a corrected composition and copied it neatly into a special exercise he was credited with 3/4d. in Rodney's ledger, and other assignments were rewarded on a sliding scale. The ledger entries were made by the seventh standard pupils, each of whom acted as accountant in turn and was given a small honorarium, not to speak of the training in elementary bookkeeping which was thrown in. At the end of every quarter Rodney would read out the totals and pay his debts: John Byrne, 1s. 10d.; Tom Magee, is. 1s 7 1/4d.; Leo O'Reilly, 2s. 01/2d.

Rodney's disregard for time extended to the school time-table, a document which he drew up carefully every year, sent to the district inspector for his approval, hung up—as the regulations demanded—

"in a prominent place in the schoolroom," and thereafter completely ignored. The two other teachers worked to schedule, but Rodney did as he pleased. If he was in the mood for geography the boys made blank maps and plasticine maps, studied railway time-tables, planned journeys (Rodney called them itineraries), and calculated the worth of the black porter which Guinness's Brewery produced in a year, a month, a week, a day, and a minute. During the geography week, or the geography fortnight as the case might be, the other parts of the programme were merely incidental and accessory. Arithmetic was geographical, history was geographical, and the reading was done from geographical magazines. When Rodney tired of geography he chose another subject, or a section of a subject, and taught it just as intensively: he might give a month to history and a full fortnight to compound interest: so the time passed pleasantly, and, on the whole, profitably.

The system, however, had some defects. It made no allowance for revision, and subjects were laid aside for months at a time, so that inspectors often found puzzling weaknesses in otherwise excellent pupils, but the amount of work done and its general merit showed that Rodney was a highly-successful teacher. Whenever he was censured for his unorthodox methods he would talk of the strange but effective methods used by teachers in China—where he had once served as a war correspondent—or discuss the school curriculum of Alsace-Lorraine, and if he was asked for drawing-copies which he hadn't got he would stroke his beard and explain that the boy who had been told to burn last year's copies had burned this year's as well. He did not get his full revenge on his censurers during his lifetime, but years after his death some of the maddest features of his school-keeping, which were really as old as Quintilian, were 'discovered' in America and quoted in European text-books as shining examples of educational progress in the great republic.

Punctuality, however, was a different matter, and one on which the Department had no difficulty in collecting evidence. Two senior inspectors arrived at twenty-five minutes to ten one morning. They asked a few desultory questions in the junior classes, and they looked at the roll-books, but it was obvious that they were waiting for Rodney: and there was no Rodney.

At ten-fifteen they decided that they would give the great man another five minutes, and at ten-twenty they gave him an extension. Just as they were preparing to go the Principal arrived, and he was never more a Principal than at that dramatic moment. He showed no surprise, no embarrassment. He merely said: "Ah, gentlemen, you have anticipated me."

The inspectors said nothing, and Rodney, looking from one to the other of them in a way which did not take from their dignity or his own, went on to explain, more with an air of a man making light conversation than of one trying to excuse himself, that he still had a touch of bronchitis, and then passed on to some general remarks about the weather, as if any more detailed account of the state of his health would insult the intelligence of his hearers and emphasize unnecessarily the obvious fact that he was a hero to be out at all. The amazing thing about the whole business, as Lehanty said to Anthony afterwards, was that Rodney was not trying to deceive; he was simply playing a part that had become second nature to him.

The senior inspector asked for the report book and wrote a mild entry recommending that the teachers of Paradise Alley should be in school at the hour laid down in the regulations, and that the Principal should give good example to the rest. Rodney caught the early train every morning for a fortnight, when a timely twinge of neuritis came to his relief. Inspectors gave him reprimands from time to time, but the Department took no serious action and evidently decided in the end to regard his unpunctuality as a congenital weakness in a servant who was in most other respects wholly satisfactory.

Teaching was a very serious business with Rodney, and the laughs of Paradise Alley were shared by Lehanty, Anthony, and Father Dunphy.

There was, for instance, Larry Lynch's famous essay on "Christmas." Anthony had told the boys to write about brown-paper parcels, fat letters slithering through letter-boxes, fat turkeys sizzling in grease, and fat Santa Clauses handing out monster shilling parcels in the big shops—and slightly more monstrous ones for one-and-sixpence. He told them also not to let the pageantry hide from them the real message and meaning of Christmas, and he wrote on the board, as a peg on which to hang the final paragraph, the sentence " We must not forget the Manger." Larry Lynch, however, finished his essay with " We must not forget the Manager," and Father Dunphy carried his message to the next diocesan dinner.

Anthony taught singing to the entire school, and so kept up contact with boys who had passed on from his own division. Once, in the hot dragging week before the summer holidays, he passed the singing half-hour by asking each senior what he was going to do when he left school. Most of them didn't know, but a few of the luckier ones had trades to go to, and he made them promise, for the fun of the thing, to give special terms to their old teacher. The cobbler-to-be undertook to mend his boots at half-price, the watch-maker arranged a special discount, and even Redser Robinson, who was to face the world as first mate on his brother's donkey-cart, said that he would "knock a juice offa every dozen coal blocks."

The last of the batch was Dan Corcoran. Dan was a stockily-built, fearless, lazy boy, and he and Anthony had never got on well together.

"Well, Dan," said Anthony. "What is it to be? Everyone has promised to help me. Maybe you'll do something for me?"

"I will, sir."

"And what are you going to be?"

A slow grin spread over Dan's face, and he laughed before he spoke.

"I'm going to be a knife-thrower," he said.

And Dan was a boy who, by ordinary school standards, was of less than average intelligence.

Paradise Alley children left school at fourteen (the statutory leaving-age for a generation lucky enough to have been born in a humane age which recognized the tremendous possibilities of popular education) and they carried with them into the adult world the vast amount of knowledge and skill which can be acquired during eight years at school, and the fully-developed intellect which, as is implied in the official regulations, every child is bound to possess "on the last day of the quarter in which he attains his fourteenth birthday." But lest the employers of Dublin might not appreciate the blessings of popular education each boy who left Paradise Alley carried with him also, as a proof of his worth, a reference from the Principal. Rodney wrote his references on printed sheets headed with the name of the school, and filled in " Good," " Very Good," or "Excellent" opposite such sub-headings as "Attendance," "Punctuality," "Character," and "General Behaviour." The final paragraph in the reference was either the bare formula "I can recommend this boy to any employer who may desire to avail of his services "or the few variants of it that could be obtained by the insertion of " heartily," "unhesitatingly," or even "with the utmost confidence."

But even this impressive passport did not satisfy all the pupils, and some of them thought it better to have in addition a less official-looking but more personal recommendation from Anthony or Lehanty. Anthony had a reputation for writing "gorgeous" references, and the parents of Paradise Alley had a pathetic belief in his powers of composition. Rodney kept carbon copies of his references, so that whenever the police came seeking further particulars they found him very helpful. Anthony kept no carbon copies, but he re-wrote a more colourful version of one of his references and kept it in his archives as a wager with fate.

It was a reference for Nedser Bolger, Nedser who wrote the wonderful essay on "Spring," who went his own way and took nothing on trust, who discomfited inspectors on examination days, who took no hurt from his schooling or his environment. This is what Anthony wrote:

"To some Unknown Greengrocer:

Ned Bolger has been a pupil of Paradise Alley National School for the past eight years. We didn't succeed in teaching him very much, and we didn't feel much need to. His stock of general knowledge will surprise you, and we can guarantee that his intelligence will be equal to any load you care to put upon it.

I hope, for your sake, that he doesn't stay with you as long as he stayed with us: if he does he will own the shop. But for whatever time he does stay with you it will be your privilege, as it has been ours, to watch the development of a very remarkable personality. It is a terrifying as well as a wonderful privilege, and you need not despair if, after a month's experience of Nedser's intelligence, you feel that you have always been inclined to over-rate your own. I warn you, envy you, and wish you luck."

CHAPTER NINE

Anthony went home to Lurgameelon three times a year- for a few days at Christmas, a week at Easter, and three weeks in the summer. The rest of his summer holiday he spun out as his purse allowed, in Kilkee the Blaskets, or Tramore. He went to the Isle of Man once with Mandy in a broiling August; it was Mandy's first and only holiday until his honeymoon. Mandy didn't see any need for holidays. He thought they only interfered with business. The sight of the sardine crowds on Douglas beach and the thronged fruit shops along the front made Mandy very unhappy. It was acute discomfort for him to see tens of thousands of potential customers and have nothing to sell them. So after his Isle of Man holiday he contended himself with a three day run to Lahardan every Christmas. But he found time for at least one other interest, and when Anthony came back from Lurgameelon in the late Summer of 1912 he found that Mandy's status in the Lenihan household had altered radically, and by October the only question to be settled was whether or not the wedding should be a full-dress affair. Mandy wanted a quiet wedding, and Anthony, who was to be best man, maintained that he wouldn't wear a tall hat for anyone, but in the end Alice, sweet Alice, had her way and was married in the white crepe gown with a train of old Brussels lace.

By this time Anthony had begun to like Alice a little better. Her statuesqueness, he found, was not the cold thing he had taken it to be; it was just the way she was made. She was kind, and good-natured, and she was in love with Mandy. Her father would have rather had her marry a man with a county name and an educated taste in wines, but Alice chose for herself and it was red-headed Mandy Logue, Fruit and Vegetable Merchant, who put the ring on her finger.

Mandy's father and mother and a sprinkling of his brothers and sisters came up for the wedding, but they refused to wear the traditional wedding garments of the upper classes. Anthony wanted to refuse, too, but he wasn't a free agent, and he had to fit himself out with striped trousers, a cut-away coat, spats, and a shiny top-hat. The indignity of wearing the things was bad enough, but that passed away with the wedding morning. What was far more hurtful was the fact that the wedding photograph, which appeared in all the papers, was cut out and preserved in the homes of Paradise Alley as a permanent record of his shame. The wedding outfit, if he had had to buy it himself, would have cost him a quarter's salary, but Mandy insisted on providing all the props and costumes, and Anthony, feeling that he had been coerced into the cast, for once made no objection.

Mandy and Alice spent a fortnight in London and Paris—a far cry from Mulroy and the road across the moor—and came back to a six-bedroomed house in Rathgar.

"Larry Lenihan would like me to start off with a bigger place," said Mandy to Anthony on the night of the first house-warming party, "but I'll creep before I walk."

"Maybe he thought you should have bought the Vice-regal. If that's what you call creeping it'll be a long time before I can put a foot under me."

"It's your own fault then, Anthony. I'm sick, sore, and tired asking you to come into the business with me. There's money enough in it for two of us, aye and to spare. If you were with me I could do twice as well—I know it. And what will you have at the rear if you stay in Paradise Alley? Where will you finish up? All you need now is digs money and a few bob for tobacco, but you must look ahead. You can't stay single all your life. I shouldn't be speaking out of my turn but I think that if you were to ask someone we both know well you could be fairly certain of getting the right answer."

"It all depends on what you mean by the right answer. Dammit you're not so long married yourself that you should think of setting up a matrimonial agency. Lenihan isn't the only name in the world. As for going into the business, well we've talked it over dozens of times. There's no use in going into it again. It's good of you to ask me, but it's not my line. I'm not a business-man, and I'll never be one."

"You could be as good a business-man as the next if you put your mind to it. I don't want you to buy or sell for me—I want you to keep your eye on things and save me from getting into a mess. And you'd like it, too, once you were in it. There's no money in teaching, and it's a worrying job."

It was not the only worrying job.

*   *   *   *

Labour unrest was growing in the city. The people of the two-pair backs, the people who lived in hunger and darkness, were asking for a little of their own. To the big employers and to the civic authorities the movement spelt anarchy and a threat to organized government. It was, of course, a tyrannical movement, and it had to be, for it was the answer to a tyranny that would not listen to argument, a tyranny whose sponsors were the spiritual heirs of the Industrial Revolution.

The philosophy of Big Business was a simple philosophy, as simple in its social views as the philosophy of the ancient Greeks, who debated first causes and thought eight slaves a fair ration for each free man. There were but two classes. The first, composed of people with property, capital, and initiative, was the mainspring of progress, the cause of prosperity. But for them there would be no ships ploughing the seven seas, no rattling looms, no invoices, no cotton frocks, no sewing machines, no plate-glass windows, no modern plumbing, no bulls' eyes, no tea in Glenties, no railway to Dingle, no prunes, no statues, no municipal galleries, no tall hats, no Spanish onions, no music recitals, no nothing. In return for all these amenities, which were due to its enterprise, traditions, and good breeding, the ruling-class was entitled to the best that a world of its making had to offer. There could be no question of sharing with the toiling masses.

At the same time it did not deny that the toiling masses could not be completely ignored. It had to have men to hew the coal and work the winches, to drive the drays and clean the sewers, and there had to be not only work but wages. The puritan ethic which regarded the pursuit of wealth as a religious duty, and was an important factor in the change from the medieval to the modern economic system saw the need for labour but not the dignity of the labourer. Wages were necessary to maintain the physical strength of the workers, and popular education was a device for inculcating discipline in their children. The schools offered an opportunity of stressing early in life the lesson that some people are born to ride to the hunt and others to clean out the stables, and their function was to produce yearly quotas of young people who would know their place and not talk back to their masters and mistresses.

This essentially unchristian philosophy, which was common in Dublin in the early years of the twentieth century, was not recognized as unchristian by these who held it and were unaware of its origins. The people who paid low wages and had never read *Rerum Novarum* were not inhuman monsters. They were, as often as not, kindly, charitable people, but they were too blind to see that the need for charity was the measure of their own guilt.

Nor were the employers all to blame. Some of them, like Mandy Logue, paid good wages, but even these distrusted the new movement and denied that the workers had the right to organize, to discuss conditions and wages, to ask for more when they hadn't enough.

"Why should they dictate to me?" Mandy said to Anthony once. "My men are well paid. Why should they be forced to join a union against their will? If I paid my men union money I'd have to dock their pay instead of increasing it. Why can't they let decent employers alone?"

"I dunno," said Anthony. "Maybe it's the rotten employers are to blame. But why not let your men join the union? What harm will it do?"

"Why should I give in to them? Am I not entitled to run my business in my own way without interference from men who don't give a tinker's curse about the workers? Who are they, anyway, these trade union leaders? Foreigners most of them—and getting a fat living out of the game. They have decent men worried and badgered, and every scamp and cornerboy in Dublin is at their beck and call."

"You'll always have scamps and cornerboys where there's trouble, but you can't explain this unrest in terms of hooliganism alone. It's bigger than that. You can't expect the leaders to be suave and spatted, and if you refuse to give them a hearing you can't expect them to argue the way a barrister argues in the court. You've left them nothing but the mailed fist, and that always means trouble."

It certainly meant trouble in the Dublin of 1913. On the one hand there were the arrogant employers, who refused to discuss or to treat, and who insisted on regarding the workers necessary for carrying on their business as a commodity which they had the right to buy as cheaply as possible; on the other was the newer arrogance born of the doctrine that all the wealth produced by the workers belonged to the workers, that the capitalist was a parasite that should be wiped out ruthlessly, that by a process of blind economic determinism the classless society was being evolved, and that religion was a soporific sponsored by the Church and the wealthy classes for their own ends. In the tremendous clash of these seemingly irreconcilable points of view those who echoed the words of Leo XIII found it hard to get a hearing and were distrusted by both parties. Neither side saw any hope of peace save in victory and defeat.

Meanwhile, in Paradise Alley and places like it, there was a great hope and a great fear: hope that the words of the labour leaders could be relied upon, that hunger, and rickets and wretchedness were doomed, that every man willing to work would be able to rear his family in comfort and put something by for his old age; fear that in the fight that was being forced upon them the little they had would be taken from them and the bearable thing called malnutrition replaced by the misery called starvation. They could paralyse the mighty port, they could stop all things that moved on wheels, they could silence the rattle of the cranes, they could pin merchandise in sheds and holds. But for how long? Who would feed children whilst stubborn fathers stood idle? What about arrears of rent and the sheriff's men? The employers could live on their fat for months. They could play a waiting game and dictate their own terms when the revolt was broken. Time was not on the side of the big battalions.

The leaders had answers for every argument. The Irish Worker was full of answers. The employers would be beaten if the workers realized their power and used it. And where there was food there need be no hunger. Food could be had for the taking, and their comrades across the channel would send them grain ships. Great issues were at stake and there could be no shirking. This was no mere local struggle but the world uprising of the toiling masses, the tang of the wind of freedom that was blowing across Europe. Workers of the world, unite.

Mandy Logue bought a revolver. Its grey-nosed bullets had butts the colour of peanuts.

"You're not going to use it?" said Anthony.

"You'd never know," said Mandy.

"Does Alice know about this?"

"She does, and she doesn't like it, but she knows that I must be ready to defend myself. They have threatened me and written about me in their paper. I'm a 'boss,' employing scab labour. I'm battening on the workers. Two scallywags were down with me on Monday saying that my men must join the union or they wouldn't be responsible for anything that might happen to me. Let them do their worst. We'll see if they can act as big as they can talk.

If they wreck my stand they'll do it over my dead body. I built up my business by hard work and sweat, and I'm not going to see it destroyed by loafers who never did a hand's turn in their lives."

A few days later, when the London North Western van arrived at Mandy's stand with a load of cherries and Kentish plums a dozen men came with it. They waited until the fruit was unloaded, and then they made a rush.

"Tumble the baskets! Down with the scabs!"

When Mandy drew his revolver they halted in their tracks.

"Tumble away," said Mandy, "but I'll shoot the first man that lays a hand on anything."

He gained his point, and no one touched his Kentish plums. But it was only a respite. The day was not far distant when plums and cherries would grow woolly beards in the London North Western sheds, when Portadown strawberries would rot in the goods yard at Amiens Street, when no one man with a revolver would face the mob.

Strikes were the order of the day. Dray-horses champed in their stables, the trams stopped running, plate-glass windows shivered into starry fragments. In the side-streets platoons of policemen waited. The police were not the enemies of the people. They were of the people. They had come from hungry, mountain farms in Kerry and Mayo, and they little thought when they went to the village schoolmasters in the evenings that their work would include clubbing people who knew a hunger that was worse than the hunger of the mountainy farms.

*   *   *   *

Anthony was caught one night in a baton charge that began outside Liberty Hall. He was one of a crowd that stretched round into Abbey Street, and he was jammed like a match in a full box. When the charge began he was carried off in the rush, but when the crowd thinned a little he was able to stand his ground with difficulty and he saw the police running and heard the thud of the batons. It was a sickening sound, and a terrifying one. One man went down near him, an old fellow with a wheezy, asthmatic way of breathing. His hat rolled from his bald head and a trickle of blood followed it.

Anthony had had an idea that the police picked their victims and distinguished between rioters and lookers-on. They didn't. They took them "out of a face"—the way a Lurgameelon man would take a burden of peats from the stack at the end of the house. And Anthony was next. He saw that clearly. He felt like protesting, explaining. He saw the baton rise over his skull, and then, remembering the wheezy old man, it occurred to him that he was desperately fond of his skull. He caught the policeman's baton arm at the wrist and, putting one leg behind him, threw him off his balance. The policeman fell on his back, though not violently, and his helmet bumped along the cobble-stones.

He wanted to pick the policeman up then, and apologise, but two more batons were making for him and he knew that they wouldn't wait on apologies. He took to his heels and panic went with him. His flight induced the frame of mind which should have preceded it. He dodged round people, he bumped into people, and he did not stop until he was in Westmoreland Street.

This was the second man he had knocked down since coming to Dublin, and again the battery was quite unpremeditated, a mere reflex action brought about by the desire to live. But he was badly scared, not for his skull, which was safe for the time being, but for something only a little less important. If the news leaked out he might get jail, might lose his job and if he lost his job because of indulgence in riot and civil commotion he might never get another. He stood for a while in College Green, getting his breath and listening to the judge.

"The position which the defendant occupies makes the offence still more serious. The teacher should, by virtue of his very office, uphold law and order on every occasion and give good example to the general public. But here we have, unfortunately the spectacle of a teacher who, instead of obeying the authorities which provide his bread and butter and which have placed him in a position of trust and responsibility, is guilty of assaulting a uniformed servant of the law. Another serious feature of the case is that some years ago the prisoner made a vicious attack on a parent who had objected to his punishing his child. There may have been some provocation on that occasion. There was certainly none on this. I have no option, therefore, but to sentence the prisoner to three months' hard labour, and I shall see that the case is brought to the attention of the education authorities."

Someone tipped him on the shoulder then, and he turned round, prepared to go quietly. It was Mollie Lenihan.

"What brings you to the city at this time of night?" He panted the words out.

"My, you're wheezing like a bellows. What on earth have you been doing?"

"I can't make any statement until I see my solicitor. Anything I say may be taken down, altered, and used in evidence against me."

"Stop being clever, Anthony, and tell me what happened."

"Come on then, while there's time. They'll be coming for me soon. Let's get to some place where we can talk."

He ordered coffee and cakes in an ice-cream shop.

"It's not the kind of place Mandy would bring Alice to," he said, as they sat down.

"Maybe not," she answered, "but it's none the worse for that. Now tell me all about it. Were you caught in the baton charge?"

"Was I caught in the baton charge! I was an incident in the baton charge. I knocked down a policeman—a real, live policeman."

"I don't believe it."

"I don't blame you. I can scarcely believe it myself. It happened in a flash. One minute he was towering over me with his baton raised and the next he was on the broad of his back. One of us had to go down, and he was the one."

"How did you manage it?"

"I just tripped him up."

"And then ran for your life."

"How did you know?"

"Well, it's what anyone would do in the circumstances. Besides, when I met you you were puffing like a winded racehorse. Did any of them follow you?"

"I didn't look round to see. Anyway it doesn't matter. A greyhound wouldn't have caught me. I was kicking hares out of my road."

"If you're arrested," she laughed, " I'll write a ballad about you. You'll be one of the felons of our land."

"There'll be no ballads written about me, Mollie. I'm not the hero breed. I don't think that the labour question will be settled by strikes or by baton charges—for they are just two different kinds of intolerance. My sympathies are with the common people, and I admire their pluck and spirit, but there must be a middle way."

"There should be, but it seems that if you want anything in this world you must be prepared to fight for it. But I haven't much time for talking. Ned O'Brien is meeting me with the trap at the far end of Thomas Street and I don't want to keep him waiting. Will you walk that far with me?"

Afterwards he walked home to Drumcondra looking up at the stars and thinking of Mollie Lenihan. He thought also of a policeman's hat bouncing along the cobble-stones. If anyone had seen him his goose was cooked.

And someone had seen him. Nedser Bolger came down to Paradise Alley next day with the news.

"Good morning, Mr. Domican," said Nedser. "I just came down to warn you that an oul' fella named Hannigan saw what you done last night and has been telling people about it. He won't tell any more about it, for I warned him that if he opened his beak I'd clock him, but the harm is done now. You know how a thing gets about."

"I do indeed, Nedser. It was good of you to come down. We'll just have to wait and see if anything happens. Tell me, how is the vegetable business going?"

"Oh, I left it six months ago to go to the grocery."

"I suppose there's more money in the grocery?"

"There's money in them all if you had a few pounds to start. I'm going to open a shop of my own as soon as I can."

"Good man. And what then?"

"Open a bigger one, sir, and maybe get a dairy as well. What else?"

What else, indeed? Nedser was eighteen then, not much bigger than when he left school, with the same bright apple-face, the same big head. His clothes were still shabby, but his eyes were bright with dreams.

Dooley, now "the Canon's man," arrived at ten o'clock to staunch a broken pane of glass with a cardboard tobacco advertisement. He slouched into the room like a conspirator.

"I heard all about it, Mr. Domican," he whispered. "Knockin' down a bobby, hawh—did you ever hear the like—I'd have given five bob to have seen it—it's what they all deserve—sure you might have knocked down a couple when you were at it. Them and their baton charges, hawh! Lave it there, Mr. Domican. Let me touch the hand that done it."

"Have a bit of sense, man," said Anthony.

Dooley winked understandingly and became even more conspiratorial than before.

"Say no more, Mr. Domican, say no more. I understand, Mr. Domican. A nod is as good as a wink to a blind horse, hawh. Leave it to me. Mum's the word, hawh, and walls have ears. No matter what happens, Mr. Domican, you can count on Dooley—aye, to the hilt. Sure all me mother's people was Fenians."

He straightened himself up then to his full height, looked as if he was about to lead his troops into battle, winked mysteriously, deflated himself again to normal pressure, and went back to his window-mending.

Rodney was the next to arrive, and Rodney was not conspiratorial. He was patriarchal, and full of the wrath to come.

"This is a terrible business, Domican—a pretty kettle of fish. Are you going to make a habit of knocking people down? If you are you should keep clear of policemen or you'll finish up in Mountjoy. What came over you?"

"How did you hear about it?"

"How did I hear about it! My good man, it's common property. The whole parish is talking about it, and probably the whole of Dublin, too. A teacher is always in the public eye. That's why he should be so circumspect. What made you get yourself into such an unholy mess? You should be more careful, for your own sake and for the sake of the school."

Anthony lost his temper.

"I'm not a congenital idiot. I didn't go looking for trouble—trouble came looking for me. What would you have done if you had seen a baton half-roads to your skull? Stopped to explain that you were a respectable citizen? Or maybe taken off your hat, bowed your head, and said an act of contrition?"

"There is no need for levity," said Rodney. "It's entirely misplaced on this occasion. This is a serious matter —possibly much more serious than you imagine. It's for your own good that I'm talking to you. You shouldn't have been mixed up in a crowd of strikers. It was no place for a teacher. Hang it all, man, if you're one of an unruly mob you're asking for trouble."

"I suppose so," said Anthony.

"But what are you going to do about it?"

"What can I do? At the moment I'm just wondering what it's going to do about me."

" I don't like it at all," snapped Rodney.

" Neither do I."

" And neither will the Canon. Wait till the Canon gets hold of you."

Anthony waited.

CHAPTER TEN

THE Canon arrived at half-past two, whistling under his breath as usual. One hand held his hat and umbrella. The other was stretched out towards Anthony. He was all smiles.

"Good afternoon, Mr. Domican. Isn't it a lovely day, thanks be to God?"

He didn't attack immediately, but made his usual feint in the direction of the boys.

"Well, boys, how is the little lah-lah doing? d r m r d-a-do-re-e-moos. Not 'muss,' boys—'moos.' Pronunciation is very important. Boys who sing sweetly never mispronounce their words. We are not bi-vocal. We use the same organs for both speech and song. Isn't that right, boys?"

"Yes, Canon," they chorused.

"And I want no absentees at Confession on Friday evening. Hands up all the boys who will be there."

He inspected the show of hands anxiously but found no heresy about.

"That's good, boys," he said then, as if a load had been lifted from his mind. "And remember—half-past four sharp." He smiled and went on: "Did you ever hear, boys, of the army sergeant who told his men to parade at ten o'clock sharp? 'When I say ten o'clock,' he told them, 'I mean five minutes to ten and not five minutes past ten '."

"My little joke fell on stony ground, Mr. Domican," he went on. "Maybe it was a little too subtle for them. That's where you teachers have the advantage. You're trained to talk to children. You speak their language. The rest of us won't grow young again until we start to dote, and then people will say that we're losing our wits. Ah me, ah me, sure the wise people of this world are the foolish ones, and the fools are wise."

"Yes, Canon." Anthony felt it was coming.

"Amn't I right now? Think of the terrible times we're living in—strikes and baton charges and hearts full of hate. The poor people! It's the women and the children who suffer most in violent times like these. God alone knows what will be the end of it."

Anthony took the bull by the horns.

"I suppose you heard what happened last night?"

"I did hear something," said the Canon." I know that you're not mixed up in this business. You have more sense. Indeed you have. But these tales lose nothing in the telling. What exactly did happen?"

He was looking out the window as he spoke, and Anthony, looking with him, could see the twisting river deep in the sand, the platoons of seagulls, the smudges of smoke out in the bay. He told his story, and the Canon said nothing until he had finished.

"You're a headstrong young man, Mr. Domican," he said then, "but I'm glad to know that this thing wasn't done intentionally. These are troubled times—and troubled times bring up the worst elements as well as the best. I'm glad you're not one of the wild fellows. The Church is often accused of being conservative, of being on the side of power and privilege, but she has a lot of experience and she knows that upheavals are often dangerous to faith and morals—that's why theologians lay down such rigorous conditions before they sanction revolutions. But I'm sure you know all this as well as I do. Anyway, don't worry too much about what happened last night. It's all over and done with, I hope."

"I hope so too, Canon."

"Please God it is. But for both our sakes be a little more cautious in future. We're both teachers, you know, and our job is to guide the people, not to lead them astray. Example is very important, and sometimes a thing which is innocent but looks wrong is as bad, as far as example is concerned, as something wholly wrong. You see what I mean?"

"I do."

"The people are having a difficult time and they hear a lot of lies. Sometimes I hear it said 'Why doesn't the Church do something?' But the Church has been preaching justice and charity from the beginning, and sure most of our social troubles boil down in the long run to want of these two virtues. When people say that the Church should do something they usually have their own notion of what she should do, and if she does the opposite they say that she should stick to her surplices and holy-water fonts."

He smiled then and rattled his umbrella.

"You had me worried for a while, young man. First you stretch Touser Kennedy and now you do the same for a policeman. Death and yourself are two great levellers."

"I must be off now," he went on, stretching out his hand. "Take care of yourself and say a prayer for me.'

He had his hand on the door-knob when he turned back.

"What's this they wrote about Goldsmith—*nihil tetigii quod non ornavit*. We'll have to change it a little to suit you. How would this do—*nihil tetigii quod non perdidit*?"

*   *   *   *

The policeman, who arrived next morning, was not in uniform, but he might as well have been: he would have looked a policeman in bathing trunks. Anthony knew him. He was a Doherty from Gweedore.

"Good day, Mr. Domican," he said. "I'm sorry to take you away from your work but I'd like to ask you a few questions."

"Come out to the hall," said Anthony, and closed the door on a class which hoped to a man that he would be handcuffed and brought off in the Black Maria.

Doherty cleared his throat.

"We have a report that on the night of Wednesday last you assaulted a policeman in the execution of his duty. Has the report any foundation?"

"I'm afraid it has," said Anthony, " but you could hardly call it an assault."

"There's more than one kind of an assault, Mr. Domican. An assault may be a blow, push, let, stay, or hindrance. So please be good enough to tell me what happened."

"Well I was caught in a baton charge and I saw people falling like ninepins all round me. So when the policeman who was making for me raised his baton I caught his arm and tripped him up. The thing was done on the impulse of the moment, and in self-defence."

Doherty shook his head, opened his coat, and dug his thumbs into his waistcoat pockets.

"It is always, Mr. Domican, if I may say so, a serious thing to interfere with a servant of the Crown in the execution of his duty. On the other hand your action was, as one might say, unpremeditated."

"It was."

"Which might," went on Doherty, "be regarded in the light of an extenuating circumstance."

"I hope so," said Anthony.

"And yet," said Doherty, with majestic impartiality and ruthless logic," it might not. We must view the case from every angle. If the assault had occurred, let us say, on degree night, the judge might be inclined to take a lenient view of it. But in my opinion the present disorder in the city exaggerates the offence."

"I suppose it does."

"It's a lucky thing for you, Mr. Domican, if I may say so, that I was sent to investigate this occurrence, and it's a lucky thing for you that Mulvany—the man you knocked down—happens to be a particular friend of mine. Mulvany and I, you might say, and in a manner of speaking, are intimate."

Anthony did his best to look like a man who might conceivably knock down a friend of Doherty's, but who in no circumstances would knock down a particular friend of Doherty's.

"So this is what I propose to do," said the detective. "I propose to report that you deny all knowledge of the alleged assault."

"But I don't," said Anthony. "How can I?"

"Now Mr. Domican, be advised by me. When a man admits an assault no one can do very much about it. But when a man denies an alleged assault, well then, in the absence of any strong evidence, and with a little assistance from the inside, so to speak, the authorities can't do very much about it."

"But what about your friend, Mulvany? Couldn't he identify me?"

"Mulvany," said Doherty solemnly, "is an understanding sort of a man, and moreover, as I said before, he happens to be a particular friend of mine. Mulvany might be asked, of course, but Mulvany might not be able to remember anything about the appearance and physical characteristics of his assailant. Let us suppose, however, for the sake of argument, that Mulvany is sent down here to see you. What happens? Mulvany goes back to the station and reports that to the best of his knowledge and ability he has never seen you before. If he does, then the might of the law can do no more."

"It's very good of both of you, Mr. Doherty."

"Ah, well, it would be a poor world if a fellow couldn't do a turn for a countyman of his own. But you were lucky, Mr. Domican. You were lucky. If a Kerryman or a Cork-man had been in charge of this inquiry, or even, for that matter, a Connachtman, things might have been different. You might have got into serious trouble. You might have got into very serious trouble. Do you see what I mean?"

"I can see that, and I'm very grateful to you."

"For nothing, Mr. Domican. How is Mr. Logue keeping?"

"Fine."

"There's a man has got on well in the world. A fine tidy business he has. Well, I'll be moving along. And make your mind easy. Mulvany and I will see you right."

That evening, when Anthony was going home from school, he saw Touser Kennedy leaning against the window of a publichouse. The big fellow straightened up immediately, whispered something to the men who were with him, touched his cap, and shouted: "More power, Mr. Domican."

The fall of a policeman always pleased Mr. Kennedy, but the fall of Constable Mulvany gave him a special delight, since it recovered for him most of the face he had lost on the day he was carried unconscious from Paradise Alley National School. It was no disgrace to be clocked by a man who could hold his own against the Dublin Metropolitan Police.

*   *   *   *

The strikes dragged on. The strikers pawned their blue serge suits, their brown boots, their china mantel-dogs, their bedclothes. They fought hunger by going hungry.

They saw themselves not as the complement of capital but as its hereditary enemies. They waylaid scabs and threw bricks at policemen. They marched and demonstrated; they listened to fiery speeches; they read the fiery papers. They gathered in groups at night outside the ever-open doors of tenements and wondered when the end would come and what it would bring with it.

The old, inevitable questions gnawed at them, and they saw one answer in the faces of their children. Is it worth it? Have we the right to make them suffer? How long will it take us to empty the pawnshops and get back our few bits of furniture? They were on the march to the promised land, but they remembered the flesh-pots.

Anthony saw two sides to the question: on the one hand the injustice of the employers, on the other the barren philosophy that social and economic history was an evolution that men might hasten but not impede, that the struggle between money and muscle was beyond compromise or adjustment and would never be resolved until the blind forces that had brought it into being shaped out the classless society. It was a philosophy which denied the primacy of the spirit, which left no room for free, will, for revealed religion, for the duties of the created towards the Creator.

Anthony saw two sides, but Mandy saw only one.

" It's diabolical," he said one day when Anthony called to see him in the market. " The whole idea is diabolical."

" It may be," said Anthony, " but it is opposed to another thing almost as diabolical—the puritan, money-making ethic. There is tyranny on both sides, but the tyranny of the workers is the tyranny of desperate men. You refuse to discuss things with them on a proper basis, and when they let off steam and break a few windows you call out the police."

"What should we do? Give in to them? If we do there'll be nothing but strikes and no end to increases in wages. And in the long run who pays for increases? The consumer, of course. If wages go up prices follow. It's a vicious circle."

"Prices follow wages because so many employers are in business for the sole purpose of making money."

Mandy opened his eyes in horror. 'And what else would a fellow be in business for only to make money? We're not in it for our health, surely?"

"It's all a question of values, Mandy. There must be profit, certainly, but if the profit motive is the only one then it's good-bye to fair prices and decent wages."

"Nonsense, man. Prices fix themselves—supply and demand—if your stuff is too dear no one will buy it."

"And if your wages are too low no one will take them, I suppose. Everything is regulated by iron economic laws. There is no such thing as justice or injustice. Next thing you'll be saying is that the seventh commandment applies only to house-breaking."

"Commandments! What about all this destruction of property? What about interfering with a man's business? Are these fellows not breaking all the commandments that ever was made? Sure they might as well put their hands in my pockets."

The strike was costing Mandy money. The salerooms of Liverpool were stacked with stuff that he was itching to sell—American apples, Spanish onions, bananas from Jamaica and the Canaries, tufted pineapples from Calcutta. His supplies were not cut off completely, but the little he could handle under police protection wouldn't fill his ledgers. The Glasgow trade, too, had dwindled to nothing. The farm labourers were on strike, the carters were on strike, the dockers were on strike, and in Kimmage and Rialto cabbages were going to seed or rotting in the ground. And though Mandy did not know it at the time, the Glasgow trade was gone for ever. The strike of 1913 did not merely interrupt it: it killed it. Ayrshire rubbed its eyes and saw the market it was missing, and after that no more green stuff sailed up the Clyde on the Burns and Laird boats.

*   *   *   *

The English trade unions sent food to Dublin to feed the strikers and their families—flour and meal, rice and potatoes, tea and sugar. But they couldn't send enough, and their support was more a gesture than an organized relief scheme. Later on some Dublin children were taken to Liverpool and lodged in institutions there at the expense of the English unions. Dublin welcomed this charity at first, but soon had reason to fear that it was the old, old kind of charity.

"We must stop the children going away," Canon Dunphy told Anthony.

"No one can defend hunger and the things that bring it about, but there are some things worse than hunger."

The Canon organized pickets of men to watch the Liverpool boat. It was a risky business, for things were at their ugliest and the strikers were in no mood to put up with opposition, or with anything that looked like opposition, and they formed their own pickets.

Anthony was one of the watchers on the night the first clash occurred. Forty or fifty children were to go away that night, and the Canon's men spoke to the mothers and warned them of the dangers of proselytism. The mothers wanted their children fed, but they weren't prepared to pay as high a price as this. Some of them started to turn home again.

"Confraternity-men and craw-thumpers!" shouted the leader of the strikers' picket. "Into the river with them! Why shouldn't the children go to England and get some food into their stomachs? They won't get much food in the churches—only scabs and hypocrites. Into the river with them."

He was a small, wiry man, with a voice that could make itself heard above a hurricane. He mounted a packing-case and spoke without opposition for two minutes. Then someone got up on another packing-case—a small man with a quiet voice. It was Canon Dunphy.

"I'm not blaming anyone," said the Canon. "I'm not a fighting man, nor a shouting man. I'm not even a clever man—like our friend here. I don't pretend that I know how all this bitterness and hatred can be brought to an end. All I can tell you is that wiser and more Christian men than I am have laid it down that every worker should have a living wage. That's all I'll say about the strike."

"Why can't you let the chislers go where they'll get enough to eat?" shouted a voice.

"Because I don't know where they're going," said the Canon. "The best and safest place for any child is his father's house."

"Listen to him," shouted the man with the voice like a gale of wind." What kind of houses have the fathers and mothers of Dublin? Rooms without a stick of furniture in them—grate without fires—beds without bedclothes—and larders without a bite in them. Is this kind of a home the best place for a growing child? Judge for yourselves, mothers of Dublin?"

"Judge for yourselves, mothers of Dublin," echoed the Canon, with a new fire in his voice. "Judge for yourselves, but think for a moment of the terrible responsibility that is yours. Remember your forefathers and the bad times when there was grim starvation throughout the length and breadth of Ireland—when there was no porridge, no bread, no potatoes—when every parent saw hunger in the eyes of his children. There was only one way then of taking the edge off that hunger, only one way of giving the stomach what it craved for—and that was the black, devilish way of souperism. They did their best to take our children from us then. They are doing their best to take them from us now. They built schools and institutions for them. But they failed. They failed dismally. Are they going to succeed now? Are you going to lose the fight that your fathers won? Are you going to sacrifice your children's Faith for your children's stomachs? Are you going to sell the pass?"

"Ask them rather," shouted the man beside him, "are they going to dash food from the mouths of their children. This priest preaches history to you, but the one lesson of history is that the Church is the prop of capitalism—both need slaves, and both decay where men are free. Don't let the priests make you give in to the bosses. Don't be traitors to the cause. It's easy for him to talk about hunger, because he knows nothing about it."

"There is no need to tell me what hunger is," said the Canon. "I live and work in the middle of it. I see it all about me—and I know that the anger of the just God comes sooner or later to those who keep food from the people. The things that have produced hunger in Dublin today are just as black and devilish as the things that produced hunger a hundred years ago in Kerry and Roscommon, in Connemara and Donegal—and they are the things that the Church has grown hoarse denouncing—injustice, and tyranny, and oppression—everything that grinds the faces of the poor.

"I'm willing to argue the whole question out with our friend here any time he pleases. I'll show him what Leo XIII has said about the rights of workers and the duties of employers. But I can't go into it all here on this draughty quayside. The Church's teaching on these matters is so clear and so rooted in justice that even a stupid parish priest like myself would find no difficulty in defending it anywhere against anyone.

"Though perhaps it would only be waste of time to defend it against people who don't want to believe anything but the worst of the Church, and I don't flatter myself that I could convince my friend in the next pulpit. The lie that the Church is the enemy of liberty, progress, and democracy is an old and hoary one, and it is based on ignorance and prejudice. I'm willing to argue, but this isn't the place or the time for argument. I'm here to expound, to warn, to appeal. Don't let your children be taken from you. It is your duty to keep them."

The little man with the big voice began again when the Canon finished, but he seemed to have lost his grip and the crowd melted away from him. Only three children sailed on the Liverpool boat.

The strike finished at last and the men drifted back to work. But many of them had no work to go back to. They would never cross a footplate or turn a trolley again, and the strike-breakers who had taken their places in signal cabins and on drivers' platforms were not displaced.

It was a famous victory, but no one seemed quite clear which side had won. Big Business had gained its point, and lost it. Trade Unionism had tasted power and forged a new technique.

CHAPTER ELEVEN.

ALFRED MENDELSSOHN RODNEY was a man of many activities. He was a member of the Stephen's Green Antiquarian Society, the Acme Dramatic Society, and the Shakespeare Lovers' Study Group: and he was Principal of the Erin Academy, an evening school which prepared a few pupils for civil service examinations and a much larger number of pupils for the King's Scholarship—a generous bounty which enabled boys and girls to train as teachers without being too much of a burden on their parents, and helped them into a profession in which they would be a considerable burden to themselves. In country districts, where the national teacher, being a little better off than the small farmers, who were only drawing clear of the Penal Laws, was looked upon as a man of means, parents of clever children regarded the King's Scholarship as the door to a career of quiet opulence: and so, year after year, batches of young people who, had the king been less anxious to get good teachers at bargain prices, might have become police inspectors, bank officials, cattle dealers, or farmers' wives, came up to Dublin and did a few months hard work at the Erin Academy. They were young, clever, and ambitious: they were prepared to work hard for the King's bounty: and in due course the best of them saw their examination numbers in the official result sheet and their full names and addresses in the prospectus of the Erin Academy.

But Rodney's parents had been a little optimistic when they gave him his middle name; for though the standard in tonic sol-fa expected of King's Scholars was exceedingly merciful it was far beyond Alfred Mendelssohn. Indeed, had the programme been confined to the first five notes of the major scale it would still have been far beyond him, for he was capable of repeating a note and thinking that he had gone down a couple of tones, or of singing an augmented fourth under the impression that it was an octave. So although he taught, at various times, mathematics, history, French, and Latin, and although his prospectus offered "tuition in Chinese," he could not teach singing. It was his one blind spot.

Anthony taught the singing at the Erin Academy, replacing a shabby old violinist who knew nothing about discipline, despised tonic sol-fa, and was drunk three evenings out of five. Anthony was not a musician, but the Erin Academy did not ask much from its music-teacher. If he could manage the modulator, give a few ear-tests on the piano, and drive home by sheer repetition the three songs which every King's Scholar who could sing at all was expected to keep on tap against the examination day, Alfred Mendelssohn was perfectly satisfied to pay him seven shillings and sixpence a week.

There were six teachers on the staff, for the Academy was thriving, and Rodney, who in its early days had done all the work single-handed, took only an occasional class and gave most of his time to drafting advertisements for the provincial papers, collecting fees, and answering letters.

Tom Lehanty taught English as a main subject and geography as a fill-in.

"I don't teach essay-writing," Lehanty used to say to Anthony. "I unteach it. I cross out. Of all the recreations with which human beings are won't to fill their leisure hours none delights me more than swimming and I make them write 'I like swimming.' If they came to me with only their mother-wit to guide them—but they don't. They come with their heads buzzing with echoes and they burst their braces trying to work in tripe like 'In the glorious and ever-relevant words of William Shakespeare, the bard of Stratford, and the author of several masterpieces, the man that is not moved by concord of sweet sounds is fit for treasons, stratagems and spoils'."

Lehanty had a special diet for word-spinners. "Bread and water for a fortnight, Burke," he would say, and Burke would get his instructions: not more than ten words to a sentence, five sentences to a paragraph, and four paragraphs to an essay. The diet worked wonders. It taught the likes of Burke to prune and economize, to write parsimoniously, simply, directly. It did away with quotations and discursiveness, and it produced crisp essays that read like telegrams. When Burke was put on normal diet again he was so chastened that his old teacher would have disowned his workmanlike English.

After a time Anthony taught algebra as well as singing at the Academy, and his part-time income rose to fifteen shillings a week. He felt like a man of substance then, and managed to put a few pounds in the bank. And because he had only three free evenings in the week the few shillings he allowed himself for pocket-money stretched further, so that he no longer needed to smoke his pipe to the last sour shreds of the dottle.

On his way home from the Academy one night he went into a shop for a box of matches. It was a tiny shop in a side-street and so brand new that its owner was still putting up some shelves. The owner was Nedser Bolger. He came down from his ladder all smiles.

"Be the janey, Mr. Domican, is it yourself? How are you at all? What do you think of the joint?"

"So it has come at last, Nedser. You have a shop of your own."

"I have an' all." Nedser grinned proudly and indicated the shelves that were stacked with jars of sweets, bottles of sauce, tins of polish, packets of candles, and boxes of biscuits, and decorated with three or four banner-posters on which was written "Bolger's for Service—Quick Sales and Small Profits."

"Good for you, Nedser. How did you manage it?"

"It's a long story, Mr. Domican. Would you think bad of me if I asked you to have a drink? I'll be closing up any time now!"

"I never think bad of anyone who asks me to have a drink. But sell me a box of matches first, and a packet of cigarettes while you're at it."

"Hansel, Mr. Domican. May your money bring me luck."

They made a striking contrast as they stood together at the publichouse counter. Anthony was tall, slim-waisted, broad-shouldered; Nedser small, stout-legged, barrel-chested. Anthony had fine, regular features, black hair, and kindly eyes; Nedser had a pippin face, a snub nose, dun-coloured hair, and eyes that looked prominent because they were popping with excitement. Mandy was a different type of business-man. His shrewdness was hidden, his optimism did not show. But Nedser's eyes gave away his faith in himself and his zest for living.

"Here's good luck, Mr. Domican." Nedser raised his pint.

"All the best, Nedser, and success to your new venture."

"Now for the story," said Anthony. "How does one become a shopkeeper all of a sudden?"

"It wasn't so sudden at all, Mr. Domican. I'm eight years left school now. I'm twenty-two past. Yes, it's eight years."

"It's not such a long time as you think, Nedser."

"It's long enough when you're working for other people —though I wasn't working for other people all the time."

"No?"

"I started in the milk business over a year ago."

"And why did you give it up?"

"I didn't give it up." Nedser was enjoying his recital.

"Lar—the brother—is doing the milk for me now. I have about fifty customers."

"Begin at the beginning.' Anthony was a little bewildered. "How did you get into the milk business?"

"Easy enough, Mr. Domican. You know the cattle lairs at the North Wall? Well any cows that's there for the night must be milked. For a long time any one that liked was let milk them—chislers, oul' wans—anyone who had a can and knew how to milk—and sometimes ones that hadn't cans and didn't know how to milk."

"So that's how you get your milk?"

Nedser drank down a laugh and wiped his mouth.

"It is and it isn't. What you'd get by fighting your turn wouldn't wet your tea. But there's no more free milking now. I went to the foreman and offered him ten shillings a week to let me milk all the cattle. He made me pay twelve-and-six, but it was worth it."

"So the chislers and the oul' wans don't get free milk any more?"

"They don't." Nedser looked only a little repentant. " But sure if I hadn't done it someone else might have done it."

"I forgot myself, Nedser—I should have remembered that there's no room for mercy in business."

"Ah, don't be so hard on me, Mr. Domican."

"I couldn't be hard on you if I tried, Nedser. But tell me this—did the others object?"

"Object!" Nedser's eyes lit up still more. "They were for throwing me into the Liffey at first. I got a few black eyes, and I gave a few. But they don't mind now, and it wouldn't make a bit of difference if they did. It wasn't a gold mine, but it gave me cheap milk and I wasn't long working up a round of me own. I carried the cans on a bicycle at first, but we have a pony and an oul' yoke now."

"May you have ten before you're finished, Nedser. This calls for another drink. What'll it be? A pint?"

"Make it a bottle of stout, Mr. Domican, if you don't mind. I'm not much of a drinker."

"I'd be thinking not, Nedser. You couldn't have much time for drinking."

"Nor much money either. I put by every bob I could lay my hand on."

"I'm sure you did. Do you get a regular supply of milk at the North Wall?"

"Oh, it's not regular—some days more than others and some days none at all. But I can buy all I want from the big dairies."

A thought struck Nedser then, and he looked a little bit abashed.

"I say, Mr. Domican—I hope you don't think it was cheeky of me asking you in for a drink?"

"Make your mind easy, Nedser. I thought it was very nice of you to ask me in for a drink. I'm only your old teacher, and you're the makings of a successful businessman."

"Now, Mr. Domican-"

"I'm in earnest, Nedser. In dead earnest. You started from scratch but if you don't go up and up I'll eat my roll-book. I'm backing you, and I'm proud of you."

"Thanks, Mr. Domican. It's good of you to say it. If only I had a bit of money."

"What would you do?"

"Lots of things. I'd buy a few cows and a bit of land to graze them on. I'd have my own milk then—not the watery stuff I have to buy sometimes. I'd open a good-class dairy in Rathmines or Ranelagh, and I'd sell eggs, honey, cream, butter, scones and cakes. I might open a few of them."

"Anything else?"

Nedser took the question quite seriously.

"A little tobacco shop in the centre of the city. College Green or somewhere. Tobacco—that's where the money is. No tick, no wastage, no weighing-out, no parcelling-up. Just hand the stuff out. Quick turn-over and good profits."

And this, Anthony was thinking, is one of the boys to whom I taught arithmetic. Why, he had arithmetic in his blood—like Lipton, like Rockfeller, like Mandy Logue.

Mandy had moved to a bigger house off Ailesbury Road. It was called *The Laurels*, and it had two tennis courts as far as Mandy was concerned this was two too many, but Alice was looking ahead. Anthony went there now and again, by invitation—unwillingly because of the gentlemen farmers and professional men who came to Alice's formal meals and discussed brood mares and stock exchange prices, willingly (though at first he never admitted this to himself) because Mollie sometimes came also. What he liked better was to drop in casually when Alice, no longer the hostess, sat by the fire knitting woollies for her first-born, and Mandy had a chance to talk. There was less chance of seeing Mollie on these casual visits, but when he did see her he got a bigger share of her company than he did on the formal occasions.

Mandy was making more money than ever, despite the loss of his Glasgow trade. He had a special agent in Liverpool who bought fruit for him at the big auctions and at prices much less than those his Dublin competitors paid the Liverpool wholesalers. He had contracts with strawberry growers in Banbridge and Portadown, and with apple growers in the Suir valley. He had a gas-heated banana house where the green fruit ripened to schedule. He supplied shops, hotels, and military canteens. He was making money hand over fist.

Anthony called to *The Laurels* one night shortly after his drink with Nedser and ran into yet another session of an old, old argument.

"You're pushin' on, me boy," Mandy began. " You're well into the thirties now, and it's not a bad age. And where are you getting? Teaching day and night, and what have you to show for it? Why don't you chuck it and come in with me?"

"Will you never be done harping on this, Mandy? You don't need me."

"I'm telling you I do need you. And I could pay you three times as much as you're making now."

"I wouldn't be worth it."

"If I thought you wouldn't be worth it I wouldn't be offering it to you. I know I could get a clerk or a salesman for a good deal less, but I want someone I can depend on—someone with common sense and education. I've had two robbers on my staff already, and between them they cost me the best part of a thousand pounds. I can't watch everything myself."

"It's no use, Mandy. I'm made the way I'm made, and you won't change me now. If I were like Ned Bolger, now, there might be room for me in the market. There's a business-man in the making for you! Started from scratch and has a dairy business and a shop of his own—and all in eight years."

"Ned Bolger—he's the boy you used to tell me about?"

"Yes. Nedser has plans in his skull—talks about buying cows, renting fields, opening dairies in the suburbs and tobacco shops in the centre of the city. All he needs is capital, and he'll get the capital sooner or later. If I had any money myself I'd invest it in him."

"I'd like to meet this genius some time. Maybe I would give him a bit of backing myself."

"Are you serious?"

"I'm not promising anything." Mandy knocked the ashes out of his pipe and looked cautious. "I'm not a philanthropist. But if this young fellow is all you say, and has ideas—well, he mightn't be a bad investment. Anyway it's worth thinking about. I don't get the divil a lot of interest on some of my money as it is. We might work the thing together. Haven't you a bit of money yourself?"

"I'm rolling in it," said Anthony. "I have eighty-seven pounds in the bank, not to speak of the clothes I stand up in, an old pair of football boots, a bicycle, a camera, six pipes, and a trunkful of books. Value me at an even hundred and you won't be far out."

"It's not a lot, but it's better than nothing, as Dinny the Cobbler used to say about potatoes and salt. For that matter, any time you want to back this lad—we'll watch him for a while and see how he shapes—I could lend you a couple of hundred. We might even form a wee company, and then you'd be in business in spite of yourself. You could maybe draw a small salary. I wouldn't have the time, of course, to take any active part in the management. However, we'll put it on the long finger. There's no hurry."

This was a development of the old argument. Anthony knew well what was in Mandy's mind. He wanted him to have enough money to get married on, and he wanted him to marry Mollie Lenihan. This fatherly solicitude amused Anthony, and sometimes angered him. He wanted to live his own life in his own way, and to marry whom he liked. He sensed that Alice was in the conspiracy, and that she wanted to plan her sister's life as Mandy wanted to plan his. But Alice would have to go more carefully than Mandy, for if Mollie got the notion that she was being shepherded into matrimony she would blow the roof off.

Alice and Mollie came downstairs after a while.

"Did Arthur go to bed quietly?" said Mandy.

"He was very good," said Alice. "Not a whimper out of him. Laughing and gurgling all the time."

"We got his photograph taken a while back," said Mandy, a little too casually. "Would you like to see it, Anthony?"

It was a purely rhetorical question, and before Anthony had time to answer it, Mandy was rummaging in the press.

"Isn't he a dote?" said Mollie, over Anthony's shoulder.

"A fine photograph," said Anthony. Then, feeling that this was a compliment to the photographer rather than to the parents, he added: " Arthur comes out well in it. He's the dead spit of yourself, Mandy. I never saw the resemblance so clearly before."

"Some say he's like me." Mandy poked the fire to hide his satisfaction. " But then again more say he's like the Lenihans."

Alice considered the suggestion carefully. " I think there's a touch of my uncle George in him—but he's very like his daddy."

This wasn't new ground. Anthony had been over it several times before, and he knew all the turnings.

Mollie had her father's three-pedal 1914 Ford with her, and she wanted to leave Anthony home, but he thought that such a courtesy would only emphasize his own poverty, and he made her pull up at the Pillar.

This will do, Mollie. I'll get a tram here."

"Nonsense. I'll run you right home. It's no bother at all."

"You'll do what you're told for once, woman dear. It will be late enough when you get home. Besides, what would Ma Mason and the neighbours say if a young woman left me home in a motor-car?"

"You're full of queer notions, schoolmaster."

"I am, Miss." He opened the door and jumped out. "It's in my blood. And I've got a queer notion now. Would you come to the pictures on Thursday?"

"Is that your night off?"

"Yes, ma'm, one of them. Will you come?"

"You're sure Ma Mason and the neighbours won't get to hear about it?"

"We'll risk it. Pillar at seven?"

"Right you are, Anthony. Be good till I see you."

She let in the clutch and rattled off.

It was an ideal association, he told himself—casual, intermittent, and care-free. It involved no commitments, no entanglements, and nothing that the whole bench of bishops couldn't see and hear. But he liked Mollie Lenihan. She had good looks, good sense, good humour, and he liked them all. He liked to sit beside her and see the shape of her face. He liked the way her eyes lit up and dimmed the stars. He liked to walk in silence with her and guess her thoughts. He saw her in upper Drumcondra and in Paradise Alley, and she sat in the first seat at the Erin Academy. He saw things by proxy for her, and spoke to her when she wasn't there to hear—showed her the way the clouds changed colour down the bay on frosty evenings, pointed out the guinea-gold of the laburnum trees to her, and looked to see her laugh when one of his pupils blundered.

He was completely heart-free.

CHAPTER TWELVE.

AT first he couldn't understand it, and for a time he couldn't believe it. All the other girls in whom he had been interested from time to time had seemed to him, from the beginning, utterly peerless. He had never had any doubts, had never progressed in certainty. He could fall in love easily and instantly. It came always like a thunderbolt. But this thing came on him so gradually that it was mountain-high before he admitted its reality: and when he did admit its reality he did not know whether to stake everything on a sudden avowal and risk her bright laughter or to try, somehow, to instill a little sentiment into an association which had up to then been free from embarrassment.

In the resolving of this problem young Arthur Logue played his part.

Anthony called at *The Laurels* one night and was some time getting in. Mollie opened the door to him and explained in one breathless sentence that Mandy and Alice were at the pictures, that it was the maid's night off, and that the hope of the Logues had been roaring at the top of his voice for the best part of an hour.

Anthony went up to see the patient. The little fellow was certainly in pain, and he was making no secret of it.

Things weren't so bad when he was howling, but each time he stopped for breath Mollie thought that he had stopped for ever.

"What'll I do?" she said. " If anything happens to Arthur Alice will never forgive me."

"It's surely not a case for forgiveness. It's not your fault."

"Stop arguing, Anthony." She stamped her foot. " Tell me what to do."

Anthony didn't know what on earth she should do, and he thought of Mr. Dick when David Copperfield arrived in Dover. But he thought also of similar disturbances in Laharden years before, and he risked Mr. Dick's prescription.

"Put the kettle on and get ready a bath."

"A bath?"

"Of course. I'll phone the doctor. What's his name?"

"Dr. Clarke of Donnybrook. You'll get his number in the book."

Dr. Clarke was not alarmed. It was probably some stomach disturbance. Nothing serious. He approved of the hot bath, and said that he would be round in fifteen minutes.

"How hot?" said Anthony.

"Test it with your elbow. If your elbow can't stand it it's too hot for the child."

Anthony repeated the injunction to Mollie. She thought it was first-hand, and, in spite of her trepidation, she was impressed. Together, and not too confidently, they bathed the howling infant, dried him in terror, and laid him in a nest of blankets in front of the fire. The bath had quietened his howls a little, and by the time Dr. Clarke arrived he was merely whimpering.

The doctor's long-distance diagnosis was correct.

"A touch of colic," he said. " I'll give him a spoonful of this medicine now, and leave you the bottle. Give him another in an hour's time."

"And I thought he was dying," said Mollie. "You have a lot to learn, young woman." Ten minutes afterwards the patient was sleeping peacefully.

Anthony and Mollie sat by the drawing-room fire then, saying nothing. The clock ticked to them, and the fire made little noises. It was all very domesticated, and the environment did not echo the song in Anthony's heart. But it was a song to which words could not be fitted at once. It ventured too much. It was based on a supposition. It involved an avowal.

He took her in his arms and kissed her, and then Mandy's latchkey grated in the hall-door. The night's adventure was told in detail, and Alice went upstairs at the double to verify the happy ending. They became a committee of experts on infant diet and the dangers of sour milk.

But Mandy couldn't always be about with his latchkey, and there were many times after that when there was no one to disturb them. The song in his heart, Anthony discovered, did not venture too much. It was based on hard fact, and the avowal, which came in due course, was not too one-sided.

In her father's house, on a night when her eyes had candles behind them, he asked her to marry him.

"I don't know," she said. "I can't marry anyone who just likes me, nor anyone whom I just like. It mustn't be a sober thing. It must be mad and unreasoned."

"It's not sober, Mollie. It used to be, but now it's as mad as anyone could wish. You don't think, surely, that I would ask anyone to marry me if I were in my right senses. The fact that I did is a proof that I'm not."

"When did it start?"

"At the very beginning- it must have started at very beginning."

"I fought against it, Anthony."

"You fought against it? Why?"

"Because Alice and Mandy had it all planned. I didn't want to have my marriage arranged the way you'd arrange a hockey match. I thought at first that they might have influenced you, and if they had I'd have lost all respect for you. But I've known for a long time how you felt."

"But how could you? I said nothing."

"You didn't, you goose. I was wondering when you would pluck up your courage."

Frank Lenihan took it surprisingly well.

"I should ask you what your prospects are,' he said to Anthony . "But I'm not going to. I don't see that it matters a whole lot, provided that you have enough to live on."

"It all depends on the kind of life we want to lead. I won't be able to ride to the hunt, but if I watch myself I should be able to pay the butcher and the grocer."

"That's fair enough, Domican. As I say, it doesn'tmatter a whole lot. If Mollie says you're the man then you're the man. The College of Cardinals couldn't hold her when she gets the bit between her teeth. I had other plans for her- I won't deny that. I trotted up man after man to her, but it wasn't any good. She could have had any one of a round dozen in her time to my own knowledge, but she knew her own mind. Well, here's my hand on it."

"Thanks," said Anthony. It sounded inadequate, but it was all he could think of.

"She's a grand girl," went on Lenihan, "though it's myself that says it, and I'll miss her sorely. Aye, she's a grand girl, though like the rest of us she has her bad points. But I'm proud of her, Domican, and fond of her. Let's drink to it."

He poured whiskey into two glasses.

"Here's to you and the last of the Lenihans."

Alice, when she heard the news, regarded it as a personal victory and set about planning the wedding as if it had been her own. She drew up lists of guests, decided the shape, pattern, and material of Mollie's going-away outfit, and prepared herself for the social event of the season.

Anthony let her have her head for a while and then rebelled.

"We must get this straight, Alice. I appreciate all your good intentions, and I hate to spoil your plans, but you had better resign yourself to the fact that I'm not going to be married in a swallow-tail and topper."

"But you must." Alice could smile very sweetly. " You're being married in University Church."

"Even if I were being married in the mosque at Sofia I wouldn't wear a claw-hammer. I won't be able to decide what I'll be buried in, but I'm being married in a lounge suit.   That much is fixed, final, and definite."

"But you must consider Mollie, and Mollie wants a white wedding.   Don't you, Mollie?"

For the best part of a week Mollie had been trying to bully Anthony into a white wedding, but she did not want a white wedding of Alice's choosing, so all she said was:

"It takes two to make a wedding, and I must consider Anthony."

"But what have you against it, Anthony?" said Alice. "You wore a tall hat at our wedding."

"Loyalty, ma'm, and good nature. If you had asked me to come in pyjamas and wear a fez I wouldn't have argued. But that was your wedding.   This is mine."

"You'd better give in, Alice," said Mandy. "This fellow is as stubborn as a mule once he takes a notion."

Anthony, being a teacher, was poor, but he was not as poor as most teachers, for his salary was bolstered up with his earnings at the Erin Academy and by the twenty-five pounds a year which he got as a purely nominal director of M. Logue & Sons, Fruit and Vegetable Merchants. Mandy gave excuses for this payment by saying that Anthony had got him Devern's business and had suggested the appointment of a country traveller, but it was really a disguised wedding-gift. In addition, Mollie had a tiny private income, and Anthony did not feel too reckless when he rented a house in Clontarf at £36 a year. It wasn't a big house, but it was as big a house as he could afford, and because Mandy gave him a bedroom suite and a carpet he managed to furnish it after a fashion and have something left for the honeymoon.

The wedding was quiet, but not too quiet, for the county families turned up in strength. The only guests on Anthony's side were his father and mother, and Sullivan, the new assistant in Paradise Alley, a tall youngster with a Kerry accent and a Grecian profile. The Domican contingent was small, but it gave a good account of itself. Sullivan was a handsome groomsman, and he made the second-best speech of the morning—the best was made by a tall teacher from a little school in the shadow of Errigal.

"I am no longer a young man," said Black Donal, "and you must excuse me if I speak from the heart. Candour is the privilege of age. A wedding means the making of new ties, but it means also to some extent the sundering of an old one, and it is an end as well as a beginning. The happiness it brings is tinged with something like regret and built about a core of sweet sorrow. The young folk here to-day may not understand me, but the grey heads will; and the young folk will understand in time.

"Our children are wholly our own in the beginning, but year by year they grow away from us—thinking their own thoughts, making their own friends, living their own lives. They belong to us as nothing else belongs to us, but at times they seem like strangers. This is part of our common human story, and its unfolding is not hindered, nor may it be delayed, by love or affection. It is an old, old story, and it has a stock ending, and it is a sad as well as a happy ending. This may seem puzzling, but it means simply that even the closest human relationships are dwarfed—and threatened—by that tremendous thing we call personality, and that in the last analysis each one of us stands alone. We parents may see the picture aright if we try to think of ourselves not just as parents but also as children, and if we remember that the sense of loss which comes to us with a child's growing-up is not something new in history but is a common experience of the whole human race.

"Ladies and gentlemen, you must pardon this philosophizing, which may, after all, be a sign of senile decay. Let me ask pardon for having introduced a serious note into an occasion which has brought so much joy to all of us. Good manners keeps me from praising my son, much as I should like to praise him. Yesterday I might have praised the beautiful girl who is now his wife, but it would ill-become me now to praise my daughter. Let me be content with saying that I feel—and I know—that she is as good and wise as she is beautiful. They have my blessing, and his mother's blessing, now and always."

Anthony had always tried to hide from his mother that Lahardan, with its bustle and life, had been more of a home to him than Lurgameelon, for it seemed a kind of disloyalty to her, but he had never realized before how deeply his foster-life must have hurt his father. He had always imagined that his father's feelings for him had been simply the feelings that the commandments enjoined, and he had been deceived by the strict impartiality with which Black Donal treated the boy who was his son as well as his pupil. Now, on his wedding morning, he saw the affection that this lonely teacher had hidden too well, and he regretted that his own selfishness had helped Lahardan to rob Lurgameelon.

Lurgameelon was a lonely place for a young fellow, but it had been lonely, too, for old people, and from now on it would be lonelier than ever.

CHAPTER THIRTEEN.

ALFRED MENDELSSOHN RODNEY retired from teaching three years after Anthony's marriage, and Tom Lehanty became Principal of Paradise Alley, which by that time had acquired two new rooms (they were really one room with a partition in the middle) and two new teachers. There was a staff of five, and Anthony, as Vice-Principal, got a share of the capitation money.

When Alfred Mendelssohn retired he retired. He could have kept on the Erin Academy without much trouble, and with not a little profit, but he wanted to leave Dublin.

He did not, of course express himself as simply as this on his presentation night. He said that he was going to "shake the dust of the metropolis "off his feet and seek "tongues in trees, books in the running brooks, and sermons in stones." In addition to this communing with Nature he intended, he said that night, to write a critical survey of Restoration Drama, a branch of literature which—and he said this without turning a hair—had been surprisingly neglected. With this impressive commitment on hands he would have no time for nursing King's Scholars and he offered to sign the Erin Academy over to Lehanty and Anthony, lock, stock, and barrel, provided that they undertook to send him each half-year forty per cent of the audited profits. Anthony and Lehanty gave the undertaking quite willingly, and Alfred Mendelssohn took a single ticket to Arden with Beaumont and Fletcher.

Paradise Alley did not fall to pieces when the great man left it. It grew and grew until it had an average for two more teachers and no place to put them. The Canon said he hadn't any money, and neither had he. The Canon never had any money. Money and the Canon were incompatible. He gave it away to widows and orphans, he parted with it to every liar who had been "promised a job in Manchester "and wanted the fare, he bought boots for poor children and blankets for tenements. So the Canon had no money for building.

"Where would I get it?" he would say. "This isn't Donnybrook or Rathgar. Do you want me to bankrupt the parish? Then there's the Education Office— it only spends a certain amount on new schools every year, and I'd have to fight with the officials and beggar my poor people."

But Lehanty kept at him, pointing out that the rooms were smelly and over-crowded, and in the end the Canon gave in. But he couldn't understand how the school was growing so quickly—it was only five years since he had built the two extra rooms—and he had a notion that the long waiting list would soon melt away and that the increase was only a temporary one; so he built two lean-to sheds against the wall of the yard. The floor of the sheds was the sloping, concrete floor of the playground, and the two twilight windows—one to each shed—were so small that in more primitive times they would have been exempt from window-tax. These additions, which held about forty boys each—the way a sardine-tin holds sardines—made school organization a nightmare. No class could be expected to stay in one of the sheds more than half-an-hour at a time, so all the classes changed rooms at the end of every period and the school spent about one-eighth of the day on the march.

It was only, of course, a temporary arrangement, and it lasted a bare seven years.

Anthony's share of the Erin Academy profits came to about twenty-five shillings a week and he got another twenty-five for teaching there, so that he was, as teachers went a wealthy man. He paid his way and put a little in the bank. He could buy tooth paste when he wanted it and look his tailor in the face. All he had to do to keep his head well above water was to work day and night. He never sat by the fire in his slippers, he seldom had time to play cards or go to a theatre, and his social life consisted mainly of an odd flying visit to Mandy and Alice at *The Laurels*. Mollie complained that she was a grass widow, and warned him to mind his health. She grumbled when he brought home the Academy accounts and worked at them until the small hours. She said that he would work himself into an early grave. But he didn't. He was as strong as a horse and eager for work. The double load of Paradise Alley and the Erin Academy did not satisfy him, and the only time he was really miserable was when he had nothing to do.

Nedser Bolger called to see him one night and said that he wanted advice.

"It's like this, Mr. Domican. That shop of mine has done well, but it's only a huckster business at best. It gives me a living, and a good living, but it's not the line I want to be in."

"Still thinking of the modern dairies, Nedser?"

"I am, sir. I know there's money to be made, and I want my share of it. And amn't I right?"

"I suppose you are, Nedser. The first million, they tell me, is the only difficulty. After that it's all plain sailing."

"Don't jeer me, Mr. Domican." Nedser was deadly serious, and a little hurt. "I know what I'm talking about."

"Sorry, Nedser." He passed him a cigarette. "But why not start your modern dairy?"

"It's not so easy as that," said Nedser, lighting up. "It takes a bit of money."

"Maybe that could be managed."

"That's what I came to see you about, sir. I haven't very much ready cash. Most of my money is in the shop and in the milk business Lar is running for me. We have a few cows now and three yokes on the road. I only bought the last one a month ago, and between the mare and all it ran me eighty pounds. I got married last year, too, and that costs money."

"Whom are you telling it to, Nedser? Well, let us get down to hard figures. How much would you need to start this modern dairy of yours?"

"I need a lot. You see, I don't mean ordinary dairies." His eyes lit up as he spoke. "I mean the kind of dairies I saw in London one year—clean as Lipton's shops—all white marble and glass cases. Dairies with honey, butter, eggs, cheese, home-made jam, good-class cakes and confectionery."

"Wouldn't one dairy be enough—for a start?"

"That's the whole point," said Nedser. "One isn't enough. You can buy cheaper for two shops than for one, and for three than for two. It stands to reason. No, Mr. Domican, I'll start with two shops or with none at all."

"I don't see why one wouldn't do."

Nedser became dogmatic.

"If you want to buy well you must buy big. It's the only way. The small man stands a very poor chance."

"How much would you need for two shops?"

"Let me see." Nedser pretended to consider. Say five hundred pounds."

"Five hundred!"

Nedser smiled at Anthony's ignorance.

"It's not so much after all. The shop fitting will cost a power of money for a start-the kind of fitting I want. Then there's the stock. I want to be able to buy for cash,

And at the right price. I'll need ovens, too-the wife's sister is a pastry-cook, and she was one herself before she got married-so the cooking will be all right. No, I don't think five hundred is too much. It might even take six, and I'd feel safer if I had seven or eight."

Anthony laughed and filled his pipe.

"I don't know what to say, Ned, I'm frightened of big figures. But tell me-how much money have you yourself?"

"In hard cash not more than a couple of hundred. I don't want to leave myself too short for fear I'd cripple the milk business."

"So you'd need about four hundred?"

"In or about. I was wondering whether I could get it from a bank. That's what I came to see you about."

You're a liar, Ned, Anthony was thinking. Whatever you came for you didn't come to get my advice about banks. You know more about banks than I'll ever know.

"I don't think so, Ned," he said aloud. "Banks lend money to people with money. If I had a thousand pounds in gilt-edged securities the bank would lend me five hundred – provided that I give them the custody of the securities and the deeds of my house as well – and if I had all that I wouldn't need to borrow five hundred. Banking, Nedser, is a mystery which brings about wars, famine, and suicides. Little men like you and me better keep away from it until we can speak its language. No, I think we can rule out the banks."

"I was wondering, sir,"—Nedser looked very humble as he said this— "I was wondering if you could put me in the way of getting the money."

Anthony wasn't surprised, though he pretended to be. He was doing some rapid calculations. He had something over two hundred pounds in the bank; blood money, earned in laborious days and laborious nights, money that stood between his children and poverty, money that he hadn't the right to risk and couldn't afford to lose. On the other hand, he had believed in Nedser's ability from the very beginning, and he believed in it now more than ever. If he wanted an investment, where would he get a better?

The delay made Nedser a little despondent.

"I only thought, like," he said apologetically, and left it at that.

"I'm a teacher, Ned, not a business man," said Anthony.

"But I'll have a chat with a friend of mine who might possibly put up the money. I can't promise anything but I'll talk things over with him and I'll put up as good a case as I can."

"I know I have a brass neck asking you, Mr. Domican, but I wouldn't ask at all only I'm certain I could make it pay. And anyway the milk business is a sort of security."

"The best security of the lot is your own instinct- that's what I'm banking on. This is Tuesday-I'll have word for you one way or another before this night week. Will that do?"

"Fine, Mr. Domican. I won't forget it to you."

Anthony called in to the market next day to see Mandy.

"It seems a good idea," said Mandy, " and if this fellow Bolger has the right stuff in him it would be a fair gamble."

"You can take my word on Bolger, Mandy. I'm absolutely certain of that. But somehow I don't like risking the few pounds I have."

"I'll tell you what I'll do," said Mandy. "If I have a talk with Bolger and like the look of him I'll put up the four hundred or whatever he needs. But I won't lend it to him—I'll lend it to you. You can give me two per cent on it—that's more than I'd get in the bank."

Anthony shook his head.

"Nothing doing, Mandy. It's bad enough risking money I have, but I'm certainly not going to risk the money I haven't."

"You're a queer fellow, Anthony." Mandy grinned at him. "Stubborn as a Clonmany goat when anyone wants to do you a favour. The best thing I can do is to have a talk with Bolger.   I'd like to meet him."

They met a few nights later in Anthony's house: Mandy fat, rather dull-looking, with a sizeable stomach and red hair that was losing its colour and thinning a bit on the top: Nedser low-sized, round-faced, red-cheeked, and perky as a town sparrow: Mandy the successful business man who looked as if he wouldn't drive a hard bargain with his bitterest enemy; Nedser, with his major battles still to win, looking as if he wouldn't drive a soft bargain with his best friend.

Nedser did most of the talking. He built his pyramids of honey jars on shelves of veined marble, he flicked eggs deftly into paper bags, marshalled rock buns fresh from the oven on window-trays, and showed how Rathmines was languishing for the want of an up-to-date dairy. A hucksters shop was only a huckster's shop. This was an idea and he decked it out like a poem.

"I can see it all. Mr. Logue. The thing is cut and dried in my head—it's been there for years."

Mandy nodded. Mandy understood. Mandy remembered the young man from the north who had planned his attack on the Dublin vegetable trade like a campaign. He had a fellow-feeling for Ned Bolger, and in that little corporal of commerce he saw the marshal that was to be.

The plan was drafted in the rough there and then, and the details were ironed-out at two meetings held in the office of Mandy's solicitor. Anthony and Nedser were to put up two hundred and fifty pounds each, and Mandy was to bring the capital up to a thousand. Shannon Dairies, Limited, was born and christened, and Mr. Edward Bolger was named as managing director. One shop was to be opened in the Rathmines district as soon as suitable premises were found (though Nedser had found them already) and another in Donnybrook as soon as the first was well under way.

Nedser, however, did not hand over his dream to his backers. He saw, not two Shannon dairies, but a dozen or more, and he had a clause inserted in the agreement giving him the option of supplying up to three-fourths of any extra capital that might be needed if new branches were opened later on. Nedser did not know where the money would come from, but he knew that it would come: and he knew also that Shannon Dairies, Limited, would grow and grow. Looking into the future he could see sandwich rolls in Clontarf, cream cartons in Phibsboro', and veined marble shelves in suburbs yet unborn.

CHAPTER FOURTEEN.

ANTHONY DOMICAN had two families. The one that was housed in Paradise Alley was depleted every year by the fourteen-year-olds who left to carry grocer's baskets or ride messenger bicycles, and reinforced by the plasticine brigade that marched in, hopefully or tearfully, every first of July from Sister Mary Augustine or Sister Mary Seraphine: the one that was housed in Crescent Terrace, Clontarf, on the other side of the little bay, grew more slowly, but it grew steadily, and by the time he was eight years married there were four on the roll—Christopher, Mary Margaret, Brigid Ann—who was christened before anyone thought of her initials—and Denis Patrick.

Christopher was a Lenihan to his finger-tips. It was not just a vague resemblance, something that might be admitted with reluctance and reservations. It was a startling resemblance not to the Lenihan family but to one particular Lenihan. He was his grandfather over again. Anthony claimed that Brigid Ann was a Domican, and he argued that Mary Margaret—who had reddish hair, big brown eyes, and her mother's way of laughing—was nine-tenths Fanad Logue. He could see something of himself in Denis Pat, but he could make nothing of Christopher, who was Frank Lenihan even in the cradle.Christopher had fair, curly hair, and blue eyes, and he had Anthony's heart from the beginning. Tom Lehanty used to chaff him about it.

"And you're telling me about this wonderful baby of yours! Me with my houseful. Wait until you have nine pairs of boots needing protectors and you'll know something about rearing a family."

Anthony knew something about psychology, but it didn't help him to understand Christopher, and his experience in Paradise Alley was no help in Crescent Terrace. If anything, it was the little family that helped him to understand the big family, taught him to think of children as individuals, as little folk who might be sickening for measles or weary after a night of coughing, taught him to see more and more clearly that a child is not a test-tube jumble of ancestral abilities and characteristics, and that God's image is not bestowed lightly. In the beginning he saw Christopher as an extension of himself; saw his child depending on him for thoughts and ideas the way he depended on him for dinners and woolly vests. He wanted to mould and shape him, to whittle his mind.

Mollie saw things more clearly. She had intuition to guide her, and her mind was not cluttered, as Anthony's was cluttered, with a tangle of psychological nonsense.

"You can't do it, Anthony," she used to say. "You can't train up Christopher the way you train a rose-bush in the garden. You can't map his life the way you map out a syllabus. You can't dominate him completely, and he'll hate you if you try."

Anthony was a long time learning.

Grandfather Lenihan was very fond of Christopher. He was fond, too, of Mary and Denis and Brigid, but none of them displaced Christopher: he liked Mandy's family-—Arthur, John, Nuala, Joseph, and Charlie—but Christopher came first. He called for Christopher in his old Ford (and later on in the new one that took its place) and carried him off to the Zoo, or the seaside, or home to *Sycamore Lodge*. Sometimes he brought Alice and Mollie and sometimes two or three of his other grandchildren, but this was just to take the bare look off the thing. And because *Sycamore Lodge* was so far from Clontarf Christopher was given a special bedroom there later on so that during the school holidays or at week-ends he could spend a night or a night or two with his adoring grandfather.

This open worship wasn't good for Christopher, and Anthony did his best to discourage it, but the subtle flattery behind the old man's preference often got the better of his judgment. Then there was Mollie to think about, and he had to go carefully. Mollie was inclined to resent the suggestion that *Sycamore Lodge* wasn't good for Christopher. She saw no harm in lending Christopher now and again to an old man who had never had a son of his own.

Christopher liked going to *Sycamore Lodge*. He had a pony and saddle there, a room of his own, and a housekeeper to dance attendance on him. He dined on roast duck and peaches and got as much lemonade as he could hold. He was scolded sometimes in Crescent Terrace, and whacked when he needed it, but in *Sycamore Lodge* his word was law. In Crescent Terrace he lived in community, subject to prohibitions and sanctions: but in *Sycamore Lodge* his whims were encouraged and monotony was the only crime.

Grandfather Lenihan spent money on Christopher and gave Christopher money to spend. He brought him to pantomimes and to the pictures. He got him invitations to parties in big country houses, and bespoke admiration for him everywhere they went. When they had nothing more exciting to do they went to *The Laurels*. Christopher fixed his standards early in life, and he fixed them far above Crescent Terrace, which had no tennis courts or football fields, and which didn't give away half-crowns without good reason.

He was spoiled from the beginning.

Anthony was uneasy about it all, but he found it hard to rationalize his misgivings. And Mollie gave him no help. She told him not to be selfish. It did a boy good to meet other children and see other homes. You couldn't tie a child to your apron-strings, and there was no use in trying. Children grew up, and they grew out and away from you as well as up. It hurt a little, but it couldn't be helped. Not till years afterwards did she admit that in Christopher's case it could have been helped, and then it was too late to do very much about it.

All Anthony could do was to make sure that the same mistake—and at the time he did not know how big a mistake it was—would not be made with the others. Mary and Brigid and Denis would not be weaned from Crescent Terrace with ponies and presents. They would not be ceded to *Sycamore Lodge* to give a foolish old man a family out of season. They would stay at home and eat bread-pudding. They would have to make the best of Crescent Terrace. There would be no more fosterage.

Mary and Brigid and Denis were fine little people, not any more unselfish than they should have been, perhaps, but contented enough with Crescent Terrace and happy in its protection. They were lovable children and they had their own gifts; Mary had her gold hair and quick laughter, Denis his manliness and boisterous good nature, Brigid her serious little ways and her dainty movements. But Christopher had something more magical—a charm which could not be explained by his good looks, a knack of winning everyone to his side; and Anthony, though at first he did not admit it even to himself, loved him more than any of the others, and suffered accordingly.

His love for Christopher seemed at times stronger far than his love for Mollie, for his love for Mollie was as much a part of him as his eyes or limbs, and it lost its sharp outlines in the happiness which it engendered. It was so stable, changeless, and balanced so perfectly by her love for him that he took it, as he took chairs, and books, and pictures, as part of the furnishing of his home. It never decreased, but it remained somewhere at the back of his mind and seldom obtruded itself into the sharp focus of consciousness. It was calm and comforting, like health or a clear conscience, and its real intensity was hidden by its effects. But his love for Christopher stabbed him like a pain. It was always in the forefront of consciousness. It never eased or abated, and it seemed, almost all the time, unrequited. Anthony made all the advances. Christopher was respectful, but he kept his distance.

Long afterwards, when he could look at things more dispassionately, he was to realize that the fault had not all been Christopher's, and that his own efforts to win his son's affection had helped in the losing of it. Anthony wanted to unload his knowledge on to Christopher, to form his interests, to dictate his mental background. He was never harsh, or unkind, but he tried always to turn their common experience to Christopher's advantage. Christopher went to the sea and the hills, to Guinness's and the Museum, to lectures and music recitals, and he went with a tutor by his side.

But in spite of everything Christopher grew up his own way. He fiddled with chemicals and steam engines, he rigged-up electric bells, he took watches to pieces: and these things were not in the tradition of the Domicans. Since the time of Anthony's grandfather, the poor scholar who had come home from Salamanca unpriested, the Domicans had been book-men. They were not practical, and they grudged the time they had to spend on practical things. They were in the Renaissance tradition—vir ille vere civilis non alius quam orator. They lived with words and let others put grease on the cart wheels.

So Anthony tried, very quietly, to kill Christopher's mechanical bent. He dosed it with Latin and English, tried to sublimate it into a love for pure mathematics—for mathematics unsullied by wheels and pistons, loads and forces. But Christopher wasn't interested. He left the classics unread and spent his pocket-money on potassium permanganate.

In Paradise Alley Anthony's teaching was more successful, though his success there was no consolation for his failure in Crescent Terrace. In Paradise Alley he took his material as he found it and did not try to alter the terms of the problem; in Crescent Terrace he was not so wise. He could laugh at himself in Paradise Alley, could see how all his efforts might be nullified by stupidity or stubbornness on his pupils' part, or by blindness on his own, so that he sometimes learned as much as he taught and thereafter taught the better for it: but in Crescent Terrace he did not see his own failings till the harm was done.

*   *   *   *

He couldn't do much harm to boys like "Weh" Cunningham. He could not take from them the resourcefulness that hardship bred in them, nor impair the gamin confidence that misery had left unbroken: and he could teach them to say their prayers, sign their names, and count their wages.

The light of intelligence glowed very dimly in "Weh." He was a sprawling, lanky fellow, with little flesh on his bones. His eyes were bland and dull-looking; his ears were almost fused with his head. His nick-name was a contemptuous one. It suggested the cry of a sick sheep. He was promoted year after year, not because he deserved promotion, but because, being as much of a passenger in third as in fourth, as much of a dead-weight in fifth as in sixth, he might as well finish up at the top as at the bottom. Had he been left in first standard all his life he would have been a despised whale amongst nimble minnows, and a new handicap would have been added to his congenital failings. So "Weh" got his chance and finished up at the top of the ladder. He became a docker afterwards and earned just as much as his brighter colleagues. Life reversed the verdict of the school and graded him as worth his keep.

"Tell me this, Joseph," said the Canon to him one day. "Could I say Mass?"

"Yes, Canon."

"Could Mr. Domican say Mass?"

"No, Canon." Weh was beginning to look pleased with himself.

"Very good, Joseph," purred the Canon. "Very good indeed. And now, like a good man, elaborate a little. Why couldn't Mr. Domican say Mass?

Weh didn't hesitate. This was a simple one.

"Because he doesn't know how, Canon."

The Canon rallied his forces.

"Joseph, I'm going to ask you another question."

"Yes, Canon."

"Could I baptize a baby?"

"Yes Canon."

"Quite right, Joseph—because I'm a priest. I have baptized thousands of babies in my time. I even baptized you. But now for a harder question—could you baptize a baby?"

Weh smiled. This was one of the questions to which he knew the right answer. It had been dinned into him week after week, year after year, and—possibly because it certified that in one respect at least he was as good as the next—it had stuck.

"Yes, Canon," said Weh. "I could baptize a baby if it was dying and they hadn't time to go for you."

"Precisely," said the Canon. He was all smiles, for he didn't expect much from Weh and was content with little. "In that case you could act as my vicar. You're doing very well, Joseph, and I have only one more question to ask you. Could Mr. Domican baptize a baby?"

"Of course he could, Canon," said Weh. "Sure he learned us! "

Late that afternoon, when Anthony wanted a few minutes' peace to finish a wall chart, he gave the class a piece of transcription to keep them quiet. But it didn't keep Weh quiet. Weh bristled with questions.

"Sir," he asked first, "will I write me name at the head of the page?"

"Where do you usually write it?" said Anthony. "On the roof of Farrelly's coal-shed?"

Weh got down his name, and then a fresh doubt assailed him.

"Will we write the date, sir?"

When this question was decided for him he wanted to know what date it was (though the date was written on the blackboard), and a little later, discovering that his ink-well was nearly empty, he asked permission to fill it. And he wasn't satisfied even then: he wanted to know if he could fill all the ink-wells.

"Listen, Cunningham," said Anthony. "Put that ink-can back in the press. Then sit down. And keep sitting down. And keep your mouth tightly shut. If you ask as much as one question between now and three o'clock I'll warm your palms for you."

There was no grace of movement about Weh. He lumbered over to the press, replaced the ink-can, tumbled a box of pencils, gathered them up again, and stumbled back to his place with that unsteady walk of his. Then he hitched up his trousers, sat down, twisted his body into the cramped position he adopted whenever he put his soul on paper, took up his pen, cocked his head to one side, let the tip of his tongue appear at the left side of his mouth, and was ready to begin. Just as his pen touched paper he whispered something to the boy beside him.

"Cunningham, didn't I tell you to keep your mouth shut? What did you say to Kelly?"

Weh looked very unhappy, but he said nothing.

"What did he say to you, Kelly?"

Kelly hung his head. "Stagging" was not popular in Paradise Alley, and it was not prudent to give information which might get another boy into trouble. But when he looked round at the others for guidance he saw that they wanted him to tell. Poor Weh was outside the schoolboy code.

"He said, sir—he said 'Honest to God, Jembo, me heart is broke'."

Anthony laughed and the class laughed. Weh looked desolate and alone. Life was too much for him. He did his best to learn, he tried desperately to please, he referred every difficulty to the teacher and did nothing without permission, but things seemed to go against him. Punishment he could have understood, but laughter like this puzzled and hurt. It set him apart from his fellows and gave him what he hated most of all—a fool's pardon. Anthony, reading all this in the poor fellow's face, called him up to his desk.

"Didn't I tell you, Cunningham, not to speak for the rest of the evening?"

"Yessir."

"And you disobeyed me?"

"Yessir."

"Very well. Get me the stick."

Weh stumbled happily to the press, tumbled the box of pencils a second time, picked them up again, and came back with the stick. He handled it almost lovingly—it was going to rehabilitate his self-respect.

It would have been no kindness to Weh to have given him a token slap, so Anthony gave him a good one. It had little effect on Weh's thick palm, but it could be classed as corporal punishment, and he went back to his seat justified.

Anthony disagreed with the Department's ideas on corporal punishment. The Department wanted every punishment recorded in a special book, and even laid down that the punishment and the offence should be well separated in time. It wanted its teachers to punish in cold blood, lest they should punish too often or too severely. Anthony could never punish a child in cold blood. It was against nature. Punishment was a rational sanction, but it should not, he thought, be administered rationally. It should be given in the flush of anger; it should follow hard on the heels of the offence. For him that was the safest way, for the first slap cooled his anger. Children understood punishment that was swift and certain. They saw an elemental justice in it, and the excuse of anger. But they hated remands, and in postponed punishments they saw only brutality and vindictiveness.

Anthony believed that mild corporal punishment was salutary and necessary both in the home and in the school, but he did not find it easy to punish Christopher. Denis took his tiny chastisements in the time-honoured way—he yelped and bore no ill-will, he suffered and soon forgot. But Christopher took punishment in a way of his own; without flinching, without tears; and he seemed to connect it, not with any particular offence, but with the emotional barrier that separated him from his father. He seemed to regard h both as a further proof of incompatibility and as a mean revenge.

These feelings were not Christopher's. They were projected into him by a father who saw the breach between himself and his son widen gradually in spite of all his efforts to narrow it. It might have been better, Anthony had to admit to himself long afterwards, if he had been content to do his own thinking, if he had given Christopher all the whackings he earned and spared him the lectures and reproaches which took their place.

But he seldom punished Christopher, even in the beginning. There was something about Christopher's bearing and about his slender, graceful body that made physical punishment seem a desecration: and Anthony's lectures and appeals were the measure, not of Christopher's offences, but of the heartbreak which his father felt at being cut off from the one he loved more than all the world besides.

CHAPTER FIFTEEN.

CHRISTOPHER failed his Intermediate examination—with a certain distinction. He got honours in chemistry, and drawing, a near pass in mathematics, and he failed by a few marks in Irish and by a wide margin in Latin. This was a clean break with the Salamanca tradition, which seemed to have passed to the dealing Logues, for Arthur Logue got a university scholarship that year and John, the second son, passed his Intermediate with honours.

Anthony made no secret of his disgust, and he gave Christopher the rough edge of his tongue.

"How could you expect to pass? All your time spent with gadgets and chemicals—and when you're not messing about with smelly test-tubes you're playing football! It's about time you grew out of toys. John Logue didn't fail. No fear! He has too much sense for that. Well, from now on, my fine gentleman, I'll keep your nose to the grindstone. I'll break every bone in your body before I let you become a wastrel."

He hated himself for saying it, but the hurt to his pride made him hit out blindly. At first Christopher made no effort to defend himself, and used no weapons but his proud, defiant look and his mirthless smile. He was almost man-size then, tanned from the sun and deep-chested from swimming and football. His fair, curly hair was brushed back from his forehead, and the long, girlish lashes above his blue eyes accentuated rather than took from his look of manliness.

The tirade kept on and on but it drew no response from Christopher.

"Don't stand there like a dummy," said Anthony. "Say something."

"I'm not the only one who failed the examination."

"I suppose you're not. You're not the only fool in the country. You have plenty of company among the failures—plenty. And look at the chance you got. You were denied nothing. Everything was made easy for you. And the money that was spent on you was hard-earned. The trouble is that you got things too easy—far easier than I ever got them, or my father before me. We hadn't just to pass a qualifying examination. We had to win our way into the training college against stiff competition."

"We can't all be teachers," said Christopher.

"Don't answer me back," Anthony blazed at him, and then took all point from his veto by continuing the line of argument which had provoked it.

"I don't want you to be a teacher. You haven't the brains to be a teacher."

He knew it was the blackest of lies, but his fury, and the love that matched it, drove him on. "I don't want to make a teacher of you. I want you to be something better than a teacher. That's why I'm spending money on your education and upbringing—to give you a better chance in life than I ever got. And what thanks do I get? What gratitude do you show? All you do is idle your time. I want to make something of you, to give you a profession."

"You want to make me a doctor or a lawyer," said Christopher quietly.

"I want to be an engineer."

"So you're going to be an engineer are you? An engineer without mathematics! So far as I can see—unless you mend your ways you'll end up by being nothing. All you'll be fit for is greasing cars in a garage or navigating a garbage lorry."

It was a blind, jagged, vicious sort of argument, and it hurt Anthony more than it hurt Christopher. It was the sort of argument they were to have time and time again, until in the end Christopher took refuge always in a maddening silence and left all reproaches unanswered. There was stubbornness in them both, and stubbornness wasn't the whole story.

Anthony could have borne with Christopher's idleness and failures if he had had his affection, but Christopher rejected all overtures. Mollie knew, and said nothing. Her love reached out two ways, and there was a stricken look in her eyes at times because it did not make a complete circuit. Once in a while Christopher would come to Anthony with stories of football and tennis matches, or with accounts of his experiments in the shed at the bottom of the garden, and Anthony would know then that Mollie had sent him and that he had come for her sake.

He still disapproved of Christopher's visits to the old man at *Sycamore Lodge*, but he could not ban them completely without adding fuel to a fire that was already big and disturbing, and Christopher still went regularly to see his grandfather; not so regularly as formerly, but too often for Anthony's liking. The old fellow still remembered birthdays and Christmases, and he had generous ideas about pocket-money.

Anthony did not disapprove of Christopher's visits to *The Laurels*, but they made him feel a little uneasy. Christopher, he felt, liked big houses and private tennis-courts.

There was a touch of Whang the Miller in him, a weakness of character that might develop into snobbery in time. The glories of *Sycamore Lodge* and *The Laurels* did not make him more contented with Crescent Terrace, and he was inclined to be a little impatient with a father who could not afford trips to Bermuda and was not on visiting terms with judges and cabinet ministers.

But Mary Margaret, with her brown eyes and gold-glinted hair, put Crescent Terrace first and her father before all men. She was two years younger than Christopher, but she was old enough to diagnose Anthony's complaint. She tried to make up for Christopher's coldness, and Anthony was glad to come to her in self-pity, licking his wounds.

Denis Patrick, who had the black hair of the Domicans and the stocky frame of the Logues, was a boisterous body—cheerful, impulsive, quick at his books and careless about his clothes. Brigid had black hair, a thin face, and big serious eyes. She was not as clever as Denis or Mary, but was very thorough in her work and she spoke with words out of books.

It was a family of which any man might be proud, and Anthony was as proud a father as the next. But although he knew that each of the others was better-natured, more affectionate, and more manageable than Christopher, though he knew that Mary and Denis were more brilliant and Brigid more steadfast, he could not help loving Christopher best—not because of anything but in spite of everything. He loved Christopher best, though he got next to nothing in return.

Christopher thought his father a poor man, but Anthony was poor only by the standards of *The Laurels* and its visitors. As teachers went he was well-to-do. He had his earnings at the Academy and his share of the profits, he had his tiny salary as a director of M. Logue and Sons, and he drew dividends from Shannon Dairies, Ltd., at eleven per cent. Shannon Dairies swelled and prospered, and Anthony, increasing his capital holding by a small amount each year, shared in its prosperity. It captured the suburbs and the good shopping districts one after another. It came in triumph to Grafton Street, George's Street, and Henry Street. It found customers in Dun Laoghaire, Blackrock, and Dalkey. It supplied rolls and sponge cakes to Clontarf and

Drumcondra Shannon Dairies grew to twelve branches in as many years, but it lagged behind Edward Bolger, its managing director and principal shareholder. Nedser had no need to go to Mandy Logue with his hat in his hand when he wanted new capital for his fast-growing firm. He got it from his bank manager, and he could have got twice as much had he wanted it. The bank manager was very nice to Nedser. He said "Good-morning " to him in the special tone he kept for customers whose overdrafts were never queried by head office. Nedser was a man of property, a man of many interests. The milk business that his brother Lar managed for him was buttressed by a tidy farm at St. Margaret's, and the Bolger herd supplied not only Lar's house -to -house customers but hospitals, hotels, and small dairies. Nedser had a large yard at the North Wall where cattle on their way to England were kept overnight at one-and-sixpence a head. He had his string of Shannon dairies —which sold almost everything but milk. He was nosing his way into the wholesale confectionery business and had two motor vans which carried rock buns, Swiss rolls, apple tarts, and sandwich cakes to city shops.

But his proudest venture was a little shop in Dame Street, a little shop that sold tobacco and cigarettes, pipes and cigars; for it was his very own. Cattle and cakes made money for him, but the little shop in Dame Street he loved for its own sake. He loved it so well that he wanted to spatter the city with replicas of it. "It's only the first," he said to Anthony the day after it was opened. And so it was.

Every *Cigs* shop had exactly the same fittings, the same sign, the same layout. Every *Cigs* shop was run by smart, well-groomed young men who gave expert advice on the blending of tobaccos and flashed cigarette lighters whenever customers fumbled for matches.

Nedser didn't approve of girl assistants in tobacco shops.

"They're nice to some customers," he used to say, "but they flirt too much. My young men are nice to all customers, and the third time a man calls they should know what he wants before he asks—it flatters a man and makes him come back again. My young men are well-dressed and efficient, and they can fill a pouch without wasting a shred. No sleepy Joes nor good-looking flappers for me."

The little shops did well, and they justified his formula of years before: " Tobacco—that's where the money is—no tick, no wastage, no bulk—quick turnover and good profits." It all came the same to Nedser—muddy lairage pens at Spencer Street, slabs of butter in Donnybrook, milk-vans, mahogany counters, cigarettes, cows, coffee cakes. There was money in everything he touched.

His mother, the poor woman, had been right when she had said that Nedser had more brains than Alfred Mendelssohn Rodney: and Anthony had been right when he filed away a reference as a wager with fate. Nedser had proved himself and justified all who believed in him.

It meant hard work, of course. Nedser rose with the lark and totted figures into the small hours. His red two-seater carried him from *Cigs* shop to Shannon dairy, from St. Margaret's to Donnybrook, from the North Wall to his office in Dame Street. He seemed to be everywhere at once, and his managers and assistants could never time his comings. He might arrive in the morning or in the evening; he might skip a day and come twice the next. He planned all his campaigns himself, dictated strategy, and trusted no one more than he could help.

He found time for everything. He went to a good tailor and learned how to dress. He went to a technical school at night to study book-keeping and English. He got an architect to plan him a house in Clonskea. He wanted to do the right things in the right way.

Once a week or so he called to Crescent Terrace. He usually came late at night, and he usually found Anthony alone with his late supper and tired after his evening's teaching. Nedser had got as far as calling Anthony by his first name, but be still looked up to him, still brought him his worries. Anthony was his business adviser—Anthony who knew nothing about business and cared less. But it was easy giving Nedser advice. All you had to do was to back up his own wild notions, and encourage him to trust his unerring instinct.

And sometimes it was Anthony who needed advice.

"I'm worried about this eldest boy of mine, Ned," he said one night. "He and I don't seem to get on well together. That may be partly my fault and partly his—I don't know. But one thing I do know—he's not working hard enough at his books, and that's his own fault."

"It could be, Anthony, that you're asking too much of him. You're a teacher. You're a clever man, and you're used to books. You know the old saying—'you can't put an old head on young shoulders'."

"I don't want to, Ned—God knows I don't. I tried that long ago and it didn't work. I'd be quite satisfied if he worked half as hard as Mary or Denis.

But he doesn't. He doesn't seem to realize the importance of work."

"Maybe you take him the wrong way?"

"Maybe I do, God help me, but I've tried every way. We just don't seem to hit it off together." He was thinking of his father's speech at his wedding. 'Year by year they grow away from us—thinking their own thoughts—living their own lives—so that at times they seem like strangers.'

Nedser broke in on his thoughts.

"I usually leave all this to the missus—though my kids are young yet and they don't give me much bother in that line. Women are better than men at this sort of thing, I think. After all, they should be. It's their job."

Anthony smiled.

"It's my job too, Nedser—the job I'm trained for, the job I've been at all my life. And I sometimes think that as far as Christopher is concerned I have made a very poor fist of it. I'm afraid I have."

"You probably see the thing as much worse than it really is. He's a fine lad, is Christopher. Nothing much wrong with him. Maybe a little bit spoiled, but as good as you'll get nowadays, and a lot better than most. Don't worry too much about him. Take things easy and stop fretting. Sometimes I think that you are working far too hard. That makes you see things all wrong. Try easing off for a while."

"That advice comes well from you, Ned. I suppose you're the biggest glutton for work in the city of Dublin."

"I work as hard as the next, I know, but it's not work like yours. Teaching all day is bad enough, but it's the divil altogether when you're at it day and night."

"It's not so hard as it looks, Ned. Teaching is the one trade I know, and it suits me. I get a kick out of it that I can't get out of anything else."

Ned took his pipe out of his mouth, as if to say something, and then put it back again.

"Out with it," said Anthony. "I know by the look in your eye that you have something to say. What is it?"

"Only this—that you're not as young as you used to be. None of us are —we're all going the one road. You're a young enough man yet, in a way, but you're creeping on, and it's time you were seeing a bit of your own fireside. This day and night business is all right for a while, but if you keep at it long enough it'll shorten your life."

"Maybe you're right, Ned, maybe you're right." Anthony puffed at his pipe. "But I'm not so sure. Some of these fellows who take things easy in the evenings don't look any the better of it. I think it all depends on the way you're built. This night work was very useful to me. It helped me to rear the youngsters; it gave me something over and above. A teacher's pay isn't as big as some people think it is, and if a man had to depend on it he wouldn't have much of a way on him."

"I know that," said Nedser. "It's a hard job and it's very badly paid."

"That's what Mandy Logue used to say to me years ago. He wanted me to go into the business with him."

"And you wouldn't?"

"I wouldn't, Ned, and I've never regretted it. I'm very glad that I stuck to Paradise Alley. It's where I belong."

Ned began to grin.

"You're a strange man, Anthony. If I had got the chance of going into Mr. Logue's business I'd have jumped at it like a shot. But you know your own mind, I suppose. You know what's best for you. But if you take my advice you'll ease off on this night work and take a bit of comfort for yourself."

Anthony lay awake that night and thought over Nedser's words. His days and nights had been so well filled that Mollie and the children had seen very little of him except at week-ends. That might have been yet another reason why Christopher had grown away from him. Perhaps, too, the ceaseless round of work had done something to himself, had dried him up a little, had made teaching his recreation as well as his work. And yet, without the Erin Academy the little world of Crescent Terrace would have been a little less prosperous. There would have been less money for clothes and holidays, for school fees and cod liver oil, for skates and football boots. But the welfare of Crescent Terrace could not be measured solely in terms of pounds, shillings, and pence, and a father had other duties besides the duty of providing for his children.

In one sense he had given too little of his time to his wife and family; in another he had given far too much.

CHAPTER SIXTEEN.

IN the year of Our Lord nineteen hundred and thirty, Canon Dunphy, parish priest of St. John's, became an Archdeacon, and Joe Dooley promoted himself a stage further in a hierarchy of his own. He had been in turn a curate's man, a parish priest's man, a canon's man, and now he had reached the heights. "That's a great honour we got," he said to everyone when the good news came. "Archdeacon, no less! "But the people found it hard to get used to the new honour. The Archdeacon was still " the Canon," and Dooley, outside his own mind, was still "the Canon's man."

The confraternity men, wishing to show the Archdeacon that they thoroughly approved of the honour which Mother Church had conferred upon him, and that they took a vicarious pride in it, decided to present him with an illuminated address and a wallet of notes. This little windfall coincided with the maturing of an insurance policy, and the Archdeacon found himself for the first time in his life with a little money in the bank. It didn't stay there long, and for once it didn't go to widows and orphans, touts, touchers, cabbies who wanted the price of new shafts for th' oul yoke, and innocent countrymen who found themselves, through no fault of their own, stranded and penniless.

"Did you hear the latest?" said Dooley one day he came down to put new boards in one of the school floors. "We're going to buy a motor car! Isn't it a good one, hawh? A motor car, no less. I think the Canon must be goin' soft in the head. Wouldn't th' oul pony and trap do him good enough, hawh? Sure he'd be time enough to buy a car when they make him an archbishop. Time enough, I'm thinking. His Grace the Most Reverend Patrick Augustine Dunphy, Archbishop of Dublin and Primate of Ireland—wouldn't it sound well? That'd be a quare one, hawh! He would need a car then, all right, and he'd have a man to drive it. But sure it's foolishness of him to be thinking of getting a car now. He'll never learn to drive it at his age. Someone must have talked him into it."

Dooley had another instalment of the story with him when he came down next day to replace a faulty washer, and he told it in his own way.

"'Oh, no, Archdeacon' says I, firm but respectful like. 'Anything in reason but I draw the line somewhere. I'll try anything once but I'm too old to learn to drive a motor.'And wasn't I right, hawh? Did you ever hear the like? 'Beggin' your pardon, Archdeacon,' says I, 'but I wouldn't attempt it not even if it was to cost me me job.' Real firm I was with him. Real firm. And wasn't I right? Wouldn't I look the right fool behind the steerin' wheel of a motor at my age? 'Oh, no, Canon,' says I. 'No motor cars for me'.'"

"And how did he take it?" said Anthony.

"Real crafty," said Dooley. "When he saw that I was as firm as a rock he tried coaxin'. We'd have great times riding round together in the new car— and wouldn't I hate to see someone else drivin' him—some stranger. After all these years,' said he.   Oh, he's a very persistful man, the Canon. A very persistful man. Powerful crafty, hawh. But he won't get round me. Bedad he won't. You can't budge Dooley once he gets the bit in his teeth."

Dooley, however, did less than justice to the Canon's powers of persuasion, for before the week was out he was registered as a student at the Acme School of Motoring and was learning not only how to drive a car but how to change tyres, clean sparking plugs, and free choked carburettors. It was a hard and hateful session, but in a way it was well worth while. While the car lasted, Dooley was free of cisterns and floor-boards, tattered maps and broken blackboards. The Archdeacon could go nowhere without Dooley; the Canon's man had become the Archdeacon's right-hand man. Dooley waited in the car at the school gate when the Archdeacon came to Paradise Alley. Dooley drove the Archdeacon to funerals and Months' Minds. Dooley and the pastor of St. John's were inseparable, and if the Archdeacon was a pillar of the Church Dooley was his flying buttress.

But before long a tiny cloud appeared in Dooley's bright sky. In the beginning the Archdeacon took his car with simple faith and childlike trust. It was a gift of God—like apple tarts, sunsets, newspapers, and wristlet watches—and he had no wish to analyse it into its constituents or dissect its magic into cause and effect. But after a month or so he began to take an interest in the mechanism of his chariot, and Dooley, quite unsuspectingly, helped to bring about his own downfall. He preached to the Archdeacon on the wonders of machinery and echoed the lessons of the Acme School of Motoring. He showed his employer how a few simple movements gave life to a dull, dead thing, how a touch of the wheel could keep it on a straight course. He showed him how the surging force of suddenly-generatedgases flowed through cranks and pistons and turned wheels with smooth power. Wonderful, it was, and simple as kiss-hands.   A child could understand it.

Dooley sa his mistake when it was too late. He tried to retract. He told the Archdeacon the split-second skill that gear-changing demanded, the difficulty of watching ten things at once, the terrible things that might happen if an absent-minded driver pressed the wrong pedal. Finally, he suggested that the language of the teachers of the Acme School was not by any means sacerdotal, and that it was only by the grace of God that he had finished the course without any serious weakening of his moral fibre. The Archdeacon was not in the least alarmed.

"Sure you can teach me, Joe. Why should I go to a motoring school? I'll be your first pupil. When I come to think of it, I've been very selfish these few weeks back. You haven't had time for anything but driving me around. The schools and the chapel are falling to bits, and arrears of work are piling up. It was very selfish of me, Joe, and you must forgive me. I should have thought of learning to drive long ago."

"Now Archdeacon! "Dooley was almost in tears. "You're making a terrible mistake. Leave the driving and the dirt to me. You just sit back at your ease and enjoy the scenery."

"Joe!" said the Archdeacon ominously.

"Yes, Archdeacon." Dooley knew then that the battle was lost, and he hung his head in despair.

"You can take it as settled, Joe, that I'm going to learn to drive. I can't command you to teach me, but I'm asking you, as a favour, to teach me. Will you do it?"

"Yes, Archdeacon."

"Thank you, Joe.   I knew you wouldn't refuse.   I'll have my first lesson in the Phoenix Park after breakfast on Monday morning. I think the Park would be the best place?"

"It's big enough anyway," said Dooley.

The Archdeacon always claimed that he learned to drive in next to no time, but in the opinion of others more qualified to judge he never learned at all. After an hour's tuition he was able to manage all right, as he said himself; after a full fortnight he was still a public menace. Cautious and conservative in most things he had neither prudence nor fear when he sat behind the wheel of his car. He drove far too fast, he didn't watch where he was going, he took both sides of the road with him, he broke all the traffic rules, he rasped his gears; he gave no warnings at turnings or crossings but sounded the horn when danger was past. Dooley sat beside him in terror—admonishing, warning, praying, but the Archdeacon would drive blissfully on, humming a little tune to himself and telling Dooley not to be excited.

Once or twice, when disaster seemed inevitable, Dooley grabbed the steering wheel, jammed on foot brake and hand brake together, and shouted

"Canon! Canon! " The man of God, being pulled up perforce, would say: "Joe, I think that even in moments of crisis I should respond more quickly if you remembered to address me as Archdeacon." He would look at Dooley out of the corner of his hedge-sparrow eyes then and Dooley would say: "Yes, Canon, yes, but I wish to God you'd look where you were going."

The car didn't last very long, and it was only the mercy of God that Dooley and the Archdeacon didn't finish up with it. Dooley told the story at the Anchor Tavern, at the Emerald Social Club, and in Paradise Alley at regular intervals and every time he told it he shut his eyes to avoid the crash.

"There we were—comin' down Raymond's Lane—and us goin' from side to side of the road. A terrible man, the Canon, hawh! God's truth. I told him to be careful, but I might have saved me breath. You might as well be talkin' to one of the loonies above in Grangegorman. Whistlin' he was, no Jess, hawh! Whistlin' the *Tantum Ergo*, and the brim of his hat down to keep the sun out of his eyes.

"'I'm doin' famous,' says he. You are like hell,' says I. In me own mind, of course. I was praying like the head of the confraternity at the close of a mission. Past Riordan's pub with us then, and us goin' like the Belfast mail—round the corner at Lanigan's and into Kilkenny Street. We took the corner on two wheels—and before I got my sight right back or had time to move hand or foot we ran bang into one of the Merchants' steam waggons—the big yokes. I thought we were finished, hawh! Says I to meself, well I died with the priest, anyway.' But be the grace of God we missed the steam yoke—that and the grab I made at the wheel. But we hit the side of it, and what was left of th'oul car bumped up on the footpath and bang into a lamp-post. That was bad enough, hawh! but it was a damn sight better than bein' under the steam waggon."

There were several versions of what happened next. The most colourful of them, which was based on Dooley's first-hand account, was compiled by Father Martin, the senior curate, amended by Father Mulligan, the second curate, and told by Canon Ryan at the next diocesan dinner. According to this version, Dooley, flung clear when the car hit the lamp-post, saw the mangled body of his employer crouched over the broken steering wheel. He hadn't the time nor the courage to take in all the details, but he did notice that the Archdeacon was covered with blood, spangled with broken glass, and minus an ear. Dooley ran screaming up the road, and returned in five minutes time with Father Mulligan, Dr. O'Neill, two policemen, and about one-fifth of the Archdeacon's parishioners. The battered car, still draped about the lamp-post, was by that time the centre of a fair-sized crowd, but of the Archdeacon there was no sign. He had gone back to the presbytery on a milk-car, it appeared, and those who went with all speed to give him spiritual and bodily succour found him sitting in his own parlour, holding on his left ear with one hand and turning the pages of the Apocalypse with the other.

The extent of the Archdeacon's injuries was never known for certain in the parish, but the injuries were much less serious than Dooley had led the mourners to believe, and the mutilation which Canon Ryan described at the diocesan dinner was, to say the least of it, a little exaggerated. The Archdeacon's left ear, right enough, showed a tiny piece of sticking-plaster when his head appeared above the pulpit the following Sunday, and he walked with a slight limp for a week or so, but he came off much more lightly than did the lamp-post and he suffered no permanent disability. Dooley sprained a wrist and got a few cuts on his face, but he got full value for his injuries in free drinks at the Anchor Tavern. The car, however, was sold to a garage man as it stood, and the Archdeacon, having only third-party insurance, never replaced it. From that on he did his parish journeys either on foot or in his tub trap.

*   *   *   *

Anthony was twenty-five years in Paradise Alley. Twenty-five crowded, exciting years, twenty-five heart-breaking, desolate years; exciting because he appreciated the high privilege that was his in being foster-father to successive generations of dockland children—heart-breaking because he could do so little for them. There were few Nedser Bolgers in Paradise Alley. The bulk of Anthony's pupils had been under-sized and under-nourished, and they had grown up to under-paid, casual employment. The sanatorium and the graveyard took their toll, and the high walls of Maryborough Jail preached the civic virtues to social misfits. A few of them were lucky enough to get fairly good jobs at home: some of the best were driving street cars in Boston, navvying in Liverpool or Manchester, stoking ships round the Cape, lying quiet in Flanders fields.

Paradise Alley had taught them the truths of their religion, linking up with the teaching of home and chapel; it had given them what character training it could against the down-dragging influence of the slums and the degradation of congenital poverty. But it couldn't raise them up and make healthy, self-reliant, self-respecting men of them. Only decent homes, unharassed parents, good food, and civilized sanitation could have done that. Paradise Alley was beaten from the start. It mattered little whether Smasher Murphy learned little or much in Anthony's "Extra Mathematics" class. What mattered was whether Smasher's uncle could get him apprenticed "to the carpentry" and so give him a trade which would take him away from the legacy of the tenements.

Paradise Alley was beaten from the start, but all dockland believed in it: all dockland believed in a mysterious thing called "book learning," which separated the classes from the masses. The children of dockland came to school long before they reached the statutory age for entering, but none of them stayed on a month after they reached the statutory age for leaving. They left at fourteen (getting jobs as messenger boys, or no jobs at all) because the State laid it down that at fourteen a boy was as far as the master could put him. The experts said fourteen and the parents took them at their word. It never occurred to them to ask at what age the children of the experts left school. Their strong suit was humble faith. A boy could learn a lot in eight years if he put his mind to it.

Most of them, of course, didn't get even the eight statutory years. Days were deducted for minding the house when mothers were sick, weeks were deducted for basket-carrying at Christmas, fruit-picking in June, and odd jobs that might turn up at any time. Bad weather, broken boots, and sickness claimed a good share of the balance. Rathmines went to school every day, but the roll-books of Paradise Alley were pitted with absence circles, and the attendance officer earned his money.

As formal education, Paradise Alley was a failure, but it wasn't a bad place to teach in and Anthony wouldn't have swopped it for Donnybrook or Rathgar. He was the window-through which his scholars viewed the world, their link with the salmon fisheries of British Columbia, the Battle of the Yellow Ford, and Keats's *Ode to Autumn*. They had neither books, nor holidays, nor the conversation of educated parents to give them a background. Their literature was the cinema, their art gallery the tattered hoarding. They depended on Paradise Alley.

Their environment was inimical, but not wholly inimical. They came from districts where neighbourliness was almost a law of nature and charity part of self-preservation. They had sympathy for suffering because they knew what suffering meant. They hankered after justice because they had experienced the effects of injustice. They lived side by side with vice, and in ways they grew old before their time; but the things that made them old before their time did not kill their innocence or their wonder. They had a sense of worldly values that made Anthony love them and pity them at once, but there was a simple goodness in them that seemed to thrive on the very conditions that should have made it impossible.

CHAPTER SEVENTEEN.

CHRISTOPHER grew up tall and good-looking. He was robust enough to play front-line forward in the school Rugby team, but he gave the impression of grace rather than strength. His fair hair had darkened a little, but it had kept its curl. One lock strayed down over his left temple, and he had a habit of throwing it back again with studied negligence. He was well aware of his good looks and given to striking attitudes. He was fond of clothes and he carried them well, affecting a slight carelessness in details and accessories, which gave him a look of distinction.

He did most things well but nothing exceptionally well. He took small parts in the school operas, he was a fair pianist, a good swimmer, a dependable debater. But in all his activities he relied mainly on his natural gifts, and his success owed little to hard work or application. He was content with easy profits.

His school reports were only average, and they should have been better than average. He worked at the subjects he liked and tailed along in the others. He did his homework regularly, but he took no trouble with it. Anthony pleaded and threatened, coaxed and admonished. Christopher went off to Clontarf Baths to get his fine body tanned and bronzed, to the football-field, or to parties at *The Laurels.*

"These things are all very well," Anthony used to say, "I don't want to shut you off from them. They're a part of life, but they don't come first. They are good things, but good only when they are earned. If they go hand in hand with mental indolence they'll make you sound in body but flabby in mind. I wish to goodness you would give more time to your books, Christopher, and get down properly to study. This is the time for it—it will be too late afterwards. You have the brains and you have the opportunities —far better opportunities than I ever had. Don't let them slip—for your own sake."

Sometimes the interviews were more acid in flavour, but even when Anthony hit hard Christopher never tried to excuse himself, never answered back. He simply smiled, and his smile said

"You're an old-fashioned schoolmaster—you want to drive me the way your father drove you—but I'll do things my own way and I'll get there just the same."

During his last year at school, and to the great surprise of everyone, he became a little more industrious, and during the three months before the leaving certificate examination he seemed to be taking his father's advice. He cut down his tennis and swimming, he sat late with his books, he got Anthony to help him with his Latin and mathematics. Mollie brought him tit-bits for his supper and warned him not to work too hard.

Christopher didn't work too hard, but he worked hard enough to wipe off some of his accumulated arrears, and he took the examination in his stride. Anthony cross-questioned him on his answering and felt satisfied that he had passed. And he did pass, with a little to spare. His good marks in mathematics, physics, and chemistry made up for his languages and secured him an honours rating.

Anthony met him in the hall the day he came home with the news, but Christopher said nothing and went straight out to the garden, where his mother was weeding. Mollie came rushing in a moment later.

"Christopher has passed with honours—isn't it great news? Somehow I felt he would do well this time. He worked so hard, the poor fellow."

Anthony shook hands with his son.

"Congratulations, Christopher. Great work! Splendid work! I'm very proud of you."

Christopher smiled and said nothing. And in spite of the smile there was a look in his eyes that stubbed Anthony's elation and brought a chill to his heart. It was like a boundary march, guarded and defiant.

Later in the evening Anthony and Mollie talked things over.

"I'm glad he did so well, Anthony, especially after failing his Intermediate—it will give him confidence."

"I'm glad too, Mollie. It's a relief to me. But it's not confidence he needs. He has buckets of confidence—too much I think sometimes. And he has brains enough, if cared to use them."

Mollie smiled.

"I know what you're thinking, Anthony. It's in your face. 'I gave him a good education—I spared him nothing —and still I can't get him to see life with my eyes.' 'Tell me the truth, Anthony—aren't you still bent on making him a doctor or a barrister?"

"What if I am? He's my own son and I'd like to see him in a decent profession."

"He's your own son, Anthony, but he's not you. You see him as a famous surgeon or a leading counsel, but it's not Christopher you see really—it's yourself. It's the great Anthony Domican showing the world what he would have done if only he had got half a chance."

"So that's what you think," said Anthony, sulkily "You seem to have a very high opinion of me."

She put down the sock she was mending and looked up at him.

"I think you're the best man in the world, Anthony Domican. That's why I married you. But that doesn't mean that you aren't a little bit blind at times."

"So I'm blind, am I?" Anthony was very much on his dignity. "And how or in what, may I ask, am I blind? In what way, for instance, have you better vision?"

"Don't get angry, Anthony. All I mean is that Christopher is bent on doing engineering and that it would be a crime to put him on for anything else."

"He can do anything he blooming well likes. All I ask is that he works hard and passes his examinations."

"He'll pass all right, Anthony. Didn't he pass this time? I'm glad that we have the money to send him to the university."

"I'm glad, too, but I don't think he realizes the chance he's getting. We have the others to think of—and we can't afford to send them all to the university—for that matter if I had only my Paradise Alley salary I don't see how we could send even one. So I wish he would choose something more elegant than engineering—it's only a big name for plumbing."

He didn't mean that, and he said it only to get some of the bitterness out of him. Christopher was under no obligation to follow the traditions of the mountainy Domicans, to like books and dreams, to draw back from life and study shadows. Christopher was a man of his age. He wanted to throw bridges across rivers, to conjure up new roads on the face of the country, to listen to the siren song of speed, to break the spell of the Domican who had come back from Salamanca unpriested.

"I'll let him do what he likes, Mollie," said Anthony after a while. "I'll not hinder him in any way. It's his own life and he must live it in his own way."

"That's better, Anthony. We're only lookers-on now. We owned him when he was in the cradle, but he's not ours now."

All the time they were talking there was a background to their thoughts, and they did not discuss it. Anthony silent from pride, Mollie from pity. Anthony had lost Christopher, but his hurt must never be mentioned, and there was no way of easing the pain that was eating his heart.

Mary knew it, too, and it heightened the affection she had for her father. She always came to him first with any news she had, and tried to make up for Christopher's silence. Anthony saw through it all and loved her the better for her staunchness, but the solace that she brought him was concerned only with the two of them. It did not reach the hurt that it was meant to lessen.

Christopher came in later, looking well-dressed in a shabby sports coat and flannel trousers. He had been to a meeting of the swimming club, and he had brought home a medal that he had won in the scratch fifty metres. He never told Anthony about his victories, but Anthony could have recited the whole list of them as unerringly as he recited his prayers. He kept the newspaper clippings in his pocket-book until they crumpled with age.

Anthony tried to talk to his son.

"How did the meeting go, Christopher?"

"Oh, very well."

"When is your next water polo match?'

"Against Pembroke on Wednesday."

"Is Pembroke a good team this year?"

"Pretty hot."

It was making conversation.

Anthony put on his hat and walked down as far as the sea wall. The tide was coming in, creeping round the Baths and making an island of the disused mine-shaft beside it. On the far side of the bay, amongst oil tanks and warehouses, cattle yards and tenements, was Paradise Alley. It was a place where a man could see his work objectively and be free from emotional complications, a place where good teaching was a matter of skill and care. He had been a success in Paradise Alley, but he had failed with Christopher.

Just a week later there was a little celebration in *The Laurels*. John, the second son, had passed leaving certificate, and Arthur, the eldest, had got his first medical with honours. Christopher and Mary went over for tennis in the afternoon; Anthony and Mollie came in time for tea. There was a dance afterwards for the young people, and Anthony and Mandy went upstairs to be rid of the noise.

Mandy poured out whiskey.

"Here's good luck to the rising generation, Anthony. We're shoving on a bit ourselves—we've got responsibilities, and stomachs, and bald patches."

"Aye," said Anthony, sipping his drink. "It's a long time now since we had that famous argument with the captain of the *Ayr Maid*—thirty years and more."

"Troth it is," said Mandy.

The phrase comes strangely from you, Anthony was thinking. It belongs to the past that you've left far behind you, to Mulroy and the purple hills. You're fat and prosperous now. One of the big business men—Chamber of Commerce, subscription lists, stock exchange reports, cruises to Madeira, and front seats at symphony concerts. The same old Mandy, with a touch of dignity added. Not purse-proud, God bless you, nor bumptious, but a wee bit smug, maybe.

Mandy tilted his pipe between his teeth.

"Good news about Christopher, eh?"

"He did a lot better than I expected. All I was hoping for was that he'd scrape through matriculation. He did a bit of work this time, though, and it helped him."

"What are you going to do with him? The university, I suppose?"

"He's talking of doing engineering."

"He could do worse, Anthony. It's the coming profession. This is a mechanical age."

"I suppose so, but I would rather see him doing medicine —like Arthur."

"Every man to his taste. We can't make doctors of them all."

"Oh, I'll let him follow his bent. All I hope is that he studies and works a bit harder than he did at school. Arthur seems to be doing well—he's a clever lad."

Mandy lit his pipe before replying, as if too ready an assent would be bad manners.

"He"s a good lad, Anthony, though it's myself that says it. But there again—I wanted him to come into the business with me. Wouldn't hear of it. There was no use in forcing him. I hope that John will come in though. I won't last for ever."

"No more than any of us."

"No more than any of us, as you say. Here, have another drop of whiskey." As he was pouring it out he added, a little too casually;   "Did I tell you they were asking me to go for the Senate?"

"The Senate?"

"Aye," said Mandy, gloomily. "The Senate. I don't want to, naturally, but they're coaxing me."

You old hypocrite, Mandy. They won't have much trouble coaxing you. And Alice would love it—'Senator and Mrs. Logue.'

"The only thing that would tempt me at all," said Mandy, "is that business isn't getting a fair crack of the whip. Labour has far too much power. Free this and free that—doles and vouchers—the country can't stand it. And the very people who are getting them can't stand it, either. It's making them think of the Government as a sort of universal provider. Unless we business men call a halt there's no knowing where things will end."

Anthony said nothing. He was thinking of the forces which had brought Labour into being, that had compelled it, in self-defence, to meet tyranny with tyranny. He was thinking of Paradise Alley and the slums about it, of boys who left school at fourteen and faced a labour market which had no room for them, of sandwich-men in flittered boots, of the recruiting station at Newry, of the whole horrible mess that was called a social system.

"What are you smiling at?" said Mandy. "At the idea of me being a senator?"

"Not that at all." Anthony shook his head. "You'd make as good a senator as the next, Mandy, and a sight better than a lot of them. No, I'm thinking of the talks we used to have in 1913 or thereabouts. And what makes me smile is to hear that business isn't getting a fair crack of the whip."

"But neither it is, Anthony. I tell you the drain on employers and ratepayers is crippling. Wages have rocketed.'

"You come to Paradise Alley with me any day, Mandy and I'll show you another side of the picture. I'll show you boys with weak chests and bare feet, under-size toddlers who are being reared on tea and bread, women who never know a minute's peace—nor anything within an ass's roar of enough to live on—from the time the first child goes to the breast to the day they bury them with penny a week insurance policies. Yes, and I'll show you men who grow old before their time trying to raise a family on fifty-five shillings a week. These are the things which no country can afford."

"The main trouble," said Mandy, "is under-production. "We pay men for doing nothing, and those who are working won't do a decent day's work for a decent day's pay. Why should they, when they can get paid for holding up the walls of the labour exchange? Under-production—that's the trouble. That's the real reason why the country can't afford improved social conditions."

"I'm not defending the dole, Mandy. I'm not defending the unions. But I think it's a strange thing that the country that can't afford to clothe and feed its people can afford all the things that rotten conditions make necessary. It can afford prisons, sanatoria, asylums, reformatories and all the rest. It can afford judges to lecture poor harassed working mothers of so-called juvenile delinquents."

"It's a pity you don't go in for politics yourself," said Mandy, drily. "You'd make wonderful speeches."

"This isn't politics, Mandy. It's Christianity. If you like you could call it business."

Mandy sat up. "And how in the name of God could you call it business?"

"Because of the markets you're losing—because the people would buy more if they had the money. Families are the real consumers. Any one of your children will eat more, waste more, wear out more in a week than you do in a month. Take a slum child from Paradise Alley with leaking boots, a half-empty stomach, and a few thin duds on his back—there's a potential customer for butchers, bakers, candlestick-makers, and vegetable merchants—multiply his needs by a thousand, ten thousand, fifty thousand, and you have a market going a-begging."

"The whiskey has gone to your head, Anthony. I suppose you have heard now and then of a thing called money? Have you ever wondered where the money is to come from to enable all these potential customers to buy all they need?"

"There's work to be done, isn't there? When so many people have to do without there must be work to be done—shoes to be made, loaves to be baked, houses to be built. Money is simply a receipt for work done, a device that enables the butcher to get bread and socks and wash-hand basins in return for the superfluity of loaves he produces. That's what money should be—a simple token system controlled for the benefit of the people. Unfortunately, it has become a most complicated system. It has become a commodity in itself. It is cheap one day, dear the next. You go into the Senate and talk sense to them. Don't preach charity, for they mightn't understand you. Preach the rashers, and boots, and milk, and woollen underwear, and school texts, and saucepans, and overcoats that could be sold if the people had the money to buy them."

"If you want that nonsense preached," said Mandy rising, you'd better go for the Senate yourself. But don't go too deeply into this money mystery or you'll end up in Grangegorman. Come on down and we'll watch the young folk for a while. The women will be wondering what's keeping us. There were ten or twelve young people there, besides Logues and Domicans, and the dance was in full swing. Mollie and Alice could play old-fashioned waltzes, Mary and Christopher played the faster modern dance music that Anthony hated. But the oldest man in the room liked the modern music and could sing its nonsensical choruses. The years lay lightly on Grandfather Lenihan, and he eased their feather-pressure with smooth shaves, sea-water baths, well-cut clothes, and manicures. He looked like the old age of a successful jockey, slightly magnified. His face had lines, but no wrinkles, and his eyes sparkled.

"How are you at all, Anthony? You're missing all the fun. Isn't Christopher looking well? I knew that he would pass his exam, with flying colours. He's the pick of the bunch."

"He did well enough," said Anthony. "And how are you keeping yourself these times?"

"Never felt better. It's younger I'm getting since I gave up market gardening and sold out to the builders. Bricks and mortar is the best paying crop I ever touched."

It was quite an enjoyable evening, for the old folk as well as for the young, and Mollie's eyes were full of Christopher.

"We must give a party some time," she said to Anthony when they got home.

"Yes, it's a long time since we had one."

"We never had one, Anthony. I mean a real party, not just a children's party. Christopher and Mary will expect it. We could ask the O'Reillys, and the Dorans, and the Logues. If we opened the folding-doors we could have plenty of room for dancing."

She went on then to plan the party as if it was to take place the following evening, had discussions with herself about trifle, and sandwiches, and wondered whether she could manage the supper in two relays.

"Dad's very pleased about Christopher," she said, after a while. "He has offered to pay all his university fees and to buy him a dress suit."

"Oh he is, is he?" said Anthony.

"Now what exactly do you mean by that?" said Mollie, aggressively.

"Nothing—nothing at all."

"Well, I think it is very good of Dad, and you might at least have the decency to say so."

But Anthony wasn't too pleased with the idea. It wouldn't be easy to pay Christopher's university fees and keep the others at secondary schools, but it was a privilege which he didn't want Grandfather Lenihan to filch from him. And Grandfather Lenihan would do more than pay Christopher's fees. He would keep him in pocket-money and spoil him completely. Anthony couldn't do anything about it without annoying Mollie, but he did not want to see his tiny hold on Christopher weakened still further. He would willingly have spent all he had on Christopher if he could have got from him in return the one thing he wanted, and he saw no reason why Grandfather Lenihan should buy a son in his dotage.

CHAPTER EIGHTEEN.

JOE LEHANTY retired on pension, received the usual presentation from his colleagues, and was wished "many happy years to enjoy his well-earned rest." But it wasn't to be a rest. Joe couldn't afford a rest, for his pension was only half his salary, and the tail end of his family was still at school. So when he left Paradise Alley he had to work harder than ever at the Erin Academy.

Anthony's promotion took place as a matter of course. He signed a new agreement with the manager, and was formally sanctioned by the Department as Principal of Paradise Alley.

Joe Dooley was the only one who used more than a sentence or two in congratulating him. Dooley was a little bit wizened by this time, and had lost all his hair and a few more of his stained black teeth. He still visited the school in the wake of the Archdeacon, but he delegated the heavier repairs to his son, who was not on the parish pay-roll but performed a filial duty by helping to keep his father on it.

"Lave it there, Mr. Domican," said Dooley on his first visit to the school after Anthony's promotion. "Me swingin' yourself! D'ye know what it is—from the day you knocked the lard outa Touser Kennedy—saving your presence—I knew you were the man for Paradise Alley."

"That's a long time ago now."

"Long or short, what does it matter, hawh? What's a few years one way or another? Ah, I knew from the beginning, Mr. Domican. When I heard how you clocked the bobby outside Liberty Hall, says I to the missus—'Julia,' says I, 'there's a man who's goin' to be Principal of the school sooner or later'— me very words. Oh, that's as true as I'm standing here."

"It was long-distance prophecy, Joe."

"Prophecy!" Dooley seized on the word. "That's what it was. Prophecy, no less. Somehow I seen it in you."

He went into a short reverie then, and finished up by shaking his head— as if to convey the futility of trying to rationalize a premonition that clearly bordered on the supernatural.

"The right man in the right place, Mr. Domican. And I'm tellin' no lie.

There's no flattery in me. I say what I think an' them that doesn't like it needn't. The right man in the right place, hawh! You'll be able to manage th'oul Archdeacon all right."

"I'm not so sure about that."

"But you may be sure, Mr. Domican—you may be sure. He's a tough man, God bless him—like a child in some ways but tough as cement when he likes. I'm only a workin' man, Mr. Domican, but I've learned a lot since I started to work for the Canon—and that's not to-day nor yesterday, hawh! If you ever want any advice or help you can count on Dooley."

"Thanks, Joe. It's very good of you."

"Divil a bit," said Dooley magnanimously. "Divil a bit. Why wouldn't I and me knowin' you so long? It would be a queer world if a man wouldn't do a turn for a friend of his. Wouldn't it, now, hawh?"

"It would indeed, Joe."

"You might sing it," said Dooley. "What's this was in the old lesson-book long ago—*Of all the gifts that God can send there's none to match a trusted friend.* Good luck to you in your new job, Mr. Domican, and don't forget to get the Canon to build you a couple o' new rooms."

"I'll do my best, Joe."

"You're the man for the job, Mr. Domican. It might be better though if you got him to build you a new school. D'ye know what I'm goin' to tell you—I'm sick, sore, and tired tryin' to keep this old place from fallin' asunder—sick, sore, and tired."

But it wasn't so easy managing the Canon, who could see questions coming and parry them before they were uttered, who could cloak his mental processes in simplicity bland but devastating. There was the day, for instance, when the deputation called on him to ask the loan of his parish hall for a whist drive in aid of the Quay Wanderers Football Club. They rose to their feet like marionettes worked by the same wire when the Archdeacon came into the parlour, and they clutched their hats for comfort. The Archdeacon named them one by one with a delight that suggested a guessing game.

"Ah, Mr. Doyle! How are you at all? I never saw you looking better. And Mr. Rafter! How are the greyhounds doing? And bless me if it's not Mr. Murphy! Wasn't it good of you all to call on me. Sit down now. Sit down."

They all sat down.

Mr. Doyle, who was a stout, red-faced, outsize of a man, looked into the lining of his bowler hat for inspiration and in began his piece.

"You'll have to excuse us, Archdeacon, for making so free as to call on you but we were sent . . ."

"It's a pleasure to have you call on me," smiled the Archdeacon. "A pleasure, gentlemen. So please don't make any apologies, Mr. Doyle, for none are necessary. And that reminds me—did you ever see my barometer? You didn't? Come on out into the hall till I show it to you."

The deputation filed out into the hall in the wake of the Archdeacon. They inspected the barometer. They praised the barometer. They tapped the barometer. When words failed them they adopted attitudes which proclaimed the deepest admiration for the barometer. After a decent interval Mr. Doyle tried again.

"As I was saying, Canon—Archdeacon, I mean." Mr. Doyle got very red then, and his companions blushed with him. "As I was saying, Archdeacon, it's terrible of us to be taking up your time, but the way it is, you see, the football club

"Ah," said the Archdeacon, "the football club. A fine game, football. I used to play it myself when I was young—with no more than a moderate amount of success. A grand game, football. It keeps a man from getting fat. But don't think you're taking up my time, Mr. Doyle. Good gracious, no. I'm delighted to have you—delighted. I only wish that my parishioners would visit me oftener. I have a grand little house here and I'd like them to see it. Did you know that I had a geyser in the bathroom?"

Mr. Doyle hadn't known. Neither had Mr. Rafter. Neither had Mr. Murphy. All three were unaware of the amenities of the Archdeacon's bathroom. So he brought them upstairs and turned on the geyser for them.

They acclaimed it together in turn. Mr. Doyle muttered something about the wonders of science. Mr. Rafter was understood to say something about the civilizing influence of the Saturday-night bath. Mr. Murphy touched the magic hot water and bore the scald without flinching.

The deputation then inspected the Archdeacons canary, his piano, his three dark, dreary oil-paintings, and his grandfather clock, and they found no fault with him. When they were finished with the grandfather clock they expected to be brought back into the parlour, but the archdeacon opened the hall-door then to show them the potted shrubs on his door step. Here Mr. Doyle made a last valiant effort.

"As I was saying, Archdeacon, we're on the committee of the Quay Wanderers Football Club...."

"Splendid!" said the Archdeacon. "Three better men they couldn't have on the committee –three sensible level-headed decent men. Good-bye now, Mr. Doyle, and don't be long till you call again. I'm always delighted to see my parishioners."

The Archdeacon stretched out his hand and Mr. Doyle took it. It was about all he was able to do. He certainly wasn't able to speak. Neither was Mr. Rafter. Neither was Mr. Murphy. None of them spoke a word until they had gone ten yards down the road, and then Mr. Rafter spoke for the three of them.

"What the hell are we going to tell the committee?"

Dooley was doing a little harmless weeding in the back garden, and the Archdeacon called him in.

"I want you to do a little job for me, Joe."

"Yes, Archdeacon."

"You know the Anchor Tavern?"

Dooley looked the Archdeacon straight in the eye.

"I think that I have noticed a place of the name in the course of my perambulations."

"Well, Joe, I'd like you to perambulate in that direction now and bring a message from me to the three sensible, level-headed men you'll find drinking pints in the snug."

"Is it Doyle, Rafter, and Murphy you mean, Archdeacon?"

"Yes, Joe."

"Only I seen them here with you, Archdeacon, I wouldn't have known them from the description. Three sensible, level-headed, decent men how are you! "

"Now be charitable, Joe."

"And what message would you be after askin' me to bring them, Archdeacon?"

"Tell them first, Joe, that I'm a little bit absent-minded at times. And tell them—with my compliments—that if the date suits they can have my little hall for a whist drive in aid of that admirable and praiseworthy institution the Quay Wanderers Football Club. I trust, Joe, that I have the name right—I think that Mr. Doyle mentioned it once or twice."

"That's the name, Archdeacon. I'll give them the message to the best of my ability. And will that be all, Archdeacon?"

The Archdeacon thought for a few seconds.

"If they should ask you to partake of some liquid refreshment, as I think is not at all unlikely, you may use your own discretion."

Dooley listened tolerantly to the three wise men.

"Who are you tellin'?" he said when they had finished

"Tellin' me about the Archdeacon? Sure I know the man inside out—and what's more I'm the only one who does-the only one in the parish.   D'ye know what I'm going to tell you?"

He looked from one to the other of them then, and in the circuit his eye caught the pint of porter that was on the counter beside him. He looked at the glass, first in surprise, as if he wondered how it had got there at all, and then belligerently, as if he resented the presence of anything that hindered his flow of conversation. Finally he seemed to dismiss it from his mind altogether, and answered his own question.

"He could tell any one of you what you had for your breakfast this morning—what you had for your breakfast, hawh!   That's the God's truth."

He reached out for his glass then, purely from memory, looked at it without emotion, and raised it to his lips. The black stuff flowed into the cavern of his mouth, and his Adam's apple moved forward to give it free passage. When he put the glass down again it was three-quarters empty— the quarter that was left said plainly that he did not want anyone to buy him another drink immediately.

"The Archdeacon is a man," he went on then, "who likes his little joke. Some people don't understand him, but I understand him. If I didn't I couldn't have stuck him all these years. He would have broken me heart, so he would, hawh! But we get on famous together. As I said already, the Archdeacon is a man who likes his little jokes"

'There's jokes and jokes," said Mr. Doyle, darkly. That's what I say," said Mr. Rafter.   "There's jokes and jokes."

Mr. Murphy put down his tumbler and looked determined.

"I should have given him a bit of my mind," he said.

Mr. Doyle echoed him in derision. "You should have given him a bit of your mind—sure you never opened your beak the whole time we were there."

"Is that so?" snapped Mr. Murphy. "Well in that case I didn't say so much less than you—and you were supposed to be the spokesman—God bless the mark! "

At this point Dooley thought it well to intervene.

"How could anyone get speakin' if the Archdeacon didn't want him to? Sure he'd take on the whole of Dail Eireann and best the lot of them—and at his dead ease. No bother to him—no bother in the wide world. Did I ever tell you what happened the day we buried Canon McGrath?"

Joe Dooley spent a very pleasant couple of hours in the Anchor Tavern, and he came away from it considerably refreshed and no lighter in pocket. Dooley didn't mind buying a drink in his turn, but on occasions like this, when he represented the Church, he was not above taking tithes from the laity.

Anthony did not find it easy to persuade the Archdeacon to enlarge the school.

"Sure I'm always building," he used to say. "Three times, no less I've added to it. The place is like a patchwork quilt. We'll have to get a new school eventually the way the parish is growing."

But a new school, he said always, was too big an undertaking for an old man like him. It was a job for a young, energetic priest.

What he really hated was fussing over plans, haggling with the authorities for a bigger grant, signing papers, getting money out of his poor parish. He was a psychologist, not an accountant, and money was a mystery to him. He kept it in his trousers pockets, so that he could give it away easily. He cleared off arrears of rent on tenement rooms, he paid fines, he advanced railway fares, he provided outfits for young fellows going away to missionary colleges. His was not indiscriminate charity by any means, but in Paradise Alley even cautious philanthropy was a costly business, and the Archdeacon never had enough to go round.

Three years after Anthony's appointment as Principal he got two new rooms that he needed badly. They were spacious, airy rooms, for once the Archdeacon got under way he bought the best that could be got and didn't spare expense: he was a slow starter, he said himself, but he had excellent acceleration. Two new rooms meant two new teachers. Paradise Alley was growing, but it couldn't grow much further. It was up against stone walls.

Many things happened during those three years. Grandfather Lenihan died, leaving Mollie the rents from four houses. He left a hundred pounds to each of his ordinary grandchildren, and two hundred to Christopher. Nedser

Bolger became Mr. Edward J. Bolger, T.D. and startled the Dail with his forcible, ungrammatical speeches. Mandy Logue got his seat in the Senate, but made no speeches at all.

Anthony's mother died suddenly in May, 1937, and her husband died in August. The two of them had lived so long together in the lonely house at the foot of Errigal that when one of them went the other followed. Black Donal was old, but he didn't die of old age. The life just ebbed out of him slowly, and he made no effort to stop it.

Anthony reached Lurgameelon the day before his father died. The old man was conscious, but he could say very little, and his mind had slipped back through the long years.

"You'll be finished training soon, Anthony," he said the morning he died. "I don't care where you teach until I'm going on pension, but I want you to come back then and begin where I leave off. There must always be a Domican in Lurgameelon."

He said nothing more, and he died within the hour.

Anthony felt then and for long afterwards that he had failed this quiet, reticent man who had loved him so well and had asked so little in return. Fosterage had spoiled Anthony Domican, had made him a Fanadman, a Lahardan Logue, so that in the end he was a stranger in his parents' house. But he had remained all the time in their hearts and in their dreams. In one way they had lost him; in another he had remained with them to the end.

When he came back from Lurgameelon and its two fresh graves he brought with him a remorse that was more bitter than sorrow, and a sense of retribution. Christopher was to him as he had been to Black Donal: Christopher was Lurgameelon's revenge. Yet the parallel was not complete. The gap that had separated Anthony from his father had been bridged at times. It made contact difficult and infrequent, but not impossible. But the gap that separated him from his son was too wide for bridges.

Mandy laughed at him when he tried to put this feeling into words.

"Have a bit of sense, man, and don't let yourself get morbid. This is just your reaction to the death. There was no gap between your father and you—except in your own imagination. When anyone belonging to you dies you think of all the things you left undone—you think that if you only had them back you'd make up for all your neglect—it's a common experience. And quit worrying about Christopher."

"I'm not worrying about him, Mandy. I'm sort of resigned to it all now. It's just one of these things that can't be helped."

"Hang it all, Anthony, what do you expect the lad to do? Hug you in public? What different is he from Arthur and John? I tell you it's all imagination—sheer imagination. No boy shows affection for his father when he gets to Christopher's age. He may feel it, but he'd be ashamed of his life to show it."

Mandy was a parent, but Mandy didn't understand. Being a parent wasn't enough. It helped, but it wasn't enough. There was no reality behind the conception of parental love in the bulk—the only reality was the love of a particular parent for a particular child.

"I know how you feel "was arrogant blasphemy. No one knew but yourself. Words could not convey it. The double barriers of personality shut it off and walled it in.

*   *   *   *

Christopher scraped through his university examinations. He passed in scraps of subjects, struggled through at repeats, gathered qualifications by instalments. He played rugby for the college, and had he tried he might have been on the first fifteen, but he was content to stay on the second. In the colourful set in which he moved industry and ambition were looked upon with disfavour, and it was bad form to pass an examination at the first attempt or to take adequate notes at lectures.

Christopher's scrappy examination record hurt Anthony's pride, but he might have sublimated the hurt, and even made capital out of it, had Christopher come any nearer to him. He might have played the part of a father who made allowances for a handsome, well-built, care-defying young man whose charm and popularity were in inverse ratio to his industry. But Christopher came no nearer. He kept his distance. He answered questions with a punctiliousness that was almost insulting, but he volunteered nothing.

CHAPTER NINETEEN.

Christopher hired a cap and gown. Christopher had his photograph taken. Anthony and Mollie went to the university one bright October morning and saw a tall, fair-haired young man shake hands with the President and receive from him the glossy paper which certified that the degree of Bachelor of Engineering had been conferred on Christopher Anthony Domican. There was nothing on Christopher's glossy paper to show that he had taken two extra years to his course. A Bachelor of Engineering was a Bachelor of Engineering.

Mollie dabbed her eyes with her handkerchief and caught at Anthony's hand.

"If Dad were only here," she whispered. Anthony's heart missed a beat and there was a tickly sensation in his spine. This was the first time that a Domican had received a degree. Not even the Salamanca Domican had done that, nor Black Donal, who spent whole winters juggling with conic sections, nor Anthony Domican, who read Tacitus for pleasure. The universities had ignored the scholarly Domicans; now they were accepting the worst scholar of the line.

I have reared up this boy, thought Anthony. I have shown him frogs sitting on stones. I have named the stars for him. I have watched him sicken for measles, and rung up doctors for him in the waste of the night. He has grown away from me but I can never lose him. I count for nothing in his life, but until the breath dies in me he will come first in mine. Nothing he can ever do to me can change me, and when I am ready for the grave he will be still in the cradle.

The ceremony was over, the last parchment awarded. The doctors and professors filed out in their coloured robes and medieval hats, the broad staircase was chock-a-block with graduates and parents. Outside, in the bright sunshine, bored Press photographers clicked their shutters.

For a full week afterwards Anthony found himself boasting.

"I was over at the university on Saturday—my eldest boy was getting conferred."

He told the teachers in the school, he told the neighbours, he told the Archdeacon; he even told Dooley.

"Great! " said Dooley. "There's nothing like a bit of education, hawh! And sure there's no need to ask where he got the brains—he didn't get them from the sun, moon, or stars. Like father like son. hawh!"

"He has brains enough, but he's not over-fond of work. He took his time getting through."

"They're a great consolation betimes, Mr. Domican, and for that again they can be a great heartscald. My Jem, now, the eldest, was good for nothing till he joined the army—that is nothing but drinkin' pints. The first of the Dooleys to ever take the shillin'. Sure me father, God rest him, would turn in his grave if he knew it. All me people was Fenians—no British Army for the Dooleys. But it's the best thing ever happened Jem. I could never make any hand of him, but the barrack square soon fixed him up and made a man of him. He's a sergeant in the Irish Guards this minute."

Even poor old Dooley, trotting round after the Archdeacon, had a son in his heart.

Mollie, too, did her share of boasting. She framed Christopher's parchment and used it for months as a conversational opening. She hung his degree photograph over the piano as a proof that Anthony's forebodings were quite unjustified.

Christopher came home rather late from the conferring dance. Mollie went downstairs when he came in and made him a cup of cocoa. Christopher was in high spirits, and he laughed so loudly on the landing when he was coming up to bed that she told him not to waken his father. But there was no fear of waking his father. His father was wide awake, and when Mollie slipped in beside him, like a conspirator, he was facing up to the situation that Christopher Domican, B.E., had learned to drink. Anthony said nothing. He kept on being asleep. And he said nothing on Sunday morning when Christopher, helped out by the entire household, got last Mass by the skin of his teeth. It wasn't every day that a Domican shook hands with the President of University College.

There had been no fuss made about Margaret Mary, a year before, when she got tenth place in the junior executive examination; nor the year before that again, when she got second in the senior piano at the Feis Ceoil. One expected these things of Mary, just as one expected Denis to get first or second in his class and Brigid to succeed solidly, if unspectacularly, in all her undertakings. Christopher was different. Christopher was born to be fussed over. He had the knack of winning people to him, and he gathered partisans effortlessly. One condoned his failures and was grateful for his successes.

Christopher had got his degree but he showed no anxiety to make use of it. He rested for a month and then spent another two making desultory enquiries and answering occasional advertisements. In the end Anthony heard of a job as clerk of works with a road-making firm and pulled strings shamelessly for the first time in his life. He got Mandy and Ned to help him, and he made Christopher a clerk of works. But he got no thanks from Christopher, who would have preferred something bigger and better. He even got no thanks from Mollie.

"I'm sure Christopher would have got a job on his own merits," she said. "After all, he's well qualified, and he has such a good manner."

"I've got him a job," snapped Anthony. "Let him get a better one on his merits."

Christopher's job was eight miles from Dublin, and he had to catch a bus from O'Connell Bridge at half-past eight every morning. Getting him out in time was a daily crisis. His mother called him at intervals from seven o'clock onwards. Mary rapped his door before she left for half-seven Mass. The maid brought him shaving water and replaced it when it grew cold. Christopher took the fuss as a matter of course, and in spite of it he often missed his bus.

Then he bought a motor car with the two hundred pounds his grandfather had left him. It's his own money, thought Anthony, and he can do what he likes with it, but he might have asked me about it. There's no harm in his buying a motor car, but he might have waited until he had saved the price of it.

"Does Christopher give you any money?" he said to Mollie one night.

"Why, of course, dear." Mollie looked surprised and hurt.

"Does he give you enough?"

"Anthony, I think you're very unreasonable. We're not poor, and I am quite satisfied with what Christopher gives me. After all, he has to keep up appearances—he has his position to consider."

Anthony smiled wryly.

"You needn't worry about appearances. Christopher won't let the family down in that respect. He buys two suits to my one, and he pays a good deal more for them than I do. But I sometimes wonder where the money comes from. He's out somewhere every night of the week, he runs a car, and yet he has only six guineas a week."

"It's not a bad salary, Anthony. I remember when you hadn't nearly as much yourself."

"So do I. It's not so long since I had less than it—and I got married when I had less than a hundred a year. But that's not the point. Six guineas a week isn't a bad salary for a young fellow starting off. In ways it's too much—and certainly a careful man could do a lot on it. But Christopher isn't careful. He doesn't know the value of money—he's never had to. I did all the worrying about money until recently. And now, when he begins to earn for himself, he is spending money like water."

"Aren't you exaggerating a little, Anthony?"

"I may be. I hope I am. But I'm not too pleased with all this running about of his—I'm afraid he's drinking."

"I'm surprised at you, Anthony." Mollie put down her knitting. "How can you say that Christopher is drinking? Aren't you ashamed of yourself for making a charge like that?"

"I don't say he's drinking too much, but I think that he has begun rather early, and I don't like these late hours. But let me ask a straight question, Mollie—how much does Christopher give you every week?"

"I'm not going to treat Christopher like a lodger. This is a home, not a boarding-house. All I take from Christopher is a pound a week. He'd give me more if I wanted it, but we don't need it."

"But you take thirty shillings from Mary?"

"Mary is different, Anthony—completely different. Christopher must live up to a certain standard. You don't seem to understand that."

Anthony lost his temper.

"I don't understand. I'm only his father. I'm only the man who clothed and educated him. But there's one thing I do understand—and that is that any fellow worth his salt would try to make some return to his parents and help to educate his younger brother and sister. We don't need his money, right enough, but he should at least give you as much as he would give a landlady. How will he ever learn the value of money if he lashes it round him now?"

Mollie stood up and burst into tears.

"You don't understand Christopher! You never have understood him! You have always taken the wrong way with him. I know he has faults, and that he's not as wise as he might be, but at the back of it all he's a warm-hearted, lovable boy.   But if you keep up this suspicious attitude you'll sour him for life. My father spoiled him a little bit and gave him more money than was good for him. But you can't blame Christopher for that."

"It's not a question of blame, Mollie. It's a question of trying to put some sense into him. I blame myself as much as I blame him."

Mollie put her hand on his arm.

"Give him a chance, Anthony. Don't say anything to him for the time being, for he's proud and headstrong. Just try to understand him."

Anthony said nothing. He had spent nearly half a lifetime trying to understand Christopher, and he saw no use trying any longer.   His relations with Christopher did not matter any more.   What mattered was Christopher himself, the weakness of character that lay beneath the glossy surface of the things that explained his popularity.

Having four children made a difference. It eased the intensity of his affection; he could switch it from one to the other. And it made time pass more quickly. While he was watching one each of the other three was growing and developing, so that changes which must have been gradual struck him as sudden and alarming, and the years seemed to telescope into one another.

When Brigid Ann finished her schooling and announced her intention of going to the university the idea struck him as incongruous. She was only a child, a dolly-and-pram girl. She was still sticky from lollypops. But she was nothing of the kind. She was eighteen, and a mature woman. A very serious little woman she was, too; pretty in a prim sort of way, with dead-black hair, a round, white face, and trim, slender body.   Brigid walked with her head erect, kept her clothes well, and never let her shoes get down at heel. She spoke slowly and carefully, and kept little notebooks of quotations. She read the best books, she went to operas and exhibitions of paintings. She forgot nothing and echoed everything.

She said she was going to do Arts and become a secondary teacher. And that was that. When Brigid said a thing she meant it. Anthony saw no reason to object. He had the money to pay for her fees, and at sixty he had realized the wisdom of letting his children choose for themselves—within reason.

But when he saw Brigid copying her lecture-notes into big, stiff-covered exercises, he had qualms of conscience. Brigid was efficient and dependable, tidy in body and mind, but there was no fire in her, no smudge of genius. It was Mary who should have gone to the university—Mary, with her quick, lively mind and her zest for living; Mary, who could have been at least a second-rate pianist or a first-rate journalist. She wrote articles for magazines and was substitute music critic for one of the daily papers. She was lost in the civil service.

"I'm sorry I didn't send you to the university," he said to her one night. "It seems unfair to give Brigid all the chances.   You could still go, you know, Mary."

"I could have gone to the university when I left school had I wanted to," said Mary. "I'm happy enough as I am and where I am."

"But would you not think of leaving the civil service and doing a university course even now?"

"You must be a thought-reader, Dad," she laughed. "I'm starting evening lectures for the B.A. next week."

"Evening lectures! Work all day in an office and go to lectures at night—it would kill you! "

"It can't be as hard as all that. Two other girls in the office got their degree this year."

"But you'll only get a pass degree. There are no honours courses at night. It seems waste of time to me."

"It all depends. A pass degree will do me well enough."

"But it won't get you promotion—it won't get you a better job—what good will it do you?"

Mary rose and closed the door. They were by themselves in the room.

"Can you keep a secret, Dad?"

"I've kept quite a few in my time.   What is it?"

"Something you mustn't tell anyone—not even mother. I'm thinking of becoming a nun. I could go now, of course, but I'd be more useful to them if I had a degree—I could do the Higher Diploma in Education and qualify as a teacher. And I'll have more time to make up my mind."

"But do you want to be a nun?"

"Of course I don't. Sometimes I hate the very thought of it."

"Then forget about it."

She laughed at him.

"You don't understand, Dad. More than half the right things to do are things we hate. You don't want to get up on cold mornings, do you? You hate the very thought of getting up. But you know that you must. It's your duty, and if you lay on, your mind would give you no peace. That's the way I feel about entering the convent."

Anthony stood up and flexed his arms.

"Do you mean to tell me, Mary, that your mind gives you no peace? If it doesn't I must be as blind as a bat."

"Sit down and relax, Dad. I'm a small authority on vocations, and I've read all the books. A vocation is not an emotional upheaval. Nor is it a specific supernatural call. It's just a kind of certainty that a particular kind of life is marked out for one. No one is bound to enter a convent, but many people do—simply because they feel the way I do. It's a perfectly rational thing, a deliberate thing, not a sudden resolve."

"But, hang it all, Mary, that seems very cold-blooded."

"That's what I'm trying to tell you, Mr. Anthony Domican. It is cold-blooded. That's what makes it hard."

He shook the dottle from his pipe and took out his pouch. "And how long has this notion been in your head?"

"Quietly for a long time, Dad, but within this last year or so it has become very insistent. I could back out of it, of course, but I don't think I will—in fact I hope I don't. You must get the children in Paradise Alley to pray for me."

Anthony said nothing. This cold logic baffled him, left him no gaps. He began to feel that in some important matters his education had been sadly neglected.

"Don't look so glum, Dad. You're not disappointed?"

"No, I'm not disappointed." He shook his head. "Just surprised, that's all. Part of me is pleased, too, I think. When I get used to the notion maybe all of me will be pleased."

"Of course you'll be pleased. What would be the use of having a family if you couldn't get at least one of them to pray for you? But don't tell anyone, Dad. I'm not going to tell anyone else until I'm sure."

"I'll tell no one, Mary. But won't people guess? Won't you have to give up dances and all that sort of thing?"

"Not at all," she laughed. "Why should I? I must give the world a fair trial before I decide to leave it."

Anthony had to tell someone or burst, so he told the Archdeacon.

"I'm a bit puzzled over the whole thing," he said. "If it had been Brigid now, I could have understood it. Brigid is quiet, prim, and dependable. But Mary is full of life, and she's by far the brainiest of the whole bunch. I can't imagine her in a convent."

The Archdeacon locked his hands behind his back and rocked himself backwards and forwards on his heels.

"And do you think, Anthony, that God Almighty wants nothing but prim and quiet ones? Sure you should think more of Him than that. He knows all about the brains and the high spirits—and why shouldn't He—wasn't it He gave them to her? What makes you think that religious are all sober, elastic-sided folk, or stupid, brainless ones—like myself? Would you call Francis Xavier stupid? Or Francis of Assisi sober-sided? Have sense, man. High spirits is one of the best signs of a vocation. No reverend mother likes moping, straight-laced novices. They never finish the course. No, from what you tell me of Mary she'll make a right good nun."

"But why didn't she go long ago? Why did she let these years pass?"

"I think I know the answer to that one, Anthony, here's no such thing really as a late vocation—in the sense of something that should have happened earlier. It's just that everything in Mary's life—if she does enter the convent—every experience she has had—has been preparing her to do—in a fixed place and at a fixed time—something that no one else could do half so well. It's all planned and fixed—though contingent on her will and co-operation. No, here's no such thing as a late vocation. It's a contradiction in terms."

"Maybe you're right."

"Maybe I am. Anyway, if a convent is the place for Mary she'll find her way there, and at the right time. If not, well she'll just forget all about it."

"I suppose that's about the size of it. It seems that Mary knows more about these things than I do. I used to think that I was rearing up children—now I know that I was rearing up men and women."

CHAPTER TWENTY.

ANTHONY gave Christopher the chance that Mollie had begged for him. He kept his fears to himself and a rein on his tongue. He heard the little two-seater chugging home in the early hours and made no comment. He listened to Christopher's suave, laconic explanations at the breakfast table and made no attempt to riddle them. He gave him his head for a year.

And before the year was up Mollie herself was worrying. She said nothing to Anthony at first, but he could read it in her face. She tried to silence her own fears and his with echoed explanations, but her efforts were not proof against the cumulative effect of Christopher's mounting record. She believed in him as long as she could—with a faith which was but an emotional outgrowth of her mother-love; when belief was no longer possible she pretended to believe; and when she grew tired of trying to deceive herself she still hoped. She might have eased things a little by talking the situation over with Anthony, but her pride and her loyalty to Christopher kept her from asking for help.

Instead, she pleaded wordlessly with Christopher. She fussed about his socks and handkerchiefs, she made him lemon drinks when he sneezed, she watched over his appetite, she pressed his dress trousers. Christopher took her valeting for granted, but he went his way. When the storm began to break it was Mollie, not Anthony, who was hardest on Christopher. Anthony had not expected much and would have been content with little: but Mollie had built her castles high, and when they toppled she became hysterical.

At first she had little definite evidence. Christopher came home late, but so did many a young man. He lay a-bed on Sundays and had to be routed out for last Mass, but this was no sign of alarming depravity. He spent all he earned, and borrowed money from Mary towards the end of each month, but this hand-to-mouth finance was a symptom of youth.

The evidence came, in bits and scraps, in hints and whispers. Christopher covered his tracks well but luck was not always with him.

Mrs. Reynolds, the mother of his friend Lar Reynolds, called at Crescent Terrace early one Sunday morning with a tale of woe. Lar had come home drunk at five o'clock. He had been out to Bray with Christopher, and his excuse was that they had had engine trouble on the road home and had had to knock up a garage-man at Cabinteely. Mollie wakened Christopher and asked him what time he had come in at. She was a long time wakening Christopher.

"What's all the fuss about?" he asked. "It was late when I got home—some time after three."

"What kept you out till that time?"

"We were at a party at Lucan and we got a bad puncture at Chapelizod. I wish you wouldn't cross-examine me at this hour of the morning, mother. I want to get a little sleep."

"You're telling me lies, Christopher." Mollie made it sound a very serious offence. "Lar Reynolds says that you were at Bray and had to knock up a garage-man at Cabinteely."

"Does he?" said Christopher. "Then why bother me? It doesn't matter where we were. We're not children."

Mollie begged Anthony to do something about it.

"What can I do?" said Anthony.

"But Christopher must have been drunk, too. And you're so calm about it."

He wasn't so calm a fortnight later when he opened a letter one morning at breakfast. It was a tailor's bill for £20 17s. 6d., and it was accompanied by a notice which read: "Failing settlement in full within seven days this account will be handed to our solicitor." He looked at the envelope again and found that it was addressed to Mr. C. Domican.

Christopher was quite unperturbed.

"He's in a great hurry with his money," he said. "Some of these fellows need to be taught a lesson."

"It's you need to be taught the lesson," said Anthony. "Why the devil do you run up bills?"

"It's not a crime is it?"

"Don't talk back to me, sir! I won't have it—and I won't have you bringing threatening letters to this house or running up bills with people."

"Hush, dear," said Mollie. "The maid will hear you."

"I don't care who hears me—this Beau Brummel of yours evidently doesn't fear publicity—he'll be in Stubbs' before he knows where he is if he doesn't watch himself."

" Calm yourself, Anthony," said Mollie. "And Christopher—you must be more careful how you speak to your father.   Why didn't you pay this wretched man his bill long ago? You have no right to get your father into such a state."

"If he didn't open other people's letters he wouldn't be getting into states," said Christopher. Anthony banged the table.

"I told you I won't have you talking back to me! If you're not prepared to behave civilly you'd better leave this house."

Christopher rose up, leaving his breakfast unfinished.

"It might be better if I did," he said. "It's more like a nursery than anything else."

He slammed the door when he was going out.

Anthony paid the bill that afternoon, and Mollie undertook to collect the money from Christopher at five pounds a month.

Anthony wondered afterwards if he had been a little too violent with Christopher, a little too ready to condemn. An unpaid bill was not, in itself, a very big thing. But it did not stand alone. It was part of the general pattern. It fitted in with everything else.

The situation worsened steadily. Mollie wouldn't go to sleep until Christopher came in, and she tensed at the sound of every late car. Sometimes, when she thought Anthony was asleep, she would slip out of bed quietly and go down to the kitchen for a cup of tea. She would wait for Christopher then and read the riot act to him in the small hours. Once or twice Anthony got up to quieten her, but he usually left them alone. There was only one cure for Christopher, and it was fifteen years too late.

Anthony tried a new approach. He spoke to Christopher quietly and told him that he was worrying his mother and giving bad example to his brother and sisters.   He told him that if he couldn't abide by the rules of the house he would be better to pack his bag and clear out.

But Mollie wasn't satisfied with these reprimands.

"You're his father," she said to Anthony once after a bout of weeping. "Have you no influence with him? Can't you do something to make him change his ways?"

"I don't think I can, Mollie. I can kick him out of the house, of course, but that's a rather desperate remedy—and it wouldn't mend matters. If he won't come to heel for your sake he won't come for mine."

"But you're so calm about it, Anthony, so matter of fact. Can't you see the seriousness of it?"

"Listen, Mollie. I saw the seriousness of it long ago. I've seen this thing coming for years. I saw it long before you did. I didn't know what form it would take, but I knew that it was bound to come—and God knows I did what little I could to avert it. And no matter how serious it is there's no use in your working yourself into a nervous breakdown."

"How can I help being worried about him? Do you expect me to sit quietly by and see my own son go to the bad?"

"He hasn't gone very far to the bad yet, Mollie, so far as we know. There's no use in exaggerating."

"How do you know he hasn't? What do these late nights mean? They might mean anything. He hasn't been to early Mass for months—and if he wasn't living at home he mightn't go at all. It's all right for you to talk—you have Paradise Alley and your night work to keep your mind off things. I have nothing. I'm here day and night where everything reminds me of him. I can't get away from it early or late. It's at the back of my thoughts all the time and I feel I can't stand it much longer."

Anthony didn't try to argue with tears and hysterics. He walked over to the window and let her cry quietly for a few minutes. Then he sat down on the edge of her chair and put one arm about her.

"Didn't you always believe in him, Mollie?"

She nodded her head, like a child wanting to be comforted.

"Well, keep on believing for a while longer. Trust your intuition. There's no use in lecturing him or scolding him—it's only waste of breath. He's just going through a wild phase and it may soon be over. Sense doesn't come to a man overnight."

"But we must do something, Anthony."

"We're doing all we can. You must keep praying for him. You must show him that, in spite of everything, you still trust him."

"You're so wise, Anthony." She reached up suddenly and kissed him. "You always say the right thing. I don't know what I'd do without you. And I know you're right—Christopher is quite good at heart—I'm sure of that. He's just a big, spoiled child. He likes to show off, to play at being a man of the world, but he's a child at heart. There's nothing bad or vicious about him—not a single thing. Sure I know him inside out."

Anthony wasn't so sure, but he said nothing.

Mollie was wrong in saying that she had nothing to take her mind off Christopher. She had Denis, and Mary, and Brigid. Christopher held the middle of her stage, but he could not hold it all the time. Denis was the first to wrest it from him. Denis said that he was going to the Jesuit novitiate at Tullabeg, and the spotlight moved from Christopher.

Mollie would have preferred Denis to go to the secular liege at Clonliffe. She would have him at holiday-time then, and after ordination he would be nearer home, Anthony didn't mind much one way or another.   He rather liked the notion of Denis's going to Tullabeg. The Jesuits were a brilliant order and didn't want dunderheads.

Denis riddled this idea. Denis, like Mary, was an authority on vocations, and Anthony's education was being completed.

"Nonsense, dad," said Denis. "The Jesuits don't look for geniuses. All they ask is that a boy should have a certain degree of education and ordinary intelligence."

"But why wouldn't you go to Clonliffe?" said Mollie.

"I don't want to go through the whole thing again after every holiday," said Denis.   "It's better to do it once and done with it."

Denis's piety was very matter-of-fact and healthy.   He was on the senior cup team, was interested in cinema technique, and was a critical reader of detective novels.   He had will of his own, and a temper that he inherited from the Lenihans.

The night before he went, Mollie cried herself to sleep. "Just think of it, Anthony," she said. "He'll never sleep in this house again—not for one single night."

Anthony made no effort to comfort her. "And if you don't have some sense no one else will ever get a wink of sleep in it either. You should be proud to have a son joining the Jesuits."

"I am proud," she sobbed.

It was good to hear her crying for someone other than Christopher.

Brigid was the next to spread her sails. Brigid, the demure, prosaic, accountant-minded, unromantic little body sought formal audience with her father and mother one evening and told them that she had an important decision to make.

"What is it, darling?" said Mollie.

Anthony put down his paper. Brigid looked very tense and determined. Judging by her intensity it looked as if she was going to join the Poor Clares at the very least. But Brigid was not going to join the Poor Clares. Brigid, it appeared, wanted to found a community of her own. She wanted to get married.

"You can't be serious?" said Mollie.

Anthony felt certain of one thing. Brigid might be foolish, or temporarily unbalanced; she might even be drunk; but she was certainly serious. And when he saw her sitting there, and heard her making this outrageous statement, he realized how much he loved her and how much he would hate losing her when the time came.

"But you're only twenty," went on Mollie. It's far too young to get married."

"I'll be twenty-one soon," said Brigid.

"Even that is far too young. It's Raymond Brophy, I suppose?"

Brigid nodded.

"Sure he's only a boy," said Mollie. "I never heard the like. What would you live on? What prospects has he? You can't get married on a few pounds a week."

"He's twenty-six." Brigid made it sound almost decrepit. "And if he hadn't enough to marry on we wouldn't be thinking of marriage. We have given it plenty of thought."

Brigid was calm and collected. She had all her answers ready. She was prepared to debate. Mollie was excited and wanted to be pontifical, so she turned to Anthony for help.

"What has your father to say to all this?"

Her father had nothing to say, but he had to say something.

"This has taken us by surprise, Brigid," he said, and thought he sounded very foolish. "You're very young, you know—very young." (This was just to collect his thoughts). "Marriage is a very serious business. It can't be entered upon lightly."

"There!" said Mollie. "Your father agrees with me. The whole thing will have to be carefully considered. We couldn't dream of making any decision just yet."

"I didn't expect you to decide at once." Brigid was very placid about it. "Raymond will come to see father On Sunday."

Anthony sat up with a start.

"What's that?"

"Raymond will call to see you on Sunday and talk things over. I believe it's usual."

"I should think it is usual," snapped Mollie, "and I hope that your father will speak plainly to him when he does come. You're both far too young. People shouldn't even dream of getting married until they have a proper way on them. Marriage needs money and security. It will be your father's duty to speak plainly."

This was more than a statement of the moral law. It was a definite instruction to Anthony, and Anthony did not feel too happy about it. Raymond Brophy was a decent young fellow, and he didn't like the thought of catechizing him.

And when Sunday came Anthony felt just as nervous as Raymond looked. So he did little or no catechizing, and listened sympathetically whilst Raymond struggled through the piece Brigid had thought out for him. Raymond explained that he was making about three hundred a year from his hosiery agency, and that his returns were increasing monthly. His business was growing, and there was no reason why he shouldn't double his income in a couple of years.

Anthony opened his mouth and listened to the words that came out. When two young people wanted each other, he said, it was his duty and privilege as a father to give them his blessing.

This was a conception of his duty which did not tally too closely with Mollie's rigid instructions, but it was soothing and satisfying. Raymond refused a drink, but Anthony poured himself a glass of whiskey and felt that he had earned it.

Mollie attacked him later and told him that he had no notion of his responsibilities. Brigid was too young to get married, and Raymond's job wasn't secure. Anthony told her that she was fussy and Victorian. What did she expect him to do? Argue about a dowry and compromise on heads of cattle? Marriage was a gamble at the best of times, and people had a right to choose for themselves.

Brigid got her engagement ring the following Monday, and she refused to let Raymond pay more than ten pounds for it. She began to compile lists of the bed-linen, cutlery, kitchen utensils, and furniture she would need in six months' time. She examined house-purchase schemes and systems of mortgage repayments. Anthony, watching all these preparations, remembered that he had explained to Brigid that marriage was a serious business which should not be entered upon lightly. His time would have been equally well employed had he tried to teach his grandmother how to suck eggs.

Mary was the next to take Mollie's mind off Christopher. Mary went off to the Dominican novitiate at Cabra as cheerfully as if she had been going to her wedding. There was no banking-down of the fire of life that burned so brightly in her, no quenching of laughter, no stern resolve. Her going involved no emotional upheaval; it was an act of will, a cheerful signing-on with a full realization of all that was involved.

When Anthony saw her a few months later, in her white and black habit, she seemed to have come of age. Her eyes were as brown and as bright as ever, but there was a new look in them that startled Anthony until he thought it out and labelled it. It was more than a look of peace—it was a look of sanity; the sanity of a person who had discovered the order behind the seemingly meaningless medley of thoughts, acts, and impressions that made up the business of living, the look of a person who, having solved her own problem, saw all other problems more clearly. That, he thought, was where the sanity came in. People in the world were self-regarding. They were tangled up emotionally. They saw all things as centered in themselves and could see nothing objectively.

Mary Margaret was missed at Crescent Terrace. It was Comforting to think of her in her black and white, chanting Vespers at Cabra—it was like paying premiums on a spiritual annuity. But the novice did not belong to Crescent Terrace. She never came home swinging her tennis racquet, never played Chopin in the gloaming. The spiritual annuity was comforting, but the installments had to be paid daily.

CHAPTER TWENTY-ONE.

"WE'RE just where we started," said Mollie. "We've lost them all one by one."

But they hadn't. They had lost only Christopher. All the others had been reared to schedule, had been supported until they were fit to lean on their own wisdom, had been dispatched in good order and condition. They could be ticked off and docketed. One could think of them with satisfaction— Mary and Denis in their monasteries, Brigid in her three-bedroomed house in Raheny. One knew where they were and what they were doing. They could be spoken about, written to, visited. They were still part of the family. Christopher wasn't. Christopher had left no links. The others went from Crescent Terrace. He went from all that Crescent Terrace stood for. And the three successes did not quite make up for the one failure.

Christopher held out to the last. There was no chink in his armour of suavity, no flaw in his self-assured acting. He became a little bit shabbier, but he always looked well-dressed, for he had the knack of wearing clothes. His collars were spotless and picture-perfect, his ties hung properly, and he could manage a closer shave in five minutes than Anthony could in twenty on the night of an annual dinner.

At Brigid's wedding he was especially decorative. He outshone the groom and out-spoke the best man. He said the right things in the right way. He planned the taxi schedule, handled the photographer, won over the waiters. He paid for his round of drinks with an elegance which solvency could not have given. Matrons smiled on him and looked at their daughters reproachfully. He was such a good-looking boy and had such perfect manners.

Brigid's wedding was a double landmark in the history of Crescent Terrace, for Christopher did not go back to work after it. He came home as late as ever at night, he rose at mid-day, he had afternoon tea in Grafton Street. He said that he had left his job, but Anthony knew that he had lost it.

Then began a series of interviews which was to remain in Anthony's memory for all time. Each one was etched there as clearly as a scene from a film. The second-last took place one evening after school. He had just finished his dinner and lit his pipe when the drum beat to battle.

"You must have another talk with him," said Mollie. "We can't sit quietly by and see him waste his life."

Christopher was shaving in the bathroom when Anthony went upstairs.

"Your mother and I would like a word with you before you go out."

"I'll be down in five minutes," said Christopher, with his eyes still on the mirror. He took fifteen, and when he appeared in the dining-room there was not a hair out of place.

"Sit down, Christopher," said Anthony.

When Christopher sat down Anthony stood up . It was an old trick of Rodney's when interviewing pupils bigger than himself.

"Your mother and I am worried, Christopher."

Christopher lit a cigarette carefully.

"I suppose you know why," went on Anthony.

"I'm afraid I don't," said Christopher.

"Stop pretending, Christopher," cried Mollie. "You know that you lost your job because you wouldn't come in in time in the mornings."

"Is that a question or a statement, mother?"

Anthony bridled.

"You'll have to change your attitude. I won't have you talk to your mother like that. She has asked you something which we have a right to know— didn't you lose your job through your own fault?"

"Yes and no," said Christopher.

Anthony counted ten, and gave Mollie time to ask: "What can you do with a boy like that?"

"I wish you would try to give us a little information," said Anthony, "—for your own sake as well as for ours. What point is there in making things still more difficult for us? I ask a straight question and you say 'Yes and no.' Stop the quibbling and tell us did you lose your job."

Christopher smiled a patient smile.

"I wasn't quibbling when I said 'yes and no,' and I can't see the point of this inquisition. I lost the job, in one sense, but I could have held it. The fact is it wasn't worth holding any longer. I had learned all it had to teach me, and there were no prospects worth talking about, so I wasn't at all pushed whether I went or stayed."

Anthony abandoned his attempt to keep calm.

"Well, will you tell me in the name of sanity why you didn't stay in this not-worth-while job until you got a better one? Will you tell me why you didn't leave decently instead of waiting to be kicked out? Did you want to wait until you got a reference saying that you were dismissed because you didn't come in in time in the mornings and couldn't do your work properly?"

"There's no need to be dramatic about it," said Christopher. "It's not the end of the world because I lose a job. I'm a fully-qualified engineer and I can get a job anywhere in the morning—with or without a reference from Smithley and Lawson."

"Don't be too sure about that," snapped Anthony. "If this war lasts for a few years there won't be many openings for engineers in this country. You might cool your heels long enough before you get another job."

"I can get a job here or elsewhere any time I like."

"You seem very confident about it all. You got things far too easily always."

"There's no need to go into that again," said Christopher, suavely. "I've heard it all before dozens of times. I have it off by heart. You've reared me and educated me. You've given me a chance in life that you never got, and this is my return for it all."

"You have no right to speak to your father like that," said Mollie.

"Oh, mother, I can't stand this continual nagging and watching. I'm like a ticket-of-leave man in this house. I'm old enough to manage my own affairs and I want to be left alone—I'm not a child. If you're worrying because I haven't a job you're wasting your time. It's my pigeon."

They heard him whistling as he put on his hat and coat, and a few moments later the hall-door closed behind him,

A few mornings later, Anthony got a note from Ned Bolger.

"Dear Anthony,

I have something I'd like to see you about. Could you give me a ring to-morrow and arrange to see me some time in the evening?

Yours,

NED."

He phoned Ned at lunch-time and called to his office in Dame Street shortly after five. Ned was proud of his office. It was small but well-equipped—as befitted the nerve centre for Shannon Dairies, Cigs., and at least three other undertakings. Ned had carpet under his feet and a throaty house telephone that gurgled out messages when he pressed a button. He had a few good etchings on the walls, and one original oil-painting.

"Sit down, Anthony, and have a smoke. Haven't seen you for weeks. How are you at all?"

Nedser fitted perfectly into the frame of his office. He wore a dark, well-cut suit, and his tie had been carefully chosen. But he showed the signs of the battle. His chin had a background of flesh now, and there were grey smudges in his hair.

"Fairly well," said Anthony. "I needn't ask how you are yourself. I haven't seen much of you recently, but you're a busy man and a member of the Dail. You haven't as much time as you used to have."

"No, indeed." Nedser liked to be reminded of his success. "I haven't had time to bless myself for months. Not that I mind it very much. If I had time on my hands I think I'd be miserable."

"Things are going well with you?"

"I haven't much to complain about. Supplies are getting a little scarce of course—especially tobacco—and if the war goes on the position will get worse and worse."

"I suppose so. Well, what did you want to see me about, Ned?"

"It's not so easy to tell you, Anthony." Nedser fell to watching his fingers drumming on the table. "I don't even know whether I'm wise in telling you or not, but I have thought it all over and I think you should know. It's about Christopher."

Anthony nodded. There was coldness about his heart.

"Three months ago or so he came to me and said that he was in a fix about money—got into a poker school that was a few sizes too big for him, and one night he had to give an I.O.U. for a hundred. The other fellow was pressing for the money, and if I lent it to him he'd pay me back as soon as he could."

"And did you?"

"Yes, I gave him the hundred."

"Has he paid it back?"

"Five pounds—he sent me that after a week."

"The young pup," said Anthony. "Things are even worse than I thought. I'll never forgive him for this—and I'll clear what he owes you."

Ned Bolger lifted his head.

"Don't misunderstand me, Anthony—it's not the money. The money doesn't matter one way or another. I'd have given him twice as much with a heart and a half and never said a word about it. Most young fellows make fools of themselves once in a while and I'd be only too glad to get any son of yours out of a hole. I owe more than that to you. No, it's not the money that's worrying me. If it was only the money I wouldn't speak at all."

"Is there something else?"

Nedser hesitated for a little while.

"I've heard a few things recently, Anthony, that make me think that money won't help him very much. Not that I believe all I hear, of course, but I'm afraid there's more than a little truth in it."

"What did you hear?" said Anthony. There was no passion in him now, no anger, nothing but the sense of having failed.

"We won't mind what I heard. But I'll tell you what I saw. One night last week I happened to be in 'The Boiled Lobster'—a fellow asked me to meet him there on business. Do you know the joint at all?"

Anthony shook his head.

"Well, it's one of those new, chromium-plated pubs where every drink costs a little extra—and it hasn't a very-good name. I wouldn't mind him being there—it's no crime—and after all I was there myself. It's the crowd he was with—a tough crowd—boozers and gamblers—Kingpin Longrave was one of them. They were a bit noisy and they had four women with them that I didn't like the look of—that's all I'll say about them. I don't know what you think but I wouldn't like to see a son of mine knocking round with a bunch like that. They're a bad lot."

Anthony filled his pipe for comfort.

"It's a shock, Nedser, the devil of a shock. I don't know what to think, and I don't know what to do. I feel like going home and knocking the stuffing out of him, but that day is gone, and I didn't do half enough of it when I had the chance. Part of the blame is mine, I'm afraid."

"All, nonsense. It's not your fault."

"Tell me, Nedser. If Christopher were your son what would you do?"

Nedser scratched his head.

"It's a hard question, Anthony—a hard question. To tell you the God's truth I don't know what I'd do."

Anthony phoned the chemist at the corner of Crescent Terrace and asked him to send word to Mollie that he wouldn't be home for tea. Then he went straight out to *The Laurels* and had tea with Mandy and Alice. Arthur F. Logue was Assistant R.M.O. in a big asylum in the west, and John was doing well in the market. There was no Christopher at *The Laurels*.

"And how is the world using you?" asked Mandy when they were alone in the study afterwards.

"Fair enough in ways, Mandy."

"You'll take a drop of whiskey?"

"Not too much, Mandy. Go easy with it."

They sipped at their glasses and sat silent for a little while.

"Mary and Denis doing well?"

"Both doing well, thank God."

"And Christopher?"

"Not so well, Mandy. That's what I've come to see you about."

"What's the trouble?"

"In the first place he's lost his job—wouldn't rise in time in the mornings, and kept such bad hours at night that he wasn't fit to do his work properly."

"That's not so good, Anthony. But it might teach him a lesson—and he won't have much trouble getting another job. He's a clever enough lad if he'd watch himself."

"It's not just the job, Mandy. He's knocking about with the wrong sort of people—a boozing, gambling crowd—and if what Ned Bolger says is right, maybe the wrong sort of women."

"Maybe things aren't as bad as you think. He's young yet. Don't worry too much." Anthony shook his head.

"What hit me hardest of all is that he's been borrowing money from Ned Bolger—from one of my ex-pupils! The humiliation of it! To pay gambling debts, he said."

"How much did he borrow from Ned?"

"A hundred pounds."

Mandy twisted the glass in his hand and finished his drink.

"A hundred doesn't mean much to Ned."

"That's not the point, Mandy. If Christopher got into some jam or other why couldn't he have come to me and made a clean breast of things?"

"Aye, that would have been more sensible, I suppose, but sometimes a father is the last person a young fellow will go to when he's in trouble. They'd rather go to the stranger."

"But I'd rather have had him go to anyone else than to Ned Bolger. It makes me boil to think of it. If he had come to you, even, I wouldn't feel so badly about it."

Some sudden intuition struck him then.

"Did he come to you?"

Mandy uncrossed his legs and twisted in his chair. "There's no use in hiding it, Anthony. He did come to me."

"When? And how much did you give him? I might as well know everything."

"Maybe ten weeks ago, maybe not so long—I have a note of it somewhere. He asked me for fifty and I gave it to him. Don't blame me for not telling you, Anthony—he asked me not to. But there's no point in keeping it secret any longer."

"What did he say he wanted it for? Was it gambling again?"

"No. He said he had backed a bill for a friend of his and that he had to stump up."

"Has he paid you anything back?"

"Not yet, but I don't mind that."

"That's a hundred and fifty between you and Ned Bolger. I wonder if that's the whole story. I wonder who else he touched. He must be up to his neck in debt—he sold his car a while back, too. It's a nice story, Mandy, no matter how you look at it. He got things too easy always, and this is the result of it."

"Don't take it too hard, Anthony. Things could be a lot worse. All he has done is to run up a few debts—it'll all right itself in due course. You'll see it will. Here, have another drink."

Anthony felt that he needed it.

He left *The Laurels* shortly after nine and was in Crescent Terrace before ten. Christopher, home early for once, was reading a book; Mollie was knitting and listening to a string quartette on the radio. She turned the music off when he came in.

"Kelly's sent up your message, Anthony. Where were you? Would you like a cup of tea?"

"No thanks—I won't have anything. I had tea in Mandy's and I'm not hungry."

"How are they all there?"

"All well."

He made light conversation for a while, and shrank from the task in front of him. Coming home in the bus he had been strict and patriarchal. Now he would rather have held his peace.

It was hard to begin, hard to smash the quietness.

"I want to ask you a few questions, Christopher," he said at last. It was a well-worn opening gambit.

Christopher looked up from his book.

"How much money do you owe?"

"Not very much—I couldn't say offhand. Not more than I can pay, anyway."

"You must have a lot of invisible assets, then." Anthony spoke quietly, wearily. " If you wanted money why didn't you come to me and ask for it— instead of shaming me?" Even as he asked the question he realized that the answer to it covered all his relations with his son.

"I suppose Uncle Mandy has been talking," said Christopher.

Mollie dropped her knitting.

"What's all this about? Who did he go to for money?"

"Yes, your Uncle Mandy has been talking," said Anthony. "So has Ned Bolger, who isn't a relation at all. It has been a rather humiliating evening. Talking with my son's creditors. Finding that he has been borrowing money from one of my ex-pupils—the only one of them from whom anyone could borrow money."

" Did you borrow money from Mr. Bolger, Christopher? Why did you do it? What will he think of us? How could you have done a thing like that to your father and mother? What made you do it?"

"I had a bill to meet," said Christopher as equably as if he was talking about the weather. "There's no need to get hot and bothered about it. I'll pay it back."

"What kind of a bill?" said Mollie through her tears. "Why didn't you come to us for the money?"

Christopher threw his book on the table and took out a cigarette.

"I backed a bill for a fellow and he skipped to England. I had to pay up in a hurry and I hadn't the money."

"Aren't you getting a little mixed?" said Anthony. "It was from your Uncle

Mandy you borrowed the money to meet the bill. Ned Bolger's money went to pay card debts, you told him."

"Have you been gambling, too?" asked Mollie.

"I did some gambling—not much, but I was unlucky. I was foolish, I suppose, but it's not a crime to play cards."

If you were only foolish, thought Anthony. If you weren't a gadabout, a liar, and all things rotten.

"He was gambling," sobbed Mollie, making it sound worse than leprosy.

Anthony asked another question.

"I believe that you frequent a place known as 'The Boiled Lobster.' Is that true?"

" Frequent' is rather a big word," said Christopher. " I've been there once or twice. Why?"

"The whole town seems to know that you have been knocking about with elegant corner-boys and their lady friends—with drunkards, gamblers, and worse. I can't trust you any more, Christopher. I can't believe a word out of your mouth. But for your mother's sake and for the sake of your brother and sisters I'm going to clean up this dirty mess as far as it is capable of being cleaned up. But I must know how bad it is. I'm tired asking questions and I've only one more to ask—how much would clear your debts?"

Christopher stood up and threw a butt into the fire.

"I suppose you'd like to have the pleasure of hearing me confess when you've got the whole story already. You want me to tell, and yet you say you don't believe a word out of my mouth. That's part of the trouble. You don't trust me—you never trusted me—I'm still a child in your eyes. What would you have said if I had asked you for money? You'd have said the old things I've been hearing for years and years. You'd have cast my rearing in my teeth, and the money you spent on me, and the chances I got. I'm tired of it all— there has been nothing but spying, nagging, questioning and sermonizing here ever since I can remember. I've never had a moment's peace in this house, and I'll be glad to get out of it. And don't make a martyr of yourself paying my debts, for you'll get no inventory from me. I'll pay every halfpenny I owe without any help from you."

Anthony slept well that night after the turmoil. Mollie cried for a long time and swore that she had been wide awake when the clock struck four. She was certainly fast asleep at half-past seven when Christopher left Crescent

Terrace for the last time. Someone saw him at the corner with his suitcase, waiting for an early bus.

Anthony paid Mandy and Ned Bolger at once, and in full, in spite of their protests. He also paid a flotilla of smaller bills that arrived during the month following Christopher's departure. In all it cost him a little over two hundred pounds. The things that money could settle were easily settled, but Christopher left more behind him than debts. Anthony could not piece the whole story together from the snippets carried to him by people who spoke from the highest motives, and with a certain amount of relish, but it seemed clear that Christopher's folly had followed the usual run of the prodigal. Mollie, too, had her share of virtuous tale-bearers, and they made her burden no easier. In her philosophy it was one thing to do wrong; it was quite another to allow one's sense of right and wrong to become blurred. She could have borne more easily with the memory of Christopher's obvious failings had she been reasonably sure that he had stood fast in the one thing that mattered most.

CHAPTER TWENTY-TWO

Anthony was sixty-three when the Archdeacon set about the adventure— big enough at any time, but heroic at his age—of building a new school. The Archdeacon was eighty-four at the time, and suffered very much from his feet. Dooley, ten years younger and a stripling by comparison, linked him into and out of the parochial trap when he went to interview contractors, civil servants, corporation clerks, architects, and solicitors. Most of these gentlemen, after a few interviews with the Archdeacon, began to have a new respect for doddering old men, for behind his simulated dotage was a mind sound as a bell.

In the beginning, Anthony tried to give the Archdeacon courage, to coax him into building a school that would make people stand and stare, but the diffident phase did not last very long. The old man was slow in starting, but once he had taken the plunge he forgot his fears and belied his age. He snapped up a site that a printing firm wanted for a factory; he encouraged the architect to be generous with space and materials; he bullied the Department without its knowing it; he followed the contractor about like a quiet terrier.

This was to be no ordinary school. It was to have windows that would make love to sun and air.   It was to have elbow-room and playing-space, and to be so far from Walls and chimneys that it could grow and grow like an expanding suitcase. It was to have towels and wash-basins, cloak-rooms and corridors. It was to have a staff-room, headmaster's office, and an assembly hall fitted for film projection.   Anthony had pleaded with the Archdeacon for years, had coaxed and exhorted him, but when he saw the final plans he began to fear that he had done his job too well.

The Archdeacon drove down to see him the day the plans were sanctioned.

"It's going to be a marvel," said the Archdeacon. "A headline for the whole diocese. Paradise Alley has come Into its own. I don't suppose I'll live to see it finished, but I couldn't ask a better headstone, and if I get it fairly under way I think I can sing my *Nunc Dimittis*."

"I can join in the chorus, then, for I don't think I'll ever teach in the new school. I'm too near my pension."

"Sure I thought you had a long time to go yet, Anthony."

"Two years. I'm sixty-three."

"I'd never have thought it, Anthony." He shook his head. "That's the way of the world. It's our school, Anthony, and we can't think of it as belonging to anyone else, but we're building it for another priest and another principal. But no, Anthony, I'm wrong. We're building it for Paradise Alley —for the children of the docks and the tenements. They're a grand people, Anthony—a grand people. Where would you find better?"

"It would be hard to equal them—in spite of their faults."

"Isn't it a great mercy now that I was never a bright, go-ahead sort of a priest—a good speaker and a spatter of degrees after my name? I might have been changed to some parish where half the congregation would be wearing spats. And now what about the whist drives?"

This was an old trick of the Archdeacon's, and Anthony countered it by looking blank.

"Don't say that I forgot to tell you about them," went on the Archdeacon. "My memory isn't what it used to be. I'm going to run a series of whist drives in aid of the new school."

"That's good," said Anthony. "I'm glad to hear it. For a moment I thought you were going to ask me to run them."

"Ah, you're very hard on me, Anthony. To tell you the truth I was thinking that you might see about the tables and the packs of cards."

"And the tickets?"

"We'll need tickets, I suppose?"

"And the prizes?"

"That's another thing. I had forgotten about the prizes."

"Ah, but then your memory isn't as good as it used to be."

"You're a hard man, Anthony, and you're hitting below the belt. Sure we must get the money some way—the whole parish is helping me. We're going to have drawings of prizes, sales of work, fancy dress dances for the children, and maybe a little carnival in the summer. What's a couple of whist drives?"

"Nothing between friends," said Anthony.

Anthony hated whist drives, but Dooley loved football matches. Football was meat and drink to Dooley, and the proudest moment in his life was when he saw the posters which announced a

Challenge Match

In aid of

Paradise Alley Building Fund

Dooley's XI. v Leinster Selected.

The Dooley mentioned in the posters was Dicky Dooley, Joe's youngest son, but the Dooley of the posters was not the Dooley who claimed the credit for having arranged the challenge.

"I'll tell you how it happened," said Dooley, when he came down to the school to get Anthony to write the first of the long series of letters in connexion with the match. "We were sitting in the parlour one day—the Archdeacon and meself—when he says, sudden like—'Dooley,' says he,

'I wonder could you get up a challenge match in aid of the new school.'

'Not at my age, Archdeacon,' says I. 'I couldn't face the bother of arranging anything. I'm past all that.' 'Dooley' says he then, 'I'm depending on you. We've done a lot of soldiering together in this parish for close on forty years, and I know you won't let me down.' When he put it like that what could I do, hawh? Sure I would have broke his heart if I had refused. I couldn't go agen him."

"You couldn't refuse," said Anthony. "That's what I say," said Dooley. "It was the way he put it."

"It was all the way he put it."

"Now do you see, Mr. Domican, hawh? I couldn't refuse—on account of the way he put it, like."

"You had no option."

"In a nutshell, Mr. Domican! In a nutshell! No option—that's what I hadn't. He's a clever man, the Archdeacon, a clever man, and he must have known about Dicky bein' the best centre-half in Leinster, hawh! Wouldn't you say so now, Mr. Domican?"

" To be sure."

"Of course when I said I was too old to face the bother of arranging a match I was exaggerating a little, hawh! It won't be much bother. Sure none of the players could refuse Dicky Dooley's father, hawh? And what's more, though I say it meself, I was a bit of a footballer in me own day."

"I didn't know that, Joe."

"I was centre-half for Strand Rovers United—you wouldn't think that to look at me now, hawh? And we never lost a match. No, not as much as one. There's a quare one for the gombeens! I had an offer from Arsenal once."

"And you didn't take it?"

"Is it me?" Dooley straightened himself. "Oh, no! No England for me. 'Here am I,' says I, when they asked me, 'and here I'll stay.' I played for Strand Rovers for years and never got as much as the price of a drink out of them— no nor didn't want it."

(Dooley had done yeoman service for Strand Rovers, Anthony discovered afterwards, but not as centre-half. He had got an odd match when someone disappointed at the last moment, but his principal job had been to carry the bag with the spare togs and liniments).

Dooley worried a lot the week before the match. He consulted the Archdeacon's barometer hourly, he got weather forecasts from seafaring men, he picked his ears at every rustle of wind. On the very last evening a few clouds came up out of the west to annoy him.

"If it's a bad day we're ruinated," he said to Anthony. "You can't expect people to get soaked. If it rains anyway heavy there won't be a sinner in the bob place and no one in the stand but them that has booked their seats. I must get the ould man himself to do a bit of praying."

But it wasn't a bad day. It was a magnificent day for football. The air was brisk, the wind was just strong enough to flutter the corner-flags, the turf was in fine fettle. The turnstiles clicked merrily at a shilling a time, but Dooley wasn't there to hear them. Dooley was sitting at home, staring into the fire, and on the table beside him was a War Office telegram.

Anthony called next evening to sympathize with him.

"Thank you, Mr. Domican," said Dooley. "Thank you, indeed. He was only thirty-eight, and he's gone before me. Six-feet-two he was, and straight as a ramrod—the best of the bunch in ways, but wild as a March hare. I could never get any good of him, but he had a heart of gold.

"If he had died here in the troubled times I wouldn't have minded so much. But he died far away and in a fight that was none of his business. Isn't it queer, too, hawh? Irishmen have been fighting in France since the days of Fontenoy. If Jem had had a bit of sense he would have stayed at home. But what's the use of talking? What's done can't be undone. God rest him and eternal light shine on him. He was wild, sure enough, but he was a good boy. Never missed his monthly Communion—thank God for that. It's a great comfort now—the only comfort we have."

Anthony was sorry for Dooley, and sorry for himself. Sergeant James Dooley was dead. Sergeant Christopher Domican was alive. Or was he? One didn't live very long in the tail of a heavy bomber. Christopher, too, was in a fight that was none of his business, and Mollie slept fitfully.

She had been a little brighter since she had heard that he was in the Air Force. It was better than knowing nothing.

Since he had joined up he had sent her three letters. Until then they had had very little to go on. Someone had seen him in Belfast. Mandy had heard that he was working in Manchester. But the proud, defiant speech he had made the night before he left home had not been prophecy. He paid no debts, he sent no money, he fulfilled no promises. He simply disappeared.

*   *   *   *

The site of the new school was cleared and levelled. The foundations were laid. The walls began to rise. All over Europe schools were crumbling overnight: in Paradise Alley, like a challenge to the mad world, one was being built.

Everything but concrete and muscle was hard to get, and the Archdeacon had a busy time of it. He fretted over delays, he grumbled when the contractors asked leave to substitute and replace. But he would have nothing shoddy. He coaxed the Department of Supplies and harried the Clerk of Works. And he came to Anthony regularly for encouragement, advice, and applause.

"It may be the last job I'll ever do," he said a dozen times, "and I'm going to do it well. I'm not the man for it—God knows I'm not—for I hate fuss and foosther, phone calls and dotted lines, bills of quantities and money on account. I'm not built for that kind of stuff, Anthony, but I'm not going to let it beat me. Paradise Alley deserves the best, and I'm going to see that it gets it. And amn't I right? Tell me straight, Anthony—amn't I right? And for an old doddering man like me amn't I doing well?"

Anthony joined in the chorus always, and the Archdeacon went away purring. Paradise Alley was going to have a school that would make a show of the wealthy parishes. It deserved it, and it had earned it. It deserved it because it needed it more than the wealthy parishes did, because the light and spaciousness it would bring would give its children a shade of conceit in themselves, because its sun-shattered windows would look out on a brighter world than the world of the tenements. It had earned it, in poverty and hunger, in coughs and rickets, behind washtubs and sewing machines, in sweat shops and factories.

The new school was going up, but it had come too late for Anthony Domican. He saw the roof going on and knew that it would never cover him. His time was coming. He would finish up with the old school and always be a stranger in the new—a visitor with certain privileges, but an old fogey who had outlived his usefulness.

The nuns had plans for the old school. They were going to build a corridor that would link it with their own school and give them space for a secondary department. They were going to tear down the rickety, death-trap sheds, and take away the playground wall. They were going to spend money on paint and plaster.

But no one had plans for Anthony Domican. There was no place for him any longer in Paradise Alley.

CHAPTER TWENTY-THREE

He gathered the roll-books into the press and locked away for the last time the sloping attendance marks that were like tombstones to the dead days. The monthly return lay on the table in front of him: 31st December, 1944. He could have read it blindfold, could have filled it in in the dark as easily as he buttoned his waistcoat.

It was the last monthly return he would ever fill. From now on it would be Sullivan's job to collect the signatures and bring it down to the Archdeacon. And the Archdeacon, before he signed his name and wrote the magic word "Yes" in the space provided for it, would make his hoary joke and say "I'm making a liar of myself every month—sure if all the rules of the Department were kept it wouldn't be a school at all, but a museum."

But the Canon, God help him (he could never get quite used to thinking of him as the Archdeacon) hadn't so many more monthly returns to sign either. The old man had a light-hearted way with the heel-chaffing years, but they would catch up with him in the long run. The Canon, like Anthony himself, like the old school, was nearing the end of his tether. They were all finishing up together.

He came home to an empty house. Mollie had left his dinner in the oven for him, and there was a note on the mantelpiece saying that she had gone over to Brigid's in Raheny. The ticking of the clock kept him company as he ate. The clock had begun to record a new sort of time. It was ticking out empty minutes that would stretch out into empty years. He had always thought that when the time came to go he would have a divided mind, that one part of him would be sorry to leave Paradise Alley and another glad of the rest. Now he knew differently. Rest was something you could take in small doses and be the better of; it was not an emptiness that knew no boundary but the grave.

Mollie came in at six o'clock, full of concern for Brigid's year-old child.

"Little Francis has whooping-cough, Anthony. Isn't it terrible! He's shooting up every feed like a water-spout—no sooner down than it's up again. I never saw anything like it."

"Indeed you did, Mollie. Sure our own four had it, and they all got over it."

"But it's very wearing on an infant, Anthony."

"Have they had the doctor?"

"They had, but he can't do very much. Told them to feed him on rice flour—it's heavy and he'll have a better chance of keeping it down. Do you know, Anthony, I think Brigid is worried."

"Ah, the child will get over it all right. Brigid is a sensible woman when she's left alone."

"There's no need to be cranky, Anthony. I said nothing to alarm Brigid— not a single thing. It's Raymond Brigid is worried about."

"What's wrong with Raymond?"

"Well, he hasn't been doing so well lately—his business has gone down a lot since the war. He finds it hard to get stuff to sell, he says. I'm afraid they are having a fight to make ends meet."

"Surely we could do something to help them?"

"That's just what I was thinking myself. There's no reason why they shouldn't give up their house and come to live with us until the end of the war."

I know you, Mollie, he was thinking. You're nearly glad that Raymond is doing badly so that you'll have Francis here all the time to fuss over. It would do you good, too. It would make you forget the emptiness of this house and keep you from listening to the clock chiming the small hours. But I'll not let you overdo it. I remember what Lahardan did to me and what Grandfather Lenihan did to Christopher.

Aloud, he said:

"They'll be welcome here any time they like to come, Mollie. There's plenty of room and we have enough to live on."

They had more than enough to live on. Anthony's pension was something less than five pounds a week, but he still had his retaining fee from Mandy Logue and Sons, and his dividends from Shannon Dairies were fatter than ever. Mollie had her investments, and the rents of the four houses her father had left her. There was a roughness of money in Crescent Terrace, but there were no children to tear the seats out of their pants on barbed wire, or bring home school bills. There was nothing to work for any more, and the annuity that Anthony had got for his interest in the Erin Academy wouldn't bring back Christopher.

Mollie took to knitting a little vest for Francis, and Anthony sat watching her. She must have grown old, but he could see no age in her. She looked happier than she had looked for a long time.

"Did you know that I finished teaching to-day?" he said, after a little while. "I'm on pension."

"Oh, Anthony, I had forgotten completely." She rose and kissed him. "Congratulations, darling. We should have arranged something—some little celebration. It's not every day that a man retires from teaching. How do you feel about it?"

"I dunno yet—it's too recent. It'll take me some time to get used to being an old man."

"But you're not old, Anthony—don't be silly. You're quite young still— you're in your prime."

"Don't kid yourself, woman. I'm in the sere and yellow leaf. Seventy will be the next milestone in my life."

"A man is as old as he feels, they say."

That wasn't the way the Department looked at it. To them a man was as old as his birth certificate, and when you reached the statutory age they threw you out. Sixty-five hadn't seemed an unreasonable retiring age when Rodney went off to write his history of Restoration Drama, but it seemed absurdly low now. Anthony admitted to himself that he hadn't the energy he used to have, nor as much enthusiasm, perhaps, but he had a patience and a humility that he hadn't brought out of the training college with him. Weighing it all in all he was a better teacher than he had been thirty years earlier, or even twenty years earlier. He had mellowed, grown wiser, was content to see results in perspective. The only blot on his record was that he was sixty-five. The experience that had made a teacher of him was his only crime. He was being pushed out, not because he had outlived his usefulness, but to make room for the newcomers, for young men who would learn in due course that everything new in the technique of teaching had been discovered hundreds of years before.

Towards the end of January his colleagues, friends, and ex-pupils entertained him to dinner at Leary's Hotel, and presented him with an illuminated address and a wallet of notes. It was quite a big affair in its way, and it got a couple of inches in the skinny, war-time papers—principally because of the presence of Senator M. Logue and Mr. E. Bolger, T.D. The speeches were full of the old tags, but the high praise which distorted the picture of his life and magnified his achievements did no violence to his intelligence, and for once he was tolerant of clichés. The speakers might not have meant everything they said, but they were utterly sincere in wanting to please him and their formality was simply the good manners of kindness.

Mandy Logue quoted Plato and worked in a Latin quotation without blushing. Sullivan, the new principal, said that Paradise Alley would never again be the same place. Ned Bolger confessed that he owed his old teacher more than he could ever repay, and that Anthony Domican was a man "who might have amassed wealth and attained the highest civic honours had he not been so closely wedded to his profession." Anthony, listening to him, was thinking of "The dandelion makes a harp of the sun's rays and the blackbird dances to the music." Nedser's vocabulary had grown a bit with the years, but he never could recapture the first fine careless rapture.

The Archdeacon was there, bad leg and all, and he made a speech that brought a lump to Anthony's throat.

"It is a long time now since I first met Anthony Domican, but I can say truthfully that from the very beginning I saw in him the man he afterwards proved himself to be. I hate to lose him, and though I have a warm spot in my heart for his successor I can't help saying that Anthony Domican's place in Paradise Alley will be hard to fill. In a way he was Paradise Alley. It was his vocation, and it took first place in his heart—as it did in mine. We worked together, Anthony and I, not just for a school but for a people. You, ladies and gentlemen, may know wealthier people, more cultured people. Permit an old man in his dotage to say that you don't know a better people.

"It was a high privilege to work with them and for them—there is at least one man in the room who will stand by me in that. Anthony Domican loved Paradise Alley, and that was the thing that most endeared him to me. It meant more than teaching ability, glowing reports, or results —all of which he had in good measure. He knew his people, and he loved them, and the traditions he has left behind him will long remain as an inspiration to those who carry on the new school which is Paradise Alley in spirit if not in name."

Anthony had a fine speech ready, but did not deliver it. Feeling dulled the edges of memory, and there was something in his throat that killed his smooth, set phrases. He floundered for a while, and then dodged the problem by praising the Archdeacon. After that the words came more easily.

"I am proud to say that I loved Paradise Alley from the very beginning, but I claim no credit for it, for even in that the Archdeacon was my teacher. This is not what is known as a good parish, and I know the Canon-the Archdeacon-could easily have got a better one. He could have got far away from the docks and the back streets if he had felt inclined that way. But he stayed where he was wanted."

"I am not going to pretend now that we always saw eye to eye, for we didn't. We had our tussles, even our stand-up fights. But even in the hottest of them I wouldn't have changed him for the pick of the metropolitan chapter—and in saying that I think I speak for every man, woman, and child in the parish.

"I am glad to see my old friend and pupil Ned Bolger here to-night. I marked out Ned from the very start as a boy who would make his way in the world, and though I have a shaky enough record as a prophet I made no mistake in Ned's case. I was proud of him in the old days—I am proud of him still. He has told you that he owes much to me and to Paradise Alley, but I can say without any false modesty that he doesn't. I take no credit for Ned Bolger. Any credit I can take—and it is precious little—is concerned with less gifted ex-pupils, with boys who made no mark in school or out of it, but who, by the grace of God, picked up in Paradise Alley something which no inspector ever tested.

"Don't think I'm boasting—the boasting has all been done for me. No teacher can help doing some good, and God knows I have done less than most. But I had one tremendous advantage in Paradise Alley—I had no spoiled children. Some of them were tough, but their failings were all on the surface and their more serious faults were due almost completely to the environment in which they lived.

"Several of the other speakers here to-night have wished me luck in my well-earned rest. I thank them for the kindly thought, but I assure them that I'm not looking forward to the rest part of the business. I don't grudge Adrian Sullivan his new school, but I'd ask nothing better than to be employed there as an unpaid monitor for the rest of my life. So perhaps, after all, I am more senile than I think.

"I have a faint hope now that my going may coincide with the beginning of a new chapter in Irish education. I look forward to a time—God grant that I may live to see even the fringe of it—when Paradise Alley will not only have a fine primary school but will share in an educational system which will prevent poverty from being what it is now—a heritage which a man passes on to his children. It was my sorrow, during my years here in Paradise Alley, to see most of my good-quality pupils leave school for ever at fourteen, and forsake books for grocery baskets and carrier bicycles. Many of them, indeed, left me for no more profitable occupation than that of holding up the nearest factory wall. I hate to go, but I could go more happily if I felt that I was the last of the old brigade and that some more democratic, more Christian concept of education was round the corner."

By the time they had come to "For He's a Jolly Good Fellow" the whiskey had gone to his head, and he was slightly fuddled when the farewells were said. But he knew everyone who shook hands with him, and next morning he was able to recall and label every compliment.

"Well, that's that," he said to Mollie, as the taxi started off.   "I've said good-bye to Paradise Alley."

She put her hands on his and kissed him lightly on the cheek.

"It was grand, Anthony. I was proud of you to-night."

"Were you, really?"

"I was indeed, Anthony. They said many nice things about you, but if they had said twice as much they would still have been short of the truth."

He sat back in his seat and patted her hands. Words and phrases were chasing one another through his head, and he wondered how near he was to being drunk.   He did not speak again until they were passing under the railway bridge.

"It's a cold night, Mollie."

"That's just what I'm thinking myself, Anthony.   I wonder if Brigid has enough bed-clothes on little Francis."

He felt a little jealous then, in spite of all the speeches.

*   *   *   *

Little Francis Anthony made a change in Crescent Terrace. He gave Crescent Terrace something to do and something to talk about. Mollie washed, ironed, and aired his clothes, polished his pram, stole in at night to listen to his breathing. She said that the child could read your thoughts, and she claimed that she could read his. She prescribed castor-oil, and comforters, and irregular feeds, and complained quietly when Brigid stood by the doctors and reminded her that Queen Victoria was dead. Brigid let her mother fuss, but she did not let her dictate. Francis was not going to be lifted every time he cried, or fed every time he was lifted, or given a soother, or allowed to have his own way. Francis was going to be reared-—and was reared—by the book.

Mollie was not in control, but she made the most of the limited control that Brigid gave her, or could not keep from her, and so was happier than she had been for months. She wheeled Francis Anthony out in his pram; she chased Raymond and Brigid out to the pictures so that she would, for a few hours, have complete charge of Francis Anthony; she took pleasure in denying herself the wireless lest she should waken Francis Anthony. She knew every cry of Francis Anthony's as the captain of a coasting steamer knows the buoys about home—she could tell the pain cry from the petulant cry, and the hunger cry from the come-and-lift-me cry. She had forgotten nothing that her own four children had taught her, and although it was many years since she had taken her degree she entered on her post-graduate course with the enthusiasm of a complete beginner.

She rose early to take her place in the wool queues. She begged wool, and bought wool, and swopped wool. But she had no wool for Anthony's socks, or for gloves and jumpers for herself. It all went into romper suits and jerseys and warm vests, and she could not have spent more time knitting had Francis Anthony been triplets.

Mollie had very rigid ideas on the rearing of children. She was of the school of thought which maintains that a baby should wear its own weight of clothes during the day and lie under a mountain of clothes at night. She thought that a baby should be fed to repletion at every meal and have a meal whenever it felt like it. She disagreed with Brigid's Spartan ideas on baby clothes and with her rigid time-table. She made very little impression on Brigid, but whenever she had Francis Anthony to herself she gave full scope to her own notions of child-rearing, so that in the end she came to believe that the ill-fortune which had cut down Raymond's earnings was a blessing in disguise as far as Francis Anthony was concerned, and that it saved her only grandson from the full, dire effects of the new psychology and its cold, orphanage-like curriculum.

It may not have been a blessing in disguise for Francis Anthony but it was certainly a blessing for his grandmother. Until the baby came to Crescent Terrace Mollie had been living in a narrow groove of thought. She wrote regularly to Denis and Mary, she saw Brigid two or three times a week, but her love for them could not banish the image of Christopher, and her happiness, even her mental health, was gambled on his return. Every day that he didn't come was a month long; every sleepless night was bordered by a dawn that might bring him.

And when news reached her that he would never come again to Crescent Terrace, Denis and Mary could not save her nor Brigid and Anthony bring her comfort. It was Francis Anthony who thawed the ice of her grief and broke through the thought-barrier that stemmed her tears.

"If I knew that he had made his peace with God I could face up to it," she said to Anthony the day the cold, official letter arrived. "But if he died with all that stubbornness in him—I'll never know peace again. And how will we ever know how he died? If I only had some news—something to hope for! "

It was ten days before news came, and it came through a Jesuit chaplain.

"Dear Mrs. Domican,

I am writing this letter in the hope that it may make your cross a little easier to bear. But it is not a routine letter of consolation, a collection of stock phrases. It deals with facts.

I saw Christopher shortly before his last flight, and I hope that when my time comes I shall be as well prepared as he was. War brings out the worst in some of us; in others it brings out the best—and Christopher was one of the others. He came to Confession regularly, and he received Holy Communion the morning he died. His faith, courage, and piety were an example to his brother officers. He was a brave boy, and a good boy. This news may not he much consolation to you now when your sorrow is fresh, but it will sustain you in the difficult clays ahead. As a Catholic mother you will be glad to know that Christopher remained steadfast to the best traditions of his Faith and country, and that he emerged unscathed from hazards that brought spiritual disaster to so many.

I shall remember him always at Holy Mass and in my prayers."

Mollie read the letter over and over again long after she had memorized it, and she cried afresh with every reading—for the consolation it brought was based on reason, and it was some time before reason got the better of emotion. But to Anthony, from the very beginning, the letter brought peace. Mollie had lost Christopher, but Anthony had found him.

ANTHONY did his best to enjoy his retirement. He rose late and went to ten o'clock Mass. He strolled through the museum and the art galleries. He went to cinema shows that finished in broad daylight. When the first buds were breaking he bought packets of seeds and dug his garden, and he walked regularly to the point of the Bull Wall and watched the ships nosing their way up the channel of the Liffey. But when he worked in the garden his mind was more active than his muscles, and though he liked watching the green waves crumbling against the Wall his eyes turned always to the smoke of the city and the low outline of Paradise Alley.

There would be no more teacher-Domicans. The line that Sean Domican had founded when he came back from Salamanca was doomed. Anthony was the last of them. If Christopher had lived, things would have been different, but Christopher was lying under a wooden cross somewhere between the Marne and the Rhine.

It was bad enough to grow old, but it was worse far to bring a name to the grave with you, to be the last chapter in the story of the Domicans.

Time moved slowly for Anthony, for he had no landmarks to measure it against. In Paradise Alley each day had had its own character, each month its own pattern of work that repeated itself like the seasons. Now the days were all alike, and the month was a succession of Sundays.

He went down once, but only once, to the new Paradise Alley. In the old days it had all been his—the tramp of the marching feet, the sing-song of the multiplication tables, the ticking of the moon-faced clock. Now he was just a stranger. Paradise Alley had not fallen to pieces when he left it, any more than it had fallen to pieces when Alfred Mendelssohn Rodney left it. Sullivan and the others told him that they envied him his good fortune, and he could not speak the thoughts that were in his heart lest they should think him a sentimental old fool.

One bright day, when the sky was blue over Howth, he turned his back on the sea and walked citywards as far as Fairview Park. It was the old road, the road to Paradise Alley. He would have liked to have gone down along the Tolka and past the old school, but he was a little ashamed of his sentimentality, a little afraid that someone might see him revisiting his old haunts and wooing the dead years. So he turned into the park and sat on a seat there, soaking in the early sunshine.

The place was full of shabby old men. They sat in twos and threes and discussed the war. He could have sat with them and talked with them—for they were as eager for company as boys, and as inquisitive as wrens—but he was in no humour for talking to strangers. He just watched the old men, and thought out stories to fit them. Each of them, he reflected, had- probably done in his time work that was just as useful to the community as his had been. They had carried builders' hods, and loaded ships, and dug drains. They had worked until they were no longer fit to work.and when they stopped they got neither illuminated addresses nor government gratuities. They lived on the old age pension—which wouldn't keep a dog in bones—and on the charity of their relatives. They carried pipes in their pockets and cadged fills from one another. They lived on sufferance in their sons' houses and spent their days on park benches discussing the tremendous advances in military science which marked off a century of civilization and progress from the dark ages which preceded it.

And, surprisingly, they were not resentful. They were simply old, and tired, and glad to be alive in a world that no longer needed them and that valued their services to the community at ten shillings a week.

Anthony sat for an hour and then began to walk about like a convalescent. Presently he would go home to dinner. In the meantime he had nothing to do and all day to do it.

Someone shouted his name.

"Mr. Domican! Mr. Domican! "

It was Joe Dooley—a little more shrunken, and thinner than ever, but the same old Dooley. Anthony was glad to see him.

"How are you, Dooley? You're looking well."

"Why wouldn't I be lookin' well, Mr. Domican? Sure I have nothing to do now but eat me grub and walk the feet off meself. It's a great life, hawh! "

"How do you like being retired?"

"Tip-top, thanks be to God. Sure I have two pensions—the old age and the few bob a week th' Archdeacon gives me. I'm living with me married daughter since the old woman died—the light of Heaven to her. She's a good girl, and she has a fine husband, but they don't want an old man like me hangin' around the house during the day, so I spend most of me time on the go. But there's not a bother on me. Never felt better."

"What would you say to a drink?"

Dooley winked and nodded his head.

"There's no law agen it, Mr. Domican. I only had one answer to a drink all me life and it never was 'no'."

"And how is the Archdeacon?" asked Anthony. They were walking out of the park then.

"Game-ball, Mr. Domican—game-ball! Of course that foot of his is giving him a deal of bother. He's not as young as he used to be."

"Which of us is, Dooley?"

"Aye, right enough. There's none of us standing still, as far as I can see. But do you know what I'm going to tell you?" He stopped then and looked accusingly at Anthony. "Do you know what I'm going to tell you? He's vexed with you."

"Vexed with me?"

"With yourself, Mr. Domican. Vexed is the word."

 "But what have I done?"

"Wait now till we get out of the way of the buses. I don't want to die for a while yet."

They crossed the road and entered a public-house. Anthony ordered two pints.

"Now go on, like a good man. Tell me the worst."

Dooley removed his hat and set it on the counter.

"This is the way it was," he said, and his tone seemed to convey that a person of Anthony's limited intelligence would find it difficult to follow the argument unless he listened attentively. "I was down with the Archdeacon yesterday. You know how it is—me havin' helped him all these years, he's sort of lost without me. So I go down to him once or twice a week to have a chat on parish matters. Do you follow?" Anthony nodded.

"Well, we were sittin' there together in the parlour, him and me, talkin' the way we're talkin' now, and says he to me, without any warnin': 'Dooley,' says he, 'what did I do on Mr. Domican?' Just like that, hawh! You could 'a knocked me down with a filleted plaice. 'Well, now, Archdeacon,' said I, real innocent, 'I don't know what you mean.'

"'Well, I'll tell you,' says the Archdeacon. 'He hasn't been next or near me for over a month. And I'm hurt.' Them were his very words, Mr. Domican! 'I'm hurt,' says he. Well, here's good luck, Mr. Domican."

He drank two-thirds of his pint, set the glass back on the counter, and waited for Anthony to defend himself.

"I suppose I should have gone down," said Anthony. "Did he seem very annoyed?"

"Bedad he did." Dooley smacked his lips on it. "Though mind you, I think his own word was the best—hurt—that's the word for it."

"Did he say anything else?"

"He said if I seen you I was to ask you to call to see him—and the very next day I bump into you unexpected. Isn't it a good one, hawh?"

"It is, indeed, and I'll go down to him this evening. I would have gone long ago, but I don't like going near the new school. It makes me kind of miserable—it's foolish, I know, but there it is. I feel that I should be inside, and I know that I don't belong there any more."

Dooley nodded his head understandingly.

"I know, I know, Mr. Domican. I felt the very same myself when Larry Malone took over me own work. It's terrible to feel that you can be done without."

This sombre thought affected him so deeply that he seemed to go into a trance, during the course of which he absent-mindedly made a good hole in his second pint.

"But can we be done without?" he said then. "That's the question. Mind you, I have nothing against Mr. O'Sullivan. Not a thing in the wide world. But there's no use in thinkin' one thing and sayin' another. Is there now, hawh? Ah, no, Mr. Domican, that school isn't the same since you left it." He shut his eyes and shook his head violently, as if to get rid of the last vestige of any impression to the contrary. "No, it's not the same place."

"Nonsense!" said Anthony.

"God's truth, Mr. Domican, and don't think I'm just saying it to your face, for many's the time I said it behind your back. It's not the same place."

"It's nice of you to say it, Dooley, but we must face facts. Sullivan is as good a man as ever I was—and maybe better. You and I are just old has-beens trying to gild the days that are gone. We find it hard to get on without Paradise Alley, but Paradise Alley has no bother in getting on without us."

"I don't know about that, Mr. Domican. The old days were good days, too.

Somehow there's not the same spirit in the people now. Did I ever tell you about the day we buried Canon McGinn?"

Dooley exhumed Canon McGinn and laid him to rest again with due reverence. He showed how Touser Kennedy fell, and shook the hand that felled the policeman. He rehabilitated the Canon's motor car and smashed it afresh beneath the giant steam waggon. The best part of two hours had passed before he refused another drink and got off the stool.

"I enjoyed that chat," said Anthony, when they were out again in the sunshine. "Do you come to the park often?"

"When it's fine I come nearly every morning."

"I must have a walk up this way now and again, then. It does me good to have a chat about old times."

"I'm always ready for a chat, Mr. Domican," said Dooley, magnanimously. "It's the way I'm built. An' I get tired talkin' to these retired policemen—they want to know everybody's business. So any time you're up this way don't pass me by—I'll be lookin' out for you. Sure I love to chat about the old school—me heart was in it."

Anthony was late for lunch, and he felt the better of it. He hadn't been late for anything for weeks.

*   *   *   *

After tea that night he went down to the Archdeacon. He did not go the short way, along the sea wall that was no longer a sea wall—for the Corporation had dumped soil and refuse inside it and stolen five acres from the estuary of the Tolka—and past the old school. Instead, he took the bus to O'Connell Bridge and walked down by the Custom House and the Burns and Laird sheds: that was the way he had gone forty years before when he first came to Paradise Alley.

The quays were almost deserted, and there were only a few boats in the river. The men and women who had snicked the heads off cabbages with big, black-handled knives were gone. But the tide still lipped against the ferry steps and gurgled under baulks of timber. The sea would never change, never grow old. It fretted itself like a living thing, but it was unlike all living things. For it there was no decay, no succession, no statutory retiring age.

Mary, the maid who had replaced old Ellen—the friend of the widda woman in Hope Street—had left her mark on the Canon's house. There was no dust in it now. It shone with beeswax, smelt of furniture polish. The only thing on which she did not leave her mark was the old man himself. He refused to be regimented into tidiness, and when he left a book on the piano he expected to find it on the piano. Mary's ideas and the Archdeacon's were incompatible, and if, in the presbytery, cleanliness was next to Godliness, it was simply a case of contiguity.

Mary was very formal with visitors.

"I'll see if the Archdeacon will see you, Mr. Domican." she said.

"Please take a seat."

The Archdeacon gave him a great welcome.

"Ah, I'm glad to see you, Anthony. I thought you had reneged me altogether. I'm delighted that you came down. Sure it must be six weeks since I laid eyes on you."

He was sitting in an armchair by the fire, and one of his feet, wrapped in red flannel, rested on a low stool beside him. At his elbow was a green card-table with books, papers, pipes, a tobacco pouch, and a cup and saucer. This little island was Church property and under the absolute control of the Archdeacon. The rest of the room was under Mary's jurisdiction and was as tidy as a convent parlour.

"Well now, Anthony, how are you keeping?"

"Splendid, thanks. And yourself?"

"Only fair, Anthony—only fair. This old foot of mine is giving me a good deal of trouble lately. Old age and bad circulation. The doctor is afraid that gangrene may set in, and if it does that may be the end of me. What's this Dean Swift says about going at the top, like a mighty oak? But in my case the decay is settling in at the other end."

"You're a long way from decay yet, thank God."

The Archdeacon set about filling his pipe. His fingers were shaky, and strands of tobacco fell into his lap.

"I don't know, Anthony, and to tell you the truth I don't care very much one way or another. I've had a long innings. Nobody likes to go, they tell me, but I have a feeling that He makes it easy for us at the finish. We all know that Christ died for us, but sometimes we stress the atonement and don't emphasise the big, important fact that He died. The breath left Him. His heart stopped. He went through the gate that we all must pass through. You might almost think that He did it to give us courage and consolation when the time comes. I wonder am I right?"

"I wouldn't be surprised if you were, Archdeacon, but I'm not a theologian. Anyway it's a nice morbid subject to be talking about on a fine evening like this."

"So it is, maybe." The Archdeacon tapped down his pipe and began to light matches. "But sure I'd be a fool to close my eyes to what's coming to me."

"Anyway there's nothing for you to be scared about. A priest shouldn't have much to regret on his death bed."

"I'm not so sure of that, Anthony. I was just reading the life of Pere Lamy the other day—and I think that I got things very soft. I had a poor parish, but he had scarcely enough to eat. I did one priest's work, but he did enough for three."

"Well now, Archdeacon, I shouldn't mind taking my chance on the merit you have piled up upstairs."

"In the long run it's a case of God's mercy, Anthony. Anyway, I have all my arrangements made—and it wasn't much bother making my will. I'm leaving a hundred pounds to Dooley, the poor man. He's a kind of responsibility to me, is Dooley."

Anthony took his cue.

" I was talking to him to-day, and he seemed in great humour. He hinted that you wanted to see me about something."

One side of the Archdeacon's pipe wasn't burning properly, so he lit another match.

"Only just," he puffed, "that I thought I'd like to have a chat with you. I wouldn't like to lose sight of you altogether just because you've retired. And tell me now—how do you like leading the life of a gentleman?"

"I don't like it."

"Now isn't that strange! " The Archdeacon raised his eyebrows. "One would have thought that you had your fill of teaching. Ah, here's Mary with the tea. Thank you, Mary. Just a cup, Anthony, and a slice of home-made cake. Bring over that little table, like a good man, and we'll take it here in front of the fire."

"A wonderful person, Mary," he went on. "She could manage anything— she even tries to manage me, but it's too late now. Well now, as I was saying,

Anthony, I thought you'd welcome your *otium cum dignitate*."

"Tell me this, Archdeacon—how would you welcome it yourself?"

"You have me there, Anthony. Sure I could have retired long ago if I had wanted to. His Grace wouldn't have minded an old man like me getting out before he cracked up. But I wouldn't have lasted a month with nothing to do—not a month. Not that I do much now—I say the ten o'clock Mass on Sundays and leave the running about to the curates. But I'm still the parochus, and I have plenty to keep my mind occupied. Have another bit of cake?"

"Mary is a good cook."

"None better. Her pastry is as light as snowflakes—and the pity of it is that I like it thick and suety. That's the way old Ellen used to make it—God be good to her."

"Yes, I have plenty to keep my mind occupied," he went on. "This Father Murphy of mine is a regular scourge."

"Don't tell me you're turning against Father Murphy?"

The Archdeacon raised one hand in protest.

"Don't misunderstand me, Anthony. He's a fine priest—one of the best in the diocese. He's full of energy, and enthusiasm, and new ideas. Fine things, I grant you, but I'm an old man. The latest thing he got me to start is this perpetual novena on Monday nights. He's always getting me to start things."

"It's time someone got you to start things," said Anthony.

"That's a rub," said the Archdeacon. "A definite rub! You're all too clever for me—that's what's the matter. But you must admit that I didn't make a bad job of the school once I got started. Honour where honour is due, Anthony. But to come back to the business of Father Murphy—he's gone clean daft recently on the boys' club—clean daft."

"I thought the boys' club was two or three years old," said Anthony.

"It is and more. But up to now it's been just rings, and billiards, and a bit of woodwork—simple stuff. Now, I believe, it's to be a sort of a university."

Anthony laughed.

"A university, no less," complained the Archdeacon. Nothing ordinary will do Father Murphy. He's full up with something he calls 'adult education.' He wants the boys taught Apologetics, and Church history, and trigonometry, and the divil knows what else. I couldn't remember the half of them. What do you make of it, Anthony?"

"It seems a bit ambitious, but it's a good idea."

"D'you say so?" The Archdeacon looked surprised, and a little bit pleased. "Well now, maybe Father Murphy is right after all. He's taking over Denson's shed as a club extension—he's going to tear down partitions, put in a new floor, and alter the whole look of the place."

"But where is the money to come from?"

" He got some from Ned Bolger, I believe, and I gave him a few pounds myself."

"But I thought you were against the idea?"

"I'm neither for it nor against it," said the Archdeacon, placidly. "I'm too old to understand these things." He looked quizzically over his glasses. "Of course I gave him a little advice."

"Naturally," said Anthony.

"In my own humble way," added the Archdeacon. "I didn't dishearten him, but I told him to go warily. 'You'll find it hard,' I said to him, 'to get men to teach all those fancy things of yours' ."

Anthony saw it all then, but he played the Archdeacon at his own game.

"You'll get men to teach anything if you pay them."

"That's just my point," cried the Archdeacon. "That's what I told him. Father Murphy, the poor innocent man, thinks that he'll get someone to do it for the love of the thing—and for the love of the parish—with maybe a little money thrown in now and again. It's nonsensical!"

"It's fantastic," said Anthony.

"That's the worst of rushing into things. 'Go quietly,' I told him, but sure he wouldn't heed an old man like me. What do you think of the war, Anthony?"

They discussed the war for the next hour.

It was after eleven when Anthony rose to go.

"Don't be so long before you come to see me again," said the Archdeacon. "I enjoyed our little chat. Now that you have time to burn you should drop in to me oftener."

"I mightn't have so much time from now on."

"And how is that, Anthony?"

"I've been offered a job."

"Well, isn't that grand. And what kind of a job have you been offered, Anthony? Don't mind an old man's curiosity."

"A funny kind of a job—it's hard to say anything definite about it. All I say is that before I begin it I must brush up my trigonometry and Apologetics. I might even have to study social science."

The Archdeacon nodded his head slowly.

"That's a full programme, Anthony. Do you think are you wise?"

"I know I'm not wise. I'm just a stupid old man—like yourself, Archdeacon. And now before I go will you tell me one thing?"

"What's that?"

"Why do you always speak in riddles?"

"I dunno, Anthony. I dunno. Maybe it's because of the job I have. You see—the whole thing began with parables."

"And miracles," added Anthony. "God forgive you for putting this foolish notion in my head."

"Now Anthony! Sure I didn't coax nor persuade you."

"Tell Father Murphy I'll be down to have a talk with him one of-these days."

He went home the short way, the old way that led pass Paradise Alley and the new school that had replaced it Men standing in tenement doorways shouted greetings to

him. He got salutes from youngsters in their teens and from children who should have been in their beds. They all knew him. They knew the very shape of him, the sound of his footsteps. He was amongst his own people again.

And he would be amongst them now until the end. He would stay with them, like the Archdeacon, until he could no longer stay, until some part of his physical mechanism gave way. He would finish his work and knit its ravelled ends together. He would smash the statutory school-leaving age, and the three R's, and the modulator. He would go on until he burst.

The boys' club extension, he knew well, wasn't just Father Murphy's idea. It was the Canon's way out for both Paradise Alley and Anthony Domican. It would bring two needs together and cancel them.

And it wasn't a money-saving idea. The Canon didn't just want a job done cheaply. He wasn't that kind of man. He wanted a job done, and he knew that Anthony was the man to do it.

Money didn't interest Anthony any longer. He could have kept on at the Erin Academy had he wanted to, but he had lost interest in that kind of teaching. It had served its purpose. It had boiled a pot that no longer needed kindling.

And if he died in the morning Mollie would have enough to live on. She had her four houses and at least two hundred a year in addition. When Mollie went, Brigid and Francis Anthony would inherit all that was going. Things would have been different had Denis and Mary stayed at home, but they couldn't have stayed at home for ever. The break would have come sooner or later, and Crescent Terrace would have emptied in time.

The thought of Christopher no longer saddened him.

Christopher had come back to him. He was more his than he had ever been in life, and that bright body of his was fixed for ever in unchangeable youth. He would see Christopher again, and know him for his own.

As he walked along the sea-front at Clontarf his eyes kept straying to the lights on the other side of the little bay. Clontarf was a dormitory, a ten-to-nine bus district, a place where people bought out their houses and earthed up their celery. But the far side never slept. Paradise Alley did not close down at five-thirty.

The electricity depot at the Pigeon House glowed with light, and the thudding of its sleepless dynamos carried across the water to him. A boat hooted as it slid down the river. There was no sleep for Paradise Alley. All night long, waggons would clank and rattle, bullocks would come padding out from railway sidings in the small hours, out-of-breath engines would whistle in the dawn. Paradise Alley and places like it were maids of all work to the city, and the port that brought salaries to Rathmines and Donnybrook was their tireless taskmaster.

During his forty years in Paradise Alley he had had little opportunity of teaching the things that really mattered. Now he was going to begin where he had left off. And even now he could do very little, for the mad venture in which he was going to share was not part of an integrated educational system. It had no backing, no authority. It was founded on charity and would live on the wind. It had no salaries, no State endowments, no nothing.

But the thought of the difficulties ahead could not depress him. He had been granted a new lease of life. He was going to teach Paradise Alley not just the things that would help it to earn a living but the things that would help it to live. There would be no inspectors, no dictated programmes, no bread-and-butter aim. The pupils would come—billiards and football would bring them—and it was up to him to hold them. And he felt reasonably sure that he could hold them, not because of anything in himself, but because of something in them, something that poverty, and under-nourishment, and bad smells could not kill.

He had always believed in Paradise Alley, and now, more than ever, he was prepared to back it against all the world.

* * * *